OUDTESTAMENTISCHE STUDIËN

DEEL XXVII

OUDTESTAMENTISCHE STUDIËN

NAMENS HET OUDTESTAMENTISCH WERKGEZELSCHAP

UITGEGEVEN DOOR

A.S. VAN DER WOUDE
GRONINGEN

DEEL XXVII

SELECTED STUDIES IN OLD TESTAMENT EXEGESIS

by

P.A.H. DE BOER

EDITED BY

C. VAN DUIN

E.J. BRILL
LEIDEN • NEW YORK • KØBENHAVN • KÖLN
1991

The paper in this book meets the guidelines for permanence and durability of the Com-
mittee on Production Guidelines for Book Longevity of the Council on Library
Resources.

BS
476
.B54
1991

Library of Congress Cataloging-in-Publication Data

Boer, Pieter Arie Hendrik de, 1910-
  Selected studies in Old Testament exegesis / edited by C. van Duin.
    p.   cm.—(Oudtestamentische Studiën, ISSN 0169-7226; d. 27)
  Includes bibliographical references and index.
  ISBN 90-04-09342-7 (alk. paper)
    1. Bible. O.T.—Hermeneutics. I. Duin, C. van. II. Title.
III. Series.
BS476.B54   1991
221.6—dc20   91-10143
                                                                 CIP

ISSN 069-7226
ISBN 90 04 09342 7

PRINTED IN THE NETHERLANDS

CONTENTS

FOREWORD

To honour Professor DE BOER on the occasion of his 80th birthday, Juni 14, 1990, arrangements had been made for the publication of a selection of his articles. Only a week before his death on August 5, 1989, he agreed with the criterion by which to select the writings that would be included in a congratulatory volume: those papers of exegetical interest which were written in Dutch or had appeared in occasional publications or in periodicals of minor circulation, and were therefore less accessible, were to be collected in this volume. In addition the bibliography of *VT* XXX (1980), pp. 513–7 was to be completed and brought up to date. Since the disablement of his last years had made it impossible for him to continue working, he deeply felt the desire to round off his active life in this way. His death did not change the project as such. The book, however, has now become a memorial volume.

While others have thrown light on Professor DE BOER's organising abilities on behalf of his fellow scholars at home and abroad[1] and on his publishing activities both as a writer and an editor, I should like, by way of introduction to this collection, to devote some words to his significance as a teacher, and to the influence of his forty years' professorship on so many generations of students of theology of Leyden University. There, in Leyden, at the *Rapenburg*, in the *gewelfkamer* (vaulted room), lay the heart and core of his professional life, of his devotion to the Hebrew texts which in his lectures he made the central issue, for both teacher and students. In spite of

---

[1] H.J. HEERING, "De Boer, de man van het Oude Testament", *NRC-Handelsblad* (15 augustus 1989);

M.J. MULDER, "In memoriam prof. dr. P.A.H. DE BOER", *MARE* (7 september 1989), p. 15;

"Professor P.A.H. DE BOER", *The Times* (September 19, 1989);

P.B. DIRKSEN, "In memoriam prof. dr. P.A.H. DE BOER", *Té-èf* 19/1 (november 1989), pp. 5–9;

P.B. DIRKSEN, "In memoriam P.A.H. DE BOER (1910–1989)", *NedThT* 44 (1990), pp. 54f.;

G.W. ANDERSON, "P.A.H. DE BOER", *VT* XL (1990), pp. 1–3;

J. HOFTIJZER, "In memoriam prof. dr. P.A.H. DE BOER (1910–1989)", *Phoenix*, Bulletin uitgegeven door het Vooraziatisch-Egyptisch Genootschap EX ORIENTE LUX, 36/1 (1990), pp. 4–6.

fashionable trends this is and always will be the classic way to a fruitful relationship between teacher and student.

For the beginning student of theology—whether he had his roots
in more liberal or in more orthodox forms of protestantism—the lectures on exegesis of the Old Testament were most literally an eye-
opener. The rights of the books of Ancient Israel, as against their
interpretation in the New Testament or as against their use or abuse
in the Church and in Christendom, were vindicated. One might say
that he stood up for the men behind the text of the Old Testament,
whose writings had no defence apart from the honesty of later generations. Texts are not utensils. Exegesis *e mente auctoris* basically
means respect for the authors of the texts, for people of earlier days.
Just as it matters to understand one's contemporaries, so it matters
to understand one's fellow men of olden time. It is not unimportant,
therefore, to know *the rights of the matter*, however trivial it may seem.
Consequently, philological acuity is an essential element of this attitude of respect for the literary legacy of former times. So Professor
DE BOER taught us to be servants of the written word—which, of
course, does not mean to be literalists or verbalists!—, prepared to
do the humble ground-work in the service of the understanding of
old texts, in order that we may perceive what had been moving
minds and hearts. For that, we honour him and his memory—we:
I am sure that I can speak on behalf of very many former students
of Professor DE BOER.

A few remarks about the selected papers may be in order. Some
of the originally Dutch articles make accessible also for his colleagues
abroad otherwise unknown aspects of Professor DE BOER's 'home-
work'. In his paper about ''A lost biblical text'' he illustrates the
meaning of text-critical work and the connection of this technical
specialism with other disciplines of theology. The didactic tone of
''In search of the meaning of Psalm li 6 (4)'' bespeaks that it was
meant originally for students of theology. His many years' engage-
ment with the text of the Books of Samuel induced him to try to
answer the question how the expression *Saul the Tyrant* found its way
to the Dutch national anthem. ''Quelques remarques sur l'arc dans
la nuée (Genèse 9,8 – 17)'' is published here as corrected by Marc
Vervenne for the 1989 reissue of *Questions disputées d'Ancien Testament*,
BEThL 33 (1974). The updating notes by Vervenne have also been
adopted. As there existed no definite version of ''Egypt in the Old
Testament: some aspects of an ambivalent assessment'', a paper

read at the meeting of the Society for Old Testament Study, Oxford, 1975[2]—Professor DE BOER had kept working on it—, this valuable treatise had to be composed out of the three or four versions the author left behind.

The lecture delivered at the Göttingen Congress of 1977, "Bemerkungen zu Jesaja xix 24 und 25", could not be included in this volume, as the author marked the file containing this paper *niet voor publicatie* (not for publication)[3].

In the bibliography the articles included in this volume are indicated with an *. There the original form of publication is recorded. In the Table of contents the (year) after the title of the article refers to the bibliography.

A considerable debt of gratitude I owe Drs. P.J. Booɪj (Amsterdam). He translated "Kingship in Ancient Israel" (1938), "An inscription from Ṣoʿar" (1956), "When David had to flee from Saul, the Tyrant . . ." (1963), "A lost biblical text" (1963), "Does Job retract? (Job xlii 6)" (1977), and improved the English of "In search of the meaning of Psalm li 6 (4)" (1969), and of "Egypt in the Old Testament: some aspects of an ambivalent assessment" (1975), of which English manuscripts were extant. He conceived his task broadmindedly and was of great help to the editor. The English translation used in these articles is the Revised English Bible, unless indicated otherwise.

Thanks are due to Dr. G. VAN DER Kooɪj (Leyden) for supplying a new photograph of the inscription from Ṣoʿar, and to Prof. Dr. W. BAARS for his approval to reprint the article about "Ein neugefundenes Fragment des syrisch-römischen Rechtsbuches" (1968).

I am much obliged to the publishers, all of whom gave permission to republish the articles in this volume.

Acknowledgments are due to Prof. Dr. A.S. VAN DER WOUDE (Groningen) for including this volume in the series of Oudtestamentische Studiën.

C. van Duin

---

[2] The title, then, was "Aspects of the double, controversial valuation of Egypt in the Old Testament".

[3] These manuscript materials have been deposited in Leyden University Library.

1
KINGSHIP IN ANCIENT ISRAEL

The information we have about kingship in ancient Israel differs from what is known about kingship in Egypt, Mesopotamia, Asia Minor, and Canaan in a major point. The Old Testament describes the beginnings of Israelite kingship, which in the case of the surrounding nations lie well before the starting-point of our historical knowledge. It may called characteristic of the human mind that in its investigations it sees the question of origins as essential to the understanding of the true nature of a phenomenon. Thus several scholars have formulated hypotheses explaining the possible origins of kingship. The two examples of Voltaire (*le premier roi fut un soldat heureux*) and Frazer (who assumes that kings initially developed from sorcerers) give rise to the suspicion that these conjectures contribute more to our knowledge of their authors' minds than to that of the nature of kingship. Only through a real understanding of the available data can we approach the nature of a phenomenon. Not unsurprisingly, however, scholars will be glad to observe that Israel's kingship is known from its beginnings. The Old Testament tells us about ''the days when there was no king in Israel and every man did what was right in his own eyes'', as is twice said in the Book of Judges (xvii 6 and xxi 25). In the Books of Samuel we have the narratives of Saul's election and his action as Israel's first king and of the establishment of the royal dynasty by his successor David. We should, however, refrain from using the lofty term ''origins'' of kingship, as there is no reference to such a thing in Israel's data either. The elders of the people come to Samuel when he has grown too old for leadership, saying, ''Appoint for us a king to govern us like all the nations'' (1 Sam, viii 5, 6, 20).

The available data present us with the following problem. Israel's kingship is not imposed by foreign oppressors, but arises from the people's own desire. It agrees with religious values which this people claims as its own and the word 'king' becomes itself the symbol of important religious values. The king is Yahweh's Anointed and the founder of the national sanctuary into which the Ark is transferred. The Davidic dynasty becomes the religious ideal. As GRESSMANN says: ''Die Messiashoffnung hängt aufs engste mit den Vorstel-

lungen vom Königtum zusammen.''[1] Both the prophets and the
wisdom poets use the word "king" in a religious sense. The psalms
are full of the intimate connection between Yahweh and Israel's
king. Yahweh is himself called "the King". In his farewell address
Samuel says, "Yahweh your God is your King" (1 Sam. xii 12).[2]
These notions did not disappear together with Israelite kingship. I
may only remind you of the function of the royal throne in the vi-
sions of Daniel, of the concept of βασιλεία in the New Testament,
of the inscription on the Cross, etc. In the Jewish world one may
point out the traditional appellation of God *mlk mlky hmlkym hqdwš
brwk hw'*. Translated literally, this means: "the King of the kings of
kings, the Holy One, blessed be He", as distinct from the title of the
King of Persia, who was called "the king of kings". In the Christian
Church, the regal title is habitually applied to God, to Christ and
to the Virgin Mary, and it is frequently used in Jewish prayer.

Yet there is substantial evidence of the influence of the surrounding nations on Israelite kingship. They were Israel's enemies, "pa-
gans", and communication with them was considered a breach of
loyalty towards Israel's God. The problem becomes clear when we
realize that besides a real appreciation of kingship there are other,
anti-monarchical sounds. The utterances of the prophets will be
mentioned here only in passing. Thus Hosea's words against
kingship—such as "They made kings, but not through me", says
the Lord (viii 4; cf. vii 3; x 3; xiii 10)—must not be isolated from
the circumstances in which they were spoken. Hosea is shocked by
the kings' wrongdoings to such a degree that he underlines the very
contrast which is at the same time the difficulty of our subject by the
words "Besides me there is no saviour"—says the Lord, who delivered Israel from Egypt (xiii 4). The prophet thus resumes the old
tradition of 1 Sam. viii (Yahweh is your King). His emotions—
which as such make it impossible a priori to draw any conclusions
about the existence of principled opposition to the monarchy—make
him say, "Where now is your king, to save you in all your cities,
and your 'judges' (saviours), those of whom you said, 'Give me a

---

[1] H. GRESSMAN, *Der Messias*, Göttingen, 1929, p. 5*.
[2] See O. EISSFELDT, "Jahwe als König", *ZAW* 46 (1928), pp. 89f. (= *Kleine
Schriften*, Bd. I, pp. 179f.); K. GALLING, *Die israelitische Staatsverfassung in ihrer vor-
derorientalischen Umwelt*, Der alte Orient 28, Heft 3/4, Leipzig 1929, esp. pp. 42f.;
L. KÖHLER, *Theologie des Alten Testaments*, Tübingen, 1936, p. 13.

king and princes'?'' (xiii 10). The mention of the so-called ''judges'' in this utterance should warn us against speaking of a Hosean or prophetic theory about kingship.[3]

More relevant to our subject is the tradition of Judges ix, the well-known ''fable of Jotham''. This Jotham, son of the judge Gideon, has escaped from a massacre by Abimelech. At the rumour that the citizens of the town of Shechem have made Abimelech king, he predicts that little good will come to the king's subjects from this useless institution. Various fruit trees are offered kingship over the trees, but they decline, asking, ''Why should I leave my good fruit, which gods and men prize in me [i.e., my useful task], to sway over the trees?'' This ''swaying'' implies instability, and according to the Old Testament, unstable things are of no use. Instability is close to unreliability. Finally the useless bramble wishes to be anointed.

This ironical satire is closely related to 1 Sam. viii. In his description of the dark side of kingship, Samuel, too, mentions the aspect of uselessness with its disastrous effects. These, he says, will be the king's ways: he will take your sons and appoint them to his chariots and to be his horsemen and also to be commanders of this army, and make them work on his fields; your daughters will have to prepare his spices and to cook and bake in his kitchen; he will claim your menservants and maidservants as well as the best of your cattle[4] and asses; he will take the tenth of your flocks and confiscate your fields, and you will be his slaves (1 Sam. viii 11ff; cf. Deut. xvii 14ff.). This aversion to the monarchy is also given a religious basis in the objection raised against the request for a king: by desiring a king, the people reject Yahweh as their king (v. 7).[5] The statement testifying to the religious weight of the word ''king'' (''Yahweh your God is your King'' (1 Sam. xii 12)), is at the same time a criticism of the request for a king in Israel and thus the clearest definition of the problem presented by our subject. On the one hand Saul is called Yahweh's Anointed (1 Sam. xi; xv 1; xxiv 7, 11; xxvi 9, 11, 33) and his ''Chosen'' (2 Sam. xxi 6), on the other Israel admits being wrong by saying, ''We have added to all our sins this evil, to ask for ourselves a king.''[6]

---

[3] The ''judges'' were undoubtedly seen as saviours sent by God.
[4] With LXX.
[5] For the religious background of the opposition to Abimelech, see p. 12.
[6] It seems hardly necessary to say that the later rupture between Samuel and

There is no lack of suggestions for a solution of the above-mentioned difficulty or perhaps even contradiction in the available data. First of all, I should mention the efforts made by the adherents of the documentary hypothesis. It is quite understandable that the principles of source criticism and later "redactional" revision, which for many people seem to solve the problems of the Pentateuch, should also be applied to the ensuing books. With his usual acuteness, BUDDE[7] tried to show that we have here two series of narratives, one of which is in favour of the monarchy, while the other is opposed to it on principle. Apart from the work of the deuteronomistic and post-deuteronomistic redactors, which is thought to be most noticeable in the passages about theocracy, the priesthood and the temple, 1 Sam. ix and x 1 – 16 (Samuel anoints Saul, Kish's son), xi 1 – 11, 15 (the expedition against Ammon to liberate Jabesh), and xiii and xiv 1 – 16 (the victory won by Saul and Jonathan over the Philistines) contain the message that Yahweh himself has decided to give the people a king. The other source, chs. vii (Samuel's victory over the Philistines), viii (the elders' request for a king), x 17 – 24a (Saul's election by lot at Mizpah), xii (Samuel's farewell address) and xv (Saul's rejection after the expedition against Amalek) shows a theocratic spirit, gives an idealistic picture of the judges and rejects kingship, which is only permitted in an atmosphere of anger. This source is to be identified with the Elohist in the Pentateuch, Joshua and Judges; the former, in all probability, with the Yahwist. In Samuel, this J source, which is also the earliest, gives the impression of being "eine vorzügliche Geschichtsquelle", while the Elohist source offers a pragmatic view of history.

LODS takes a further step and divides what Budde calls J into two sources: a "seer" source (Samuel as seer in chs. ixf.) and a Jabesh source (ch. xi). His argument, wholly rational and of great clarity in both language and construction—the secret of the French—, can be summarized briefly as follows: *aux grands maux les grands remèdes.* The political situation is perilous and so desperate that it forces the tribes to gather around one leader. The number and variety of nar-

---

Saul is not related to our problem, since another man is anointed king instead of Saul, who had been rejected and been left by the Spirit, the *rūᵃḥ* of YHWH.

[7] K. BUDDE, *Die Bücher Richter und Samuel, ihre Quellen und ihr Aufbau*, Tübingen-Leipzig, 1890; *Die Bücher Samuel*, KHC VIII, Tübingen-Leipzig, 1902; *Schätzung des Königtums im Alten Testament*, Marburger akademische Reden, 1903 Nr. 8.

ratives justifying Saul's elevation to the kingship are explained by the fact that "l'institution monarchique a été appréciée de façons très diverses selon les temps et les milieux; la personne de Saul aussi a été présentée sous des couleurs très différentes selon que le narrateur avait plus ou moins de sympathie pour la dynastie davidique."[8] The victory over the Philistines (ch. xiv) is considered by LODS to be the origin of Saul's kingship, of which his meeting with Samuel during his search for his father's asses is the legendary prehistory. Ch. vii (the victory over the Philistines ascribed to Samuel) is late and has been written from a prophetic spirit, displaying completely new ideas and an anti-monarchical viewpoint. The fable of Jotham (Judg. ix 8ff.) may not sound appropriate coming from a royal prince's lips, but the opinion on the monarchy expressed in it was probably shared by many Israelites: although they have become farmers and fruit growers, they stick to the moderate anarchism of the aristocratic Bedouin.

SMEND[9] and EISSFELDT[10] assume that there are three parallel narratives, but their views approach BUDDE's again. According to EISSFELDT, these three narratives are probably continuations of the Pentateuchal sources. His acute analysis allows for the possibility of derivations from folklore, even for his Elohist source, which is a modification in a more spiritual and clerical sense of his *Laienquelle* and Yahwist source. The deuteronomistic redaction is present, but has not made many changes.[11] CASPARI[12] attaches far more importance to the folkloristic element and rejects the assumption of the existence of independent sources. He starts from the idea of autonomous narratives of three different periods: a "novellistic", an Elohistic and a Deuteronomistic period. The linking passages and the so-called glosses explain the difficulties. He proposes a great deal of emendations and changes in the order of the text. With EISS-

[8] "Les sources des récits du premier livre de Samuël sur l'institution de la royauté israélite", in: *Études de théologie et d'histoire*, Paris, 1901, pp. 257–284, and *Israël. Des origines au milieu du VIIIe siècle*, L'évolution de l'humanité vol. XXVII, Paris, 1930, pp. 408 and 400.

[9] R. SMEND, "JE in den geschichtlichen Büchern des AT", *ZAW* 39 (1921), pp. 181–217 (published posthumously by H. HOLZINGER).

[10] *Die Komposition der Samuelisbücher*, Leipzig, 1931, and *Einleitung in das Alte Testament*, Tübingen, 1934.

[11] Thus also C. STEUERNAGEL, *Lehrbuch der Einleitung in das Alte Testament*, Tübingen, 1912, p. 339.

[12] W. CASPARI, *Die Samuelbücher*, KAT VII, Leipzig, 1926.

FELDT[13], we may call this a combination of a fragmentary and a complementary hypothesis. SCHULZ[14] and HYLANDER[15] also show a keener eye for the narrative and its motifs.

This very brief and rough survey of highly complicated matters (doesn't a scholarly work on source criticism bring back the horrors of grammar school mathematics?) has not made it possible to reach a judgment on the theories developed in source criticism. This is not really necessary for the discussion of our subject, as it is obvious that this method offers many views on the composition of the narratives, but no answer to the question of the appreciation of kingship. It describes the problem in a variety of ways and by its very diversity manifestly demonstrates the truth of the saying: "beschreiben ist schwerer als erklären". The results may bring home to us the truth that the construction of a Semitic story is not the same as that of the westerner's narratives and arguments.[16]

I said that all this does not answer the question that occupies us here. This is only partly true, as it is argued unanimously that the anti-monarchical tendency is a prophetic and consequently late form of criticism. This answer merely shifts the difficulty to another period of history and involves many new problems. EISSFELDT was the first to allow for the possible influence of ancient folk tales, even in his Elohist source. Who will provide a criterion by which to decide whether or not something is prophetic? Isn't what scholarly investigators have been doing tantamount to turning the criticism of classical prophetism against the kings of its time into a theory affirming that Priestly passages in the available sources are late, forgetting that classical prophetism did not spare the forms of worship of its time either?

---

[13] O. EISSFELDT, "Text-, Stil- und Literarkritik in den Samuelbüchern", OLZ 30 (1927), p. 657. Cf. GRESSMANN's fragmentary hypothesis. A clear survey is offered by EISSFELDT in his Einleitung (1934), pp. 303ff., and in K.A. LEIMBACH, Die Bücher Samuel, Bonn, 1936, Einleitung.

[14] Die Bücher Samuel, 2 Bde., EHAT, Münster i.W., 1919/1920, and especially Erzählungskunst in den Samuel Büchern, Biblische Zeitfragen 11, Heft 6/7, Münster i.W., 1923.

[15] Der literarische Samuel-Saul Komplex (thesis), Uppsala, 1932.

[16] It is a remarkable fact that in textual criticism, source critics like to use the Septuaginta and other ancient versions to emend the "thoroughly corrupted and revised" Hebrew text (see my dissertation Research into the Text of I Sam. I–XVI, Amsterdam, 1938), whereas in compositional research it is usually forgotten that apart from a few small-scale efforts at harmonization, the versiones antiquae show the same order as our Masoretic text.

In my judgment one should exercise caution in using the term "prophetic". The priest-judge Samuel objects against the monarchy, and so does Jotham, son of the priest-judge Gideon, but that does not make them spokesmen of the classical prophetic mind. WIESMANN[17] proposes an independent explanation. He rejects the attempts at harmonization (which, of courses, are not lacking): "In unserem Falle handelt es sich nicht um Berichte, die denselben Gegenstand behandeln und den Charakter von Varianten haben, sie sind vielmehr grundverschieden und widersprechen sich in den wesentlichen Punkten." He believes to have found a solution by relocating certain parts of the text. According to him, the story runs as follows: first Saul is elected to be "prince" (*ngyd*): Saul's first meeting with Samuel, his being anointed *ngyd* and his victory over Ammon (chs. ix; x 1 – 16, 27b – x 11). In the second part of the story, Saul is elected to be king, *mlk*: the elders' request, the choice by lot, Samuel's farewell address and the introduction of a standing army (chs. viii; x 17 – 24, 27a; xi 12 – 15; xii; x 25f.; xiii 2, 19 – 22). The motivation for the elders' request ("that our king may [. . .] go out before us and fight our battles") then refers to the war against Ammon, which is not imminent but already over. As in ancient times, Yahweh had given a liberator (xii 11). ix 16, therefore, does not refer to the people's request for a king, but to their crying for help, as so often in the period of the judges. In reply to the elders' request Samuel says, "This is wrong, for Yahweh is your king. He has governed you well and protected you from Moses' time till the present day." The two sections distinguished by WIESMANN correspond approximately to the two sources assumed by BUDDE and others, but are not seen as "doublets". In his view they are sections whose contents are totally different. That is why his hypothesis is more than a mere description. It has already been said that he distinguishes the two accounts on the basis of the terms *ngyd* and *mlk*

He sees the *ngyd* as the liberator from distress whose power is only temporary, whereas the *mlk* has permanent power. It would be impossible to give a precise definition of the office of *ngyd*, because the prompt introduction of kingship prevented the further performance of the duties pertaining to this office. In the war against Ammon the people probably learned that a closer relationship between the

---

[17] "Die Einführung des Königtums in Israel", in *ZKTh* 34 (1910), pp. 118 – 153.

tribes, as well as a standing army under a regular commander, was needed.[18]

This explanation postulates a historical development. It has, however, justly been asked how the assumed textual confusion came about.[19] Beside, ch. viii is obviously a continuation of ch. vii. Also, with regard to our problem, the question why in the anti-monarchical recensions the *ngyd* did not remain the ideal form of government remains unanswered. No attention is paid to the religious import of the term *mlk*.[20]

In his interesting book *Königtum Gottes*, Martin BUBER[21] tried to show that independently of the royal court, the Elohistic data (in his terminology a source is called a "Richtung des Schrifttums") offered a "theopolitical" interpretation of history. These data are of a prophetic nature, but yet very early. BUBER attributes the kingship over Israel to Yahweh long before the period of the monarchy. The principle of leadership that held the tribes together was inextricably bound up with the tendency towards direct theocracy. The prophets' positive attitude towards the monarchy flows from the fact that human kingship found religious acceptance in the Books of Samuel and was received as sacred in the sacramental rite of anointing. Prophetic criticism arises because of the growing lack of religion. From this criticism Buber deduces the birth of Messianism. Yahweh is "der Führer des aus Abhängigkeit in Freiheit, aus Enge in Weite ziehenden Volkes." He is the *mælæk*, "ratender Spender des Weg- und Kampf-orakels, der 'mitgehende Gott'". The cove-

---

[18] With the help of his hypothesis, WIESMANN also elucidates the following points: xi 7 "and after Samuel" is not a gloss, the *ngyd* needing the support of Samuel's authority. x 22, Saul's hiding, which for EISSFELDT is a new narrative of which the beginning has been lost (*Kompos. Sam.*, p. 7), is explained by Saul's already being *ngyd* and his not knowing whether Yahweh will confirm his "high" position or bring him down. He has no satisfying solution for ix 14 and 18. The renewal of kingship seems to him plausible, because Gilgal was important historically.

[19] In SCHULZ's critical discussion of this hypothesis in his commentary on Samuel, vol. I pp. 177f.

[20] To a lesser degree, this objection also applies to ALT's opposition of *ngyd* and *mlk* in his *Die Staatenbildung der Israeliten in Palästina*, Leipzig, 1930, p. 29 (= *Kleine Schriften* II, München, 1953, p. 22f.).

[21] *Königtum Gottes*, Das Kommende I, [1]1932, [2]1936, and "Biblisches Führertum", in *Kampf um Israel* (1933); both published by Schocken Verlag, Berlin. E. SELLIN, *Israelitisch-jüdische Religionsgeschichte*, Leipzig, 1933, agrees with BUBER to a large extent.

nant made at the Sinai is a royal treaty. "JHWH will nicht, wie die anderen Königsgötter, Oberherr und Burge eines menschlichen Monarchen sein, er will selber der Führer und der Fürst bleiben— Der eigentliche Widerpart der unmittelbaren Theokratie ist das *erbliche* Königtum."[22] Among the Bedouin one finds the same opposition to a human king. No chief would dare to call himself *malik*, he is no more than the *primus inter pares*.[23] In the light of BUBER's conception, our problem appears roughly as follows: the critical attitude we find in the data at our disposal is one that follows from the ancient image of God. The rite of anointing has a conciliatory function, as it holds on to the idea that it is Yahweh who chooses the king (cf. also Deut. xvii 15a).

Many and serious objections have been raised against BUBER's view, and not nearly all of them are refuted in the preface of the second edition of his book. His identification of the roots *mšl* and *mlk* cannot be maintained. His statement that other nations have not been able to get beyond raising a human *Führer*, "wiewohl unter gleichbetitelter göttlicher Oberhoheit", to the position of *mlk*, and his attributing an "Ernstmachenwollen" with the relation with God only to Israel imply an underrating of religious meaning of kingship and the seriousness of other people also with respect to theocracy. BUBER's undoubtedly impressive construction rightly perceives an ancient and religious motif in the anti-monarchical position. To my judgment, however, it would be an error to think that this motif can only be understood from Messianism and the prophetic criticism of kingship. Buber shares this error with many of those who distinguish different sources and thus do not seek to understand the text as it has come down to us.

A great many commentators find that kingship in ancient Israel should be seen as a phenomenon in response to the needs of the age. Those who are only interested in historical facts do not look for the background of pro- or anti-monarchical positions but only for the immediate causes which led to the election of a king. One is undoubtedly right in saying that the distress of the war made central authority necessary. I may remind you of the saying quoted above: *aux grands maux les grands remèdes*. But this does not explain the religious criticisms, nor the religious justification of the monarchy. In

---

[22] *Op. cit.*, 2nd ed., p. 139.
[23] *Op. cit.*, 2nd ed., pp. 140, 131, see footnote.

one of his excellent studies, after concluding that the formation of
the state should above all be seen as a reaction to the pressure exert-
ed by the Philistines, ALT says, "Aber so wichtig uns diese an der
zeitgeschichtlichen Lage orientierte Betrachtungsweise sein muß, so
wenig wird sie doch ausreichen, um uns den ganzen Aufbau der
neuen politischen Schöpfungen zu erschließen."[24]

The positive cannot be born from what is wholly negative,
although it may be determined by it to a large extent. In Israel war,
too, had a specific Israelitic import: the deity's providing justice for
its people. One has only to think of the ark, of Yahweh's actual
presence in the army (1 Sam. iv), of the royal sacrifices (e.g. 1 Sam.
xiv 35), and above all of the expression "the wars of Yahweh". The
available sources should be interpreted as independent, positively
religious narratives, both in their negative and in their positive judgments. The assumption of borrowings for purely practical reasons
shows unjustified contempt for the independent strength of a people
that will be pre-eminently conscious of its own religious heritage in
later history.

I should now like to point out a few particulars that to my
knowledge have not been given adequate attention in the discussion
of this subject. Theories about the arrangement of data, about
theocratic or prophetic redactions should not make us lose sight of
the texts themselves. Initially, the Israelites did not live in cities.[25]
In their traditions, one can still see that both the narrator and, consequently, his audience looked up to the city, just as in our own days
the real countryman is shy of the city and its inhabitants. The stories
of the patriarchs, in which Israel listens to its past, are rural narratives. This does not mean that Abram is not a man with power,
kabôd. In Gen. xiv he wins a victory over "kings". But he declines
even the tribute offered by the king of Salem; his God is to be distinguished from Melchizedek's El Elyon. Israel's wealth does not
come from a city god, but from Yahweh, "the God of the fathers",
i.e. the God of the farmers.[26] The book of Joshua describes the

---

[24] *Staatenbildung*, p. 16 (= *Kleine Schriften* II, München, 1953, pp. 12f.).

[25] This is confirmed by ALT's "territorialgeschichtliche Studien", e.g. *Die
Landnahme der Israeliten in Palästina*, Leipzig, 1925. See e.g. pp. 24, 25, 27 "vom
National- zum Territorialstaat ..."; 28, 29, 34 "... vor allem der Gebirge, die
an der Ausbildung des Stadtstaatensystems nur in geringem Maße teilgenommen
hatten". And esp. p. 35: "vor den Toren der Städte ..." (= *Kleine Schriften* I,
1953, respectively pp. 113–117, 118–120, 124f.)

[26] Cf. J. LEWY, "Les textes paléo-assyriens et l'Ancient Testament", *RHR* 110

sieges and conquests of several towns, but no permanent occupa-
tions of or life in those towns. In this connection, the two "spy" stories of Josh. ii and Num. xiii are typical. One of them narrates with
obvious pleasure the escape from Jericho with the help of Rahab's
clever behaviour. The other offers merely a dejected report: the cities are *b^eṣurôt g^edolot m^eʾod*, "fortified and very large" (Num. xiii
28), or, as Deut. i 28 has it, "great and fortified up to heaven". This
is a judgment given from the fields.[27] The so-called "judges" are
nearly all pictured as men of the country. Othniel is urged to ask for
a good field (Judg. i 14f.). Ehud gathers the sons of Israel in the
mountains (iii 27). Shamgar defeats the Philistines "with an ox-
goad" (iii 31). Deborah (who bears the honorary title of "mother
in Israel") lives outdoors "under the palm of Deborah between
Ramah and Bethel (iv 5). Gideon is threshing corn when he is called
by the *malʾak* of Yahweh (vi 11), his father is farmer (v. 25) and Yahweh reveals himself through the morning dew as the God of nature.
Samson is a farmer's son (xiii). According to Judg. ii 14, the Israelites can be waylaid by plunderers, which shows that they do not live
in fortified towns. The ancient song of Judg. v speaks of the righteous acts of Yahweh toward Israel, adding the word *prznw*, which
probably means "village" (v 11). V. 16 aks: "Why did you tarry
among *hammišp^etayim* [probably the stakes to which the cattle are
fastened], to hear the piping for the flocks?"

The narratives of the first Book of Samuel do not differ from those
of the Book of Judges in this respect. The sanctuary at Shiloh is attended by Elkanah, a man from the hills of Ephraim, and the death
of the priest and judge Eli is caused by the loss of the ark of Yahweh,
the attribute of the farmer's God.[28] In the narratives about Samuel
as Israel's last "judge" (1 Sam. vii and xii), he commands the deity's manifestations in nature (for Israel the thunder reveals Yahweh's power). The sacrificial meal led by Samuel as priest and judge
is held in the open, on the "high place", the place of worship, just
as the ark is kept in the house on the hill (vii 1).

Secondly, we shall have a closer look at the so-called judge's
characteristics. A *špṭ* is called by Yahweh and not by the common

---

(1934), pp. 29–65, and H.S. NYBERG, "Studien zum Religionskampf im Alten
Testament", *ARW* 35 (1938), pp. 329–387.

[27] Cf. Deut, ii 36 *śgb* and Deut. iii 5; ix 1.

[28] Cf. W.B. KRISTENSEN, "De Ark van Jahwe", in *Mededeelingen der Koninklijke
Academie van Wetenschappen*, section Letterkunde, Vol. 76, B 5 (1933), pp. 19f.

will of the people.[29] To be called by Yahweh is to receive his Spirit. In Judg. vi, the *mal²ak* of Yahweh addresses the future saviour from oppression by the Midianites with the words "Yahweh is with you!", and in the Old Testament this is the *terminus technicus* for the successful.

In Judg. xi 27 Yahweh is himself called *špṭ*, the one who will give justice to Israel, but this does not preclude Jephtah's being a liberator: the performer of Yahweh's will is the latter's substitute, as the *rûᵃḥ*, the Spirit, is on him (v. 29). By that Spirit he is a liberator, and because the Israelites are liberated, there remains an aura of charisma around him. Only in this way can the formula "he judged Israel until he died" be understood. Abimelech tries to become a ruler without having been a saviour (*mwšyᶜ*) (Judg. ix). This is the real critical intent of Jotham's fable: with the Spirit of Yahweh one is worthy to be judge, without that Spirit one is a harmful oppressor, like the kings of the cities. The critical attitude towards Abimelech culminates in the mention of his humiliating death (ix 53): a woman crushes his skull and thereby proves his foolishness, which is itself a mark of his lacking the force that comes from Yahweh gives.[30] Hereditary succession was not an issue, as far as is evident from the sources. It would therefore be wrong to seek the judge's distinguishing feature in the temporary character of his power, in his not having a right to power, as BUBER does.[31] The real criterion is: does he or does he not have the Spirit of Yahweh? Gideon's sons and Abimelech, Eli's sons and Samuel's sons are not rejected because they succeed their fathers, but because they do not act in accordance with the Spirit of Yahweh. The same is true of Saul: he was rejected because Yahweh's Spirit had left him; there is no question of hereditary succession. The essential thing is that "Yahweh is with him". This explains why the judge has a priestly function: it is he who performs Yahweh's deeds. Through him, Yahweh takes Israel's destiny in hand. About Gideon we read that he builds an altar (Judg. vi). But most of the ancient narratives refer only to the *promachos* aspect of the "judge"—Yahweh's warrior is the hero of the folk tale. Yet

---

[29] GRESSMANN's odd description in *Die Anfänge Israels*, Göttingen, 1914, ²1922, is rightly challenged by A. WENDEL, *Säkularisierung in Israels Kultur*, Gütersloh, 1934, p. 136.
[30] Cf. 2 Sam. xi 21 and Judg. iv 9.
[31] *Op. cit.*, 2nd ed., p. 178.

the word *špṭ* and its derivative *mšpṭ* point to his priestly qualities, which are particularly emphasized in the stories about Eli and Samuel. *mšpṭ* refers to the form of life that manifests itself in accordance with the divine law by which the bearer is inspired (hence his judicial capacities); to the form of behaviour that is in agreement with the inner being.[32] In 1 Sam. viii the same word is used for the "ways" of the king.[33] Thirdly, I would like to say something about the meanings of *ngyd* and *mlk*. On the basis of the available data it is not possible to consider the office of *ngyd* as an individual one. Some scholars, however, have tried to show that the term *nagid* has a more sacred character than the word *melek*. This has not been confirmed by further research.[34] The word *nagid* undoubtedly has a sacred significance. It is used several times by Yahweh in connection with the choice or anointing of the ruler.[35] It is often found in the context of the temple and its worship.[36] But the same is true of the word *melek*.[37] The use of this word to denote kings of foreign nations, which do not serve Yahweh, is no proof for its having a more profane meaning. The line that divides the sacred from the profane does not coincide with that between Yahwistic and non-Yahwistic. Moreover, *nagid* is also used as a title for foreign rulers.[38] The connection with a command given by Yahweh (*ṣwh*) and with an anointing by Yahweh's priest as his representative is frequent. Just as the

---

[32] Cf. J. PEDERSEN, *Israel, its Life and Culture*, I/II, Copenhagen, 1926, p. 350. A. ALT, "Die Ursprünge des israelitischen Rechts", in *Berichte der Verhandlungen der Sächsischen Akademie der Wissenschaften zu Leipzig*, Philologisch-historische Klasse, 86. Band, 1. Heft (1934) (= *Kleine Schriften*, Bd. I, pp. 289f.), is biased in seeing in *mšpṭm* the lay element.

[33] Cf. also Deut. xvii 9ff.; 2 Sam. xv 4. For Isa. i 26 cf. O. PROCKSCH, *Jesaja* I, KAT IX, Leipzig, 1930.

[34] Against ALT, *Staatenbildung*, p. 29 (= *KlSchr* II, pp. 22f.) (cf. W. EICHRODT, *Theologie des Alten Testaments* I, 1933, p. 239 and elsewhere). To my view ALT switches from the qal- to the hiph'il meaning too easily. *ngyd* can be an active participle meaning "Excellency" (cf. the combination *ngyd pqyd* in Jer. xx 1), not "Sager", as it is translated by J. BARTH, *Die Nominalbildung in den semitischen Sprachen*, Leipzig [2]1894, § 125e. *ngyd* can also be a passive partic., cf. *msyh*, meaning "elevated". Quite often, however, etymology does not give us an understanding of the value of a term.

[35] E.g. Isa. lv 4; 1 Sam. ix 16; 2 Sam. vii 8; 1 Kings xiv 7, xvi 2; 1 Chron. xvii 7.

[36] Jer. xx 1; 1 Chron. ix 11, 20; xii 28.; xxvi 24; 2 Chron. vi 5; xxxi 12f.; xxxv 8; Neh. xi 11; Dan. ix 25.

[37] *ngyd* synonymous with *mlk* Ps. lxxvi 13; 1 Kings xiv 7; 1 Chron. xxviii 4; Ez. xxviii 2, 12; with *śr* Job xxix 9f.; with *mšl* Prov. xxviii 15f.

[38] Ez. xxviii 2.

55

55

555

55

"judge" is called to perform his priestly duties, so the king finds himself invested with a sacred office. 1 Sam. xiv depicts Saul in several priestly functions. He exercises command over the ark (v. 18), he puts his warriors under oath (v. 24), he builds an altar and pronounces on the sacrifice (v. 34f.), and asks for a word of God (v. 37). The close connection shown in the narratives between Samuel, the central figure of the tribal sanctuary,[39] and the first king indicates the sacred character of Saul's kingship.[40] And the actual basis of the king's connection with the circle of charismatic personalities appears to be the rate of anointing, which in ch. x is therefore immediately followed by Saul's transformation into another man, ʾyš ʾḥr, by his being transferred into the world of the nᵉbiʾim: "Is Saul also among the prophets?"

Anointing is a sacral rite that is already found in ancient Israel.[41] The fact that other peoples also used this rite to enthrone a king is no reason to consider it non-Yahwistic, "borrowed" or less important. On the contrary, our data indicate that it had an independent function and was of great importance in Israel's religion.

In the elegy on the death of Saul and his sons,[42] undoubtedly an ancient song, we find a much-discussed line that if I understand it rightly provides an important indication of what anointing meant in Israel as well. After cursing the mountain fields where Saul and his companions have fallen, it says: "For there the shield of the mighty was defiled[43] [it appeared not to have protective power], the shield of Saul, not anointed with oil." Some have understood the oil here in a rational, practical sense[44] (the leather of the shield had not been made supple with oil), observing in addition that oil is used to preserve leather. It shows a great deal of ingenuity and little sense of religion to think of the presence of a purely technical argument

[39] Cf. M. NOTH, *Das System der zwölf Stämme Israels*, Stuttgart, 1930, about the sacred league or amphictyony as the bond which united the Israelites.
[40] Cf. HYLANDER's correct criticism of KÖHLER's appreciation of the priesthood, *op. cit.*, p. 224.
[41] Cf. B.D. EERDMANS, *Alttestamentliche Studien* IV, Giessen, 1912, pp. 35f.
[42] 2 Sam. i 19 f. Esp. the end of v. 21.
[43] The niph. of gᶜl remains forced. Should one perhaps read ky šmn gᶜl, etc. ("truly, the shield cast off the oil", etc., i.e.: his life force drained away)? Cf. Job xxi 10, where one should also read the qal, translating: (and does not) waste (shake off) the *semen* (sap of life).
[44] See e.g. BUDDE, *Die Bücher Samuel*, KHC VIII, Tübingen-Leipzig, 1902, and others; cf. also GESENIUS-BUHL.

in this elegy. Others, such as CASPARI[45], perceive in anointing only the attempt at warding off the evil spirits. This explanation fails to acknowledge the positive meaning of the ritual. To me the meaning of the verse seems to be that anointing with oil is incompatible with defeat, with death. The ritual of anointing gives life to the person anointed, makes him participate in the deity's life. Even if it is not quite correct, the translation in the Dutch *Statenbijbel* offers a valid interpretation of the verse by the insertion of the word *alsof* ["as though"]: "alsof hij niet gezalfd ware geweest met olie".[46] Anointing and life are connected.[47] After anointing Solomon, Zadok the priest and Nathan the prophet are to exclaim *yᵉḥî hammæłæk šᵉlomo*: "Long live King Solomon!". This is not the expression of a wish but the acknowledgement of a fact, just as the salutation formula "Let the king live for ever!" is not a wish but an expression of deference. Yahweh has chosen the king, therefore he lives (1 Sam. x 24; 2 Sam. xvi 6), therefore he is anointed (Ps. xlv 8). Jacob anoints the stone because God is alive in it: Bet-El, God who must save him from death (Gen. xxviii 18ff.; xxxi 13). Deutero-Isaiah still knows about this connection: he has been anointed and so the *rûᵃḥ*, the Spirit of Yahweh, is on him, to announce liberation from exile, life out of death (Isa. lxi 1). Yahweh is the God of life. To be anointed king, prophet or priest is to receive his Spirit, the breath of life, that protects one from defeat. This seems to constitute the religious connection between "judge", "priest", "prophet", and "king".

Before having a last look at the problem under discussion, I shall mention briefly the forms of power Israel knew from the surrounding nations[48]: the ancient Canaanite type, in which the people were ruled by an aristocratic *Oberschicht*; the Philistine type, of which we know only the military form of the common war actions; the type of the highlands, also east of the river Jordan, where areas larger in size than one city and its surroundings formed a whole; and finally the national states of Edom, Moab, Ammon, and Aram.

Our problem can be summarized as follows: how can it be explained that on the one hand Saul is called the anointed (king) of

---

[45] *Op. cit.*, p. 400.

[46] The same is found in the *Authorized (King James) Version*: "*as though he had* not *been* anointed with oil" (*translator's note*).

[47] Cf. Lev. x 7.

[48] According to the brilliant interpretation of the extrabiblical data offered in ALT, *op. cit.* Cf. also K.GALLING, *op. cit.*.

Yahweh and that on the other the request for a king provokes principled, religious criticism?

Of course, the problem is not solved completely by the above observations. Yet it seems to me that they provide some clarifica-
tion. The opposition to the elders' request arises from the Israelite
farmers' fear of oppression from the city. They knew examples of
this in the Canaanite city-states, and, worse, they had experienced
it in periods of oppression. Part of Israel is already living in towns
(the elders are the magistrates of the ancient Israelite towns), but the
rural population sticks to the only form of farmers' organization that
shows vitality, i.e. their religion: their God Yahweh had liberated
them from oppression, first from Egypt through Moses, later
through the "judges". It is their opposition to strangers, as it has
been formulated clearly in the royal law we find in Deut. xvii: "You
may not put a foreigner over you, who is not your brother." This
tradition gives the impression of being very early.

The fact that even Israel's farmers accepted the king as sent by
Yahweh, is probably due to what is explicitly stated in the narrative
tradition: the priest-judge anoints the king, makes him both priest
and king.[49] When Yahweh has shown that he saves Israel through
his anointed one, Saul is taken to the sanctuary by the people (end
of ch. xi).[50]

The Book of Samuel contains narratives that once existed independently and stem from various circles. The narratives about the
second king gradually take the character of court annals. David
gradually turns the Israelite nation into a territorial kingdom ruled
from the capital. Several data have survived that show him to us as
a king who understands about the priestly background of kingship—he acts like one of the prophets in transferring the ark to
Jerusalem, like Samuel he wears the linen ephod (1 Sam. ii 18), he
brings sacrifices and blesses the people (2 Sam. vi 18), his sons are
called priests (2 Sam. viii 18)[51]—but he is also familiar with the oppressor's rôle. It is quite remarkable that in spite of his throne in
Jerusalem, later times preferably picture him as the son of Isai, the

---

[49] The great value attached to the king's anointing appears to have been felt for
a long time in later history, cf. *Hor.* 11b (*mlky byt dwd mšyḥyn mlky yšrʾl ʾyn mšyḥyn*).

[50] For the problem of the "renewal" of kingship, see T.H. WEIR, "The Election of Saul", *ExpT* 21 (1909/1910), p. 376.

[51] Cf. Solomon in 1 Kings viii 14; also Jeroboam I in 1 Kings xii 32f. and
David in 1 Chron. xxi 26.

rural boy who grazes the cattle in the fields of Bethlehem. Yahweh "chose David his servant, and took him from the sheepfolds, from tending the ewes that had young," where he had learnt how to be a pastor of Israel, "to be the shepherd of Jacob his people, of Israel his inheritance" (Ps. lxxviii 70f.).[52]

I have tried to elucidate a chapter of the religion of the people of Israel. This attempt has failed in several respects. Firstly, the conception of nature in ancient religion in its connection with Israel's religious faith in past and present salvation has not become clear to me. And I suspect that the specific meaning of the Old Testament belief in Yahweh lies in this connection. Secondly, the relationship between Israel's king and the one whom the new Testament calls the Son of David and the Lord's Anointed[53] has not been dealt with, although it is this relationship which makes Israelite kingship important for Christian theologians.

By mentioning these two points, I have also said what I hold to be my duties. They require strict text-critical, linguistic and historical objectivity, and a self-discipline precluding one's reaching for the forbidden fruit of "results" without going the long and difficult path of exegesis *e mente auctoris*. I do not, however, accept these duties without believing firmly that "he who seeks finds".

---

[52] Cf. *Mdr. Tehillim* lxxviii 70.

[53] Χριστός; see Ch.C. TORREY, "Χριστος', in *Quantulacumque: Studies Presented to Kirsopp Lake*, R.P. Casey *et al.*, eds., London, 1937, pp. 317–324.

2

GENESIS XXXII 23-33

Some remarks on Composition and Character of the Story [1])

If anybody might think, that, with regard to the scientific examination of the data from the first book of the Bible concerning
their signification, composition and connection with each other we
have come to a certain conform issue, a contemplation of the much
divergent opinions about a passage as Gen. xxxii 23-33 may radi-
cally bowl over such an opinion. How much the conceptions differ!
Even the adherents of the documentary theory do not agree. The
authority with which scholars as Procksch [2]) and Eiszfeldt [3]) record
their results, whereby it is supposed to be irrefutable that the
differentiation accepted in other parts of the book Genesis, of a
Jahwistical and Elohistical source also holds for our passage, does
not give any certainty, when we perceive that the results do not
cover each other. A more prudent scholar of the same school,
Skinner [4]), remarks: the analysis of the passage is beset by insur-
mountable difficulties — there is the utmost variety of opinion in
regard to details. Skinner only talks of possible variants.

There is not much of a communis opinio about the connection
with the other narratives concerning Jacob too. In the hypotheses
about the nature of the narration, of Gunkel [5]) as well as of Eiszfeldt [6]), we learn more about an eventual prehistory of the passage
than about the passage as it is before us.

Robertson [7]) certainly has some right in writing: „Literary criticism by its own elaborations and meticulous subdivisions, has
already done much to upset the whole plan. When you can subdivide

---

[1]) Paper read on the International Meeting of the British Society for Old Testament
Study, Cardiff, Sept. 12th 1946.

[2]) O. Procksch, *KzAT*, Leipzig, 2 and 3 ed., 1924, pp 193s and 372s.

[3]) O. Eiszfeldt, *Die Hexateuchsynopse*, Leipzig 1922; *Stammessage und Novelle in den
Geschichten von Jakob und seinen Söhnen*, Eucharisterion, Göttingen 1923.

[4]) J. Skinner, *ICC*, [2]1930 pp 407s.

[5]) H. Gunkel, *HKzAT*, [3]1910; *Jakob*, Preuszische Jahrbücher, 1919.

[6]) O. Eiszfeldt, *Stammessage* etc., a.c.

[7]) E. Robertson, *BJRL*, Vol. 29 no 1, 1945 p. 23. For the rest this scholar is bringing
but a few data from the O.T. itself for his hypothesis about the origin of the Pentateuch,

your main documents into two, three, four or more ‚hands' the disintegration of the theory comes perilously near." Before him other scholars already put their fingers on the weak points in the documentary theory. But their conceptions about our passage in particular did not solve the difficulties of the recent text satisfactorily. Volz's [1]) acception of one source, the Jahwistical, is just for our passage giving much trouble, while Eerdmans [2]) means to have establish a double communication.

At the time Gunkel [3]) wittily remarked in his comment: „the allegoric declaration of the Christian church, ‚die uns allen ans Herz gewachsen ist' is a clear evidence of the religious strength to appropriate alien goods, give ancient data a new meaning and ‚make gold out of snails'." Not all commentators however from conservative corner honour such an alchemy. Eising [4]) in a circumstantial argument is trying to explain the text by way of the form-historic method, to defend his unity and to establish his place in the whole of narratives. Böhl [5]) is looking for greater association with the documentary theory and supposes an originally mythologic information to become a national tale by folk-etymology and wordplay, which in its turn, was worked up prophetically, religious-ethically.

These contemplations so far agree, that they see in the man, wrestling with Jacob, the one and only God.[6]) This supposition however does not find any support in our text.

Pedersen [7]) also advocates the unity of the passage. In his books however we do not find any detailed treatment of the text. Later on I am going to talk more in particular about his susception of the meaning of the passage.

---

[1]) P. Volz, in: Volz and Rudolph, *Der Elohist als Erzähler, ein Irrweg der Pentateuchkritik? BZAW* 63, 1933, pp. 116s.

[2]) B. D. Eerdmans, *Alttestamentliche Studien*, I, Giessen 1908, pp. 61, 85.

[3]) H. Gunkel, *HKzAT*, ³1910, p. 365.

[4]) H. Eising, *Formgeschichtliche Untersuchung zur Jakoberzählung der Genesis*, Emsdetten 1940. The frame of the supposed „Rahmenerzählung" appears to be much bigger than the story itself!

[5]) F. M. Th. Böhl, *Volksetymologie en Woordspelingen in de Genesisverhalen, Mededeelingen Kon. Akad.*, Amsterdam 1925 and *JPOS*, 1926.

[6]) Comp. G. von Rad, *Das formgeschichtliche Problem des Hexateuchs, BWAuNT*, 4, 26, Stuttgart 1938, pp. 54s. „Die Erzählung Gen. 32, 23ff läszt ja keinen Zweifel daran, dasz in und hinter jenem Gespenst Jahwe an Jacob handelt".

B. Jacob, *Genesis*, Berlin 1934, joins the *misdrash Ber. r.* that concepts the *mal'ak* as the heavenly ruler of Esau. Jacob is wrestling with his guilty past.

[7]) J. Pedersen, *Israel, its life and culture*, London/Copenhagen I/II 1926, p. 524, III/IV 1940, pp. 503s, 716s.

After this short summary of the different handling and conception it becomes me to speak of *some remarks* only. Although I think our insight into the text and his meaning may be enriched by taking style and character of the story as a starting-point of a contemplation of our passage I do not know a satisfying answer to all questions. Nor do I expect you to be persuaded in every way by the remarks to be made by me. I do think however that the here chosen way may open new perspectives.

My thesis is: there is an important argument to be derived from the narratory form for the unity of the narrative; in this way a surmise is justified about the signification and, in relation to Hosea xii, about the connections with other narratives concerning the ancestor Jacob.

I

First some remarks about the narrative in old Israel.

The interest of the literator Gunkel originated especially, according to his well-known comment on Genesis and to his articles about the stories of Jacob and Joseph [1]), with the way of telling, in our narratives only dimly perceptible, but really that of the legend, which has to be accepted after the text known to us. In a sagacious analytical article Eiszfeldt [2]) identified these precursors of our stories, with him originally no legends of the tribes, but novelettes, with the sources of the documentary theory.

The edition of legendary stories from Palestine of the beginning of this century, attended to by Schmidt and Kahle [3]), asked the attention for the story itself. An important article from another field of research, of the Danish scholar Olrik [4]) about the epic laws in the legendary story from 1909 was also fruitfully used in the studies of Schulz [5]) about the art of relating in the Books of Samuel, and of Baumgartner [6]) about the relating style. Baumgartner discerns very clearly the casting vote, which is of the style in the matter of text-critics, exegesis, confirmation of hiatus or adjuncts and

---

[1]) H. Gunkel, in: *ZDMG* 76, 1921.

[2]) O. Eiszfeldt, *a.c.*

[3]) H. Schmidt und P. Kahle, *Volkserzählungen aus Palästina*, Göttingen 1918.

[4]) A. Olrik, *Epische Gesetze der Volksdichtung*, in: *Zeitschr. f. deutsches Altertum und deutsche Literatur*, 51, 1909.

[5]) A. Schulz, *Erzählungskunst in den Samuel-Büchern, Bibl. Zeitfragen* XI, 6/7, Münster i. W. 1923.

[6]) W. Baumgartner, *Ein Kapitel vom hebräischen Erzählungsstil*, in *Eucharisterion*, Göttingen 1923.

source-division. It is remarkable that the source-division is not only made subject to the investigation of style by him, but is mentioned in the last place as well.

Did Baumgartner involve the whole Old Testament in his inquiry Palache [1]) placed his landmarks still more extensive. In his first lecture as professor in Oriental languages at the University of Amsterdam this most estimated member of the Dutch Society for Old Testament Study, who has been murdered by the Germans in 1944, treated the story in the Old Testament in connection with the 'agada, ḥadith and tesh'ita.

When, comparing the characteristics of the story enumerated in these studies, an unanimity strikes us about the impotence of the Oriental for using abstract notions. This may also be the cause that all through the centuries we notice a great love for the story and for the resemblance to word a thought.

The various scholars also much agree about what Olrik called ,,einsträngigkeit'', about being concerned in one object only, where the leading character is drawing nearly all attention. Some of them are speaking of a clear characterstudy of the persons. Others point (and rightly as seems to me) the failing of a real character drawing or personal character development. As to that we can speak of typifying carried out in black/white, where there is no lack of a certain mind for contrasts. Palache, whose study while published in Dutch did not require as much publicity as it should, proved that the story does not know any immutability but is quite open to the reality and tradition. By this freedom and by interest in the detail there are growing inconsequences into the image. Only when the story has become tradition and the idea of the ,,holy writ'' is ripening, the mind for harmonisation arises, whereby can be referred to the corresponding phenomenon with the Moslim theologians with the ḥadith, while the immutability, the stabilisation into one form is coming on.

Relying on some examples I will refer to some, as far as known to me, not quite sufficiently noticed outlines of the Old Testament narrative. The repetition is not always an epic expedient, but also a demonstration of the pleasure, that narrator and audience got from the information. In this way the two first chapters of the first Book of Kings repeat the main subject frequently. This is done to emphasize the main subject, but also to increase the tension. Such

---

[1]) J. L. Palache, *Het karakter van het Oud Testamentische verhaal*, Amsterdam 1925.

a repetition is not servilely literal, but free in choise of words and stage-managing.

There is still said to be a certain rule in the free story. The course of the narrative is often defined by wordplay, punning with the consonants and vowels and associations of other kind. So Gen. xxx 23 and 24 contain a double wordplay: And she conceived, and bare a son: and said, *'elohim* hath taken away — *'asaf* — my reproach: and she called his name Joseph, saying, Jhwh add — *josef* — to me another son.

By using *sham* and *shem* in Gen. xi 1-9 the whole story is concluded: ,,They found a plain in the land of Shinar and they dwelt *there*" — *sham* —, vs 2; ,,Let us make us a name (or token)" — *shem* — vs 4; ,,Let us go down, and there — *sham* — confound their language", vs 7; ,,So Jhwh scattered them abroad from thence" — *sham* — vs 8 and vs 9; ,,Therefore was the name — *shem* — of it called Babel", vs 9. [1])

The story of Jacob's dream in Gen. xxviii 11-19 is partial to the word *makom* whereby the local character of the deity is accented. The xxxii^d chapter of Genesis contains a plural wordplay with the name Mahanaim.

The story sometimes shows a certain closeness, while beginning and end correspond. Gen. iii starts by telling of the snake that ,,he was more subtil than any beast of the field", and ends with the curse, ,,cursed art thou from among all cattle and from among any beast of the field", with a pun *'arum-'arur*. In Gen. xxxii the passage vv 14-22 (Rev. Version vv 13-21) forms such a closed unity, ,,And he lodged there that night", vs 14; and at the end ,,he himself lodged that night in the company", vs 22.

No more than the wordplay as well as the chiasmus are style figures only occurring in the story is the phenomenon of correspondence from beginning to end limited by this kind of literature. So we find, e.g., in Zech. viii 9-13 such a closed unity. After the well-known introducing words of the prophetic message we read, ,,Let your hands be strong" and in vs 13 the same words return as the end of the divine message.

It is commonly known that the gist of a story is often formed by an aphorism or proverb, a rhythmically united entirety. The main contents of the story are often in such aphorisms, the surrounding story being then a kind of relating explanation or application of

---

[1]) P. A. H. de Boer, *Genesis XI* 1-9, in: *Nw. Theol. Stud.*, XXIV, 1941.

the contents of the aphorism. In this way Gen. iii 22s is clearly the explanation with the words, the style of the story what the preceding aphorism of the 'adam is referring to. [1]) Sometimes however it is not be granted whether the aphorism or the story has priority. In addition to this phenomenon we sometimes come upon a short sentence at the beginning of the story that can be characterised as the story in a nutshell. Sometimes such a sentence is lucid, another time it is more like a ḥida, enigma. In Gen. ii 7 we read, ,,And 'elohim formed man of the dust of the ground''. In this verse the following story is typified and narrator and audience already learned the indication of the sad course of the story. The fragilitas of the 'adam made out of earth and who is going to be sent back from the garden with the trees of life to that earth, where he came from, is already coming forth in this first verse concerning the chief person of the story. [2]) We find another example in Gen. xxvii 1, ,,And it came to pass, that when Isaac was old — and his eyes were dim, so that he could not see — he called Esau'' a.s.o. The parenthesis, and his eyes were dim, so that he could not see, is already anticipating the story and here with typifying the coming narrative: namely Isaac calling his son Esau for the blessing is the blind Isaac, the man who is going to be deceived. The leading motive of the stories about Esau and Jacob is already tersely indicated after the news that Rebekah conceived, ,,And the sons struggled together within her''. So the novelette of Joseph is entirely typified by what Gen. xxxix 2 is already alleging to: ,,And Jhwh was with Joseph and he was a prosperous man''. This chapter is a rich example of the characteristics of the Hebrew story as appears from the process of repetition. In several nuances the scene with Potiphar's wife is repeated. And the position of Joseph in the house of Potiphar finds a simular repetition in his position in prison, vv 21s.

The story of Cain and Abel in Gen. iv also possesses such a heading in its first sentence: Eve said, I have gotten the man of the mark of Jhwh''. Jhwh pointed a sign for Cain and therefore it is usual to speak about the sign of Cain. But it is not the sign of Cain, it is the sign of Jhwh *for* Cain. A sign, a token, here and everywhere in the Old Testament comes from the deity and its meaning and value are determined by the deity who is giving it, never by the man who receives the token. I have tried to argument in an article

---

[1]) P. A. H. de Boer, *Het verhaal van den hof in Eden*, Leiden 1941, pp. 15s.

[2]) P. A. H. de Boer, *ibidem*.

in 1942 that we must read *ḳaniti 'ish 'ot-Jhwh* and not *'et-Jhwh.* [1])
The end of the story brings the solution of this enigmatic heading.

We often come across such anticipations. So they often form an
interrogative sentence, which at the same time is mentioning the
answer. [2]) Look at, e.g. David's inquiring of Jhwh in 2 Sam. ii 1,
,,Shall I go up into any of the cities of Judah? And Jhwh said unto
him, Go up''. Gen. xix 12 ,,And the men said unto Lot, Hast thou
here any besides? son in law, and thy sons, and thy daughters...''.
This prolepsis in the line of thoughts is of the same kind as the
mentioning of an order without mentioning the execution where of
particularly Baumgartner in his already mentioned article enumerates clear examples. In the story of the messenger who comes to
tell the death of Saul and Jonathan to David, 2 Sam. i, we come
upon the question for giving new details to the story, e.g., vs 5,
,,And David said unto the young man that told him, How knowest
thou that Saul and Jonathan his son be dead?'' whereupon the
details follow. I want to give another example of pregnant and
anticipating use of a word predominating the coming story. In Gen.
xxix 4 Jacob addresses the shepherds at the well in the field as
,,My brethren'', אחי, although he does not even know who they are.
In the family relation however is the nucleus of the tale, compare
vv 10, 12, 14 and 15. Jacob is Laban's brother, Laban said to him,
Surely thou art my bone and my flesh.

With good reason the play-character of the story is pointed to.
A story is acted as a play by every narration. Therefrom we often
find the dialogue with the relating explanations of fixed gists. In
the vivid delineation the direct oration is very popular.

I think there is some sense in remarking at the details which often
add lustre to the story by this vivid forming, that the problem of
historicity of such stories does not get a positive answer by such
details. In the evolution of the stories, e.g. in the *midrash*, we just
see the details increase. Do compare the love for detail in the least
historical of the four Gospels, the Gospel according to S. John.
During the years of our occupation, when the story, carried orally,
again acted a big part in our primitive society, I myself witnessed
such a legend-formation round a true happening. During an arrest

---

[1]) P. A. H. de Boer, *Kain en Abel*, in: *Nw. Theol. Tijdschr.*, XXXI, 1942.
[2]) Cf. J. Wellhausen, *Reste arabischen Heidentums*, Zweite Ausgabe, Neudruck Berlin
und Leipzig 1927, S. 132 ,,Die Fragen enthalten immer zugleich die Antwort'' — on
asking for an oracle.

I happily escaped at the occupiers. When two months later I heard the story of this escapation from someone, it appeared to be almost all fiction except the fact of escapation, with for an outsider credible details however.

II

After this short contemplation of the story I want to put before you a translation of the passage Gen. xxxii 23-33 whereby I accounted for the fact whether the outlines of the story provide us with a new light in some of the cruces of this well-known pericope.

23   And he rose up and took his two wives and his two women-servants and his eleven children and passed over the ford (of) Jabbok;

24   — that is: he took them and sent them over the brook and sent over that he had, —

25a   thus Jacob remained behind alone.

וַיָּקָם in vs 23, followed by a waw consecutive, points out the beginning of the action, mentioned by the following verb. It does not indicate in this construction the rising out of a sitting or lying position. I have omitted the corrupted expression בְּלַיְלָה הוּא that severs the combination וַיָּקָם וַיִּקַּח. בְּלַיְלָה הוּא I think an inaccurate dittography out of vs 22, that has maintained its position in the tradition, because the fight of our narration takes place before the coming of dawn, perhaps too as a secondary link with what precedes. By this restoration we get away from the difficulty: an improbable crossing of the ford by night with family, flocks a.s.o. Skinner in his comment, o.c., already has remarked the insufficientness of Wellhausen's explanation: by apprehension of an attack of Esau. Jacob put his people and possessions on that side of the river on which they were exposed to attack!

Vs 24 cannot be read as an independent one. It goes into details of the tale. The two principal verbs — not קוּם! — of vs 23 are repeated and used more exactly to the point, while also Jacob's possessions are mentioned.

These two verses end into the information aimed at by the narrator: Jacob is alone in the coming story. The vv are clearly meant to be an introduction. They do not call the principal person of our narration, who is the subject of their verbs. They hurry on towards the information of Jacob remaining alone. And at the end of his narration the narrator neither mentions Jacob's reunion with his family and possessions. Such introductory vv do not possess an independent narrative quality of their own and must not be understood as an historian record *verbatim*, but only *ad sensum*.

So we know three facts, the place of the scene, Jabbok; the principal character of the drama, Jacob; and his position, alone. After this the proper story begins.

25*b*   And a man wrestled with him until the coming of the dawn.
26   When he saw then that he prevailed not against him, he touched
          the hollow of his thigh;
          and the hollow of Jacob's thigh was hit
          as he wrestled with him.

Here we have the summary of the story. In the first words we have the heading sentence, the title that brings the tale in a nutshell: וַיֵּאָבֵק אִישׁ. In these words, a man wrestled, the name Isra'el is heard. The *'ish* is indicated as *'el*. Besides that the unusual verb אבק is chosen on account of an association with Jabbok and Jacob, to which is repeatedly pointed, a synonym is found in it of שָׂרָה as well as of עקב. Thus the verb in this expression וַיֵּאָבֵק אִישׁ is the connective link with Jacob and Isra'el. And the identification of these two names is the leading motive of our narration. The name Jacob must have had to the ears of narrator and audience the meaning: he who comes last and nevertheless becomes first. Noth [1]) and other scholars take for granted on ground of etymologic derivations that the name originally meant, (God) may protect. Although the original meaning may not leave us indifferent, for our purpose, the conceiving of the narrator's meaning, is it much more important which associations the narrator and his audience have by the name. They associate with the substantive עֲקֵב, Gen. xxv 26, and with the verb וַיַּעְקְבֵנִי Gen. xxvii 36. Jacob is the second-comer who is successor, comp. the Arabic *'akb* that also means, son, successor; but this second-comer is becoming the strongest one by deception. He hold on Esau's heel. It appears from Jer. ix 3 that the stem עקב is considered a parallel of the stem רכל, to act as a רכיל, a pedlar, to go about with slanders.

As for the stem שָׂרָה Nöldeke [2]) supposed a connection with the Arabic stem *sharıja*, to be brisk, lively, sly. The same Arabic stem has forms with the meaning to quarrel, to answer back, and, to

---

[1]) M. Noth, *Die israelitischen Personennamen im Rahmen der gemeinsemitischen Namengebung*, Stuttgart 1928.
[2]) Th. Nöldeke, *Neue Beiträge z. sem. Sprachw.*, Strassburg 1910, p. 75, note 3.

sell. Here we are in the sphere of the oriental world of commerce. Slyness, a little boasting and impudence are characteristics of the pedlar, the marketman and salesman. He acts aggressively, he quarrels with his clients and he often gets the better of them.

„And a man wrestled." Herewith the story is straightly tersely indicated. To the insider the unknown *'ish* is herewith already indicated as an *'el*. There are no arguments to possibly decide whether an old story about a fight of Jacob is the cause for the name identification or the wordplay with existing names produced the story of the fight, such as is left to us. The essential place of the wordplays in our passage makes me suspect, that the second possibility is more likely to be the right one than the one first mentioned.

The vv 25b and 26 are closely linked together. Beginning and end correspond and so do the two intermediate sentences. This strong construction makes a distribution over sources improbable.

I will still make some suggestions on a few words out of this principal sentence of our passage.

The fight lasts until the coming of the dawn. It is pretty commonly known that an indication of the nature of the *'ish* can be read here. The *'el* appearing at the river Jabbok should be a nightspirit who fears the dawn. This is possibly right but as our story has come down to us the remark about the coming of the dawn and also the night being the time of the fight, has another meaning. The coming of the dawn is a computation of the time, working as a tensile element in vs 27. The *'ish* already presumes the in the gist announced end of the wrestling. Should Jacob succeed in earning a victory? The end of the fight is already in sight! And the night as time of the fight can hardly be anything else than the augmentation of the thought of Jacob's critical position: he is not only alone but it is night as well. The dangerous situation, where Jacob is in, cannot be drawn more sharply. The night is the time of distress. The sun, rising at Jacob's passing of Pni'el, is the sign of his rescue from death.

The verb יקע is nowadays often rendered by ‚to be strained'. Jacob represents himself again in this meeting with a by nature more powerful adversary as the clever fellow, the sly dog, who knows to lay hold of a victory. Thus he got the better of Esau, of Isaac, of Laban. The *'ish* acknowledges Jacob's clever strength. This acknowledgement consists of the touching of Jacob's thigh, by which he becomes a touched, a struck one. Jacob is a *baruk*, look at his thigh, he has a limp. The *'el* sacred, consecrated his thigh. The verb יקע also has this cultic meaning in the Hiph. in Numb. xxv 4 and 2 Sam. xxi 6 and 9, Hoph. vs 13. The rendering of these verbs by 'to hang up' as well as by ,to throw down' does not find any support in the stems akin to our verb, נקע; תקע, to knock; רקע, to stamp, to beat; בקע ,to break through, to split; פקע, to split, to break forth. Comp. also קעקע Lev. xix 28, cuttings in your flesh. In Numb. xxv and 2 Sam. xxi it is about: sacrificing, where the sacrificed are all dedicated, without being buried, to the deity. Jeremia, vi 8, and Ezechiel xxiii 17 and 18, use the Kal of the verb with מן and מעל. The usual meaning, to depart from, in my opinion does not fit very well. The *nephesh* of Jhwh was hit, whereupon he acts against the people, see Jer. vi 11 and 12; against Jerusalem, Ez. xxiii, because they have sinned. In the same way Jerusalem's *nephesh* is kindled because of Babel's allurements, Ez. xxiii 17.

Jacob's thigh is Jacob's progeny. Comp. the remark of Van Arendonk, to be found at Pedersen [1]), Der Eid bei den Semiten p. 151, who פחד יצחק explained with the Arabic *faḥid*, thigh, clan.

After this summary of the narration follows its explanation in a vivid dialogue. The vv 27-30 bring the ins and outs and the meaning of the story.

27   And he said, Let me go, for the day breaketh.
        But the other said, I will not let thee go unless thou giveth me a blessing.
28   Then he said to him, What is thy name?
        Jacob, said the other.
29   Whereupon he said, Thy name shall be called no more Jacob but Isra'el, for thou strove with *'elohim* — and with men — and prevailed.
30   And Jacob asked as follows, Tell me, I pray thee, thy name.
        But he said, Wherefore is it that thou dost ask after my name?
        So he blessed him there.

The dialogue raises the tensity of our tale: Will Jacob get his blessing? The *'ish* calls already the end of the fight, the break of day! But Jacob holds on.

The asking after the name is an introductory question, meant to give the possibility to what is coming and to direct the attention

---

[1]) J. Pedersen, *Der Eid bei den Semiten*, Strassburg 1910, p. 151.

on what is following. ‚And with men' may be a growth of the narration — not yet known in Hosea's days, see below — or a growth of the text.

Jacob's asking after the name of the *'ish* is a repetition, however with a meaning of its own. It will be an introduction to the answer of the *'ish*. This answer is a warning not to do it. The question of Jacob is the question of the auditory, curious of the name of the *'el*. The narrator shows some hesitation to identify this *'el* with Jhwh. It is better not to ask after my name, the *'el* is made to say. If this opinion is right this verse is of the time of identification of the gods of the patriarchal stories with Jhwh.

‚So he blessed him there', the end of verse 30, recapitulates what precedes. The use of the little word שָׁם, there, shows evidently that this short final sentence relates to the whole preceding story of the Jabbok. This very little word gives occasion to the name-giving of the place, the *shem* Pni'el.

31 Then Jacob called the name of the place Pni'el, for I have seen an *'elohim* face to face and my life preserved.

32 And the sun rose as he passed over Pnu'el and, behold, he had a limp in his thigh.

33 Therefore the sons of Isra'el do not eat the weak nerve, which is upon the hollow of the thigh, unto this day, because he touched the hollow of Jacob's thigh, the weak nerve. [1]

The meaning of the name Pni'el will have been sufficient occasion to mention it in addition to this story. Its position at the other side of the Jordan may have assisted in this addition.

הַצֹּלֵעַ is the one who comes last. Micha, iv 6, and Sephanja, iii 9, use the expression parallel to הַנִּדְחָה, the one who is driven away. It is as though the narrator likes to say, Mark you, I pray thee, what is improbable, here becomes a reality: Jacob, the last comer, the limping, becomes, yea *is* Isra'el, the bearer of blessing, the conqueror, the גְּבִיר (Gen. xxvii 37).

The thigh bears the token of the blessing. Therefore Jacob's progeny does not eat this touched, this consecrated part.

This local deity cannot easily be identified with Jhwh. Therefore it is also comprehensible that this food-taboo is not handed down in the orthodox documents of Jhwhism.

---

[1] The precise meaning of גִּיד הַנָּשֶׁה is uncertain. I suppose that the word contains the stem אָנַשׁ, to be weak. Comp. the Syriac rendering *gᵉjada dᵉneshaja nervus muliebris*.

The story forms in itself a whole. The principal idea of the equalization of Jacob and Isra'el is winning through by means of this narration.

Before I make some more remarks on the meaning of the passage and on its place in the stories about Jacob ,I must call your attention to the twelfth chapter of Hosea, where we find an evident quotation of our passage.

III

A quotation of a place is already of itself an information of great value, the more so as the quotation is to be found in a scripture to be dated with certainty. But even this rose has thorns. We perceive this when trying to give a translation of Hosea xii 4 and 5.

4 (*a*)   In the womb he had hold on the heel of his brother;
           (or: he overreached his brother)

  (*b*)   in his prime he strove with an *'elohim,*

5   namely he strove with a *mal'ak* and prevailed;

  (*c*)   he wept
           and he made supplication to him, in Bet'el he found grace,
           for there he spake with him.

There are a lot of difficulties in these few lines. It is no time now to enter upon many questions. [1]) The question especially holding our attention is whether or not Hosea has known another recension of our story. Skinner accepts in his comment, that we already find in Hosea a still more refined interpretation of what the Jahwist and the Elohist have given when they have the story incorporated in the national epos as part of the history of Jacob and made the local deity to Jhwh.

Procksch [2]) takes the liberty to lift out of Hosea all he can use for a reconstruction of a Jhwhistical and Elohistical story. Why should you take on about the Hoseanic text giving more in a comment on Genesis? I want to respect all liberties, but I cannot succeed with this one. This mutilation of the Hoseanic text in order to change the sense of the passage in Genesis and to restore the supposed old documents J and E creates a new problem: Hosea in his

---

[1]) I like to refer to Th. C. Vriezen, *Hosea* 12, in: *Nw. Theol. Stud.*, xxiv, 1941, and: *La tradition de Jacob dans Osée xii*; in: *OTS*, I, Leiden 1942. Cp. also I. Engnell, *Israel and the law*, *Symb. Bibl. Upsal.* 7, Uppsala 1946, pp. 28 s., who brings an other suggestion on Hos. xii, 5.

[2]) O. Procksch, *o.c.*

days has been able to quote with just a word a story about Jacob so that this story must have been commonly known at that time. Why should this story, which to the opinion of most people is dealing with a weeping and imploring for grace at the Jabbok give place to our story in Genesis, that does not know any weeping Jacob?

I think that the use of the verba in Hos. xii 4 and 5 suggests us the means to discern the quotations of the prophet. Hosea calls, in my opinion, special attention to three events out of Jacob's life. These three events he quotes with a verb in the perfect. After the perfect verb of the last two quotations he adds consecutive subordinate sentences with imperfecta. The third quotation is clearly mentioning the name of place Bet'el. [1]) Jacob wept — perhaps בכה possesses a connection with the אלון בכות out of Gen. xxxv, 8 — and implored for ḥen, grace. The following verb continues this thought. מצא חן repeatedly occurs in the stories about Jacob. Gen. xxx 27, xxxii 6, xxxiii 8, 10, 15, xxxiv 11. Does not it go without saying that the suffix of ימצאנו should be conceived as this grace for which Jacob implored? In the passage Gen. xxxv Jacob finds grace in Bet'el. As appears from the end of Gen. xxxiv Jacob is in imminent danger, at the beginning of Gen. xxxv the most radical measures are taken, the gods are buried and refuge is taken with the 'el of Bet'el. This 'el of Bet'el is talking to him, xxxv 11 and 15. [2])

The god of Bet'el is in the eyes of Hosea the god of the House of Idolatry. He connects the deceit of the people, ,,They make a covenant with Assyria, and oil is carried into Egypt'', vs 1, with the cult in Bet'el. The god of Bet'el is the god of Jacob who overreached his brother, who strove with an 'el, who wept and asked for grace in Bet'el. Just like the idol is a god who is not reliable, just so the people of the cult of this god are not trustworthy.

Hosea must have known an order of stories about Jacob and must have been able to suppose this known by his audience. In this order the passage at the Jabbok had its place and that before the story of Jacob's return to Bet'el.

---

[1]) In spite of the studies much worth to be read of R. Dussaud, *Les Origines cananéennes du Sacrifice Israélite*, Paris 1921, and of O. Eiszfeldt, *Der Gott Bethel*, in: *AfRW*, xxviii, 1930 I am not convinced that there consisted a God named 'House of 'el.

[2]) I translate, as G, 'with him', but I do not alter the masoretic text. I suppose, with reservation, that we must read עמנו, ʿimmennu, as an intentional similarity in sound with ימצאנו. We also find -an- in the prepositions min-an-hu ממנו and taḥt-an-ha תחתנה, Gen. ii 21.

The prophet denies that Jacob's god is Jhwh. He has, therefore, known stories about Jacob without the god Jhwh. He declaims against the syncretism popular already in his days, which identifies the god of Moses with the gods of the patriarchs.

IV

Cassuto [1]) thinks our passage in Gen. xxxii to be an example of the later entry of Isra'el into Canaan, and of the fight against the gods of Canaan. Pedersen [2]) also means that the position of our passage is conditioned by the fact that the fight must take place before Jacob enters Canaan. On Hos. xii he says, „The prophet knew a story like this with a few different features. Curiously enough the prophet uses it as an accusation against the people". Pedersen thinks that our story is a reminiscence of stories of the fight of Jhwh against the *Ba'alim* of Canaan. Jacob should act here in virtue of Jhwh's protection. 'A wrestling contest with the God who appeared in the border country settled the matter, and everything was then put into the hands of Jacob.'

With this conception Hosea's attitude remains not only curious, but utterly incomprehensible. This difficulty disappears when the non-Jhwhistic character of our passage is admitted. Hosea just quotes our story as one of the arguments of non-Jhwhistic religious practices. Moreover our passage does not mention the name of Jhwh.

The *'el* with whom Jacob was wrestling creates by the blessing a lasting cult. It should be incomprehensible that the trace, the token of the conquered God becomes a lasting cult-object amongst the Jhwhistic believers.

Our recension of the first Bible must be of a time when a mild syncretism identified the family gods as well as the local Canaanitic gods with Jhwh. An interlude in the cyclus about Esau and Jacob like our passage from Gen. xxxii keeps some outlines of an older picture of Isra'el's religious life which by means of the data from the 8th century of Hosea vaguely shows.

August 1946

---

[1]) U. Cassuto, *La Questione della Genesi*, Firenze 1934.
[2]) J. Pedersen, *Israel, o. et l.c.*

3

SOME REMARKS ON EXODUS XXI 7—11
The Hebrew Female Slave

The beginning of Ex. xxi regulates the privileges which the Hebrew slave enjoyed above those enjoyed by the slave of foreign origin. Privileges which are shown in the possibility of freedom after a certain fixed time. What now follows deals with the position of the female Hebrew slave with regard to these privileges. For her other rules must be followed as her position differed from that of the male slave. The female slave is not only a worker for her master, but as a woman she is also his property. The master can take her as his wife, vv. 8 and 10; he can also give her in marriage to his son, vs. 9; or to one of his slaves, without thereby losing his rights of property, vs. 4.

As a Hebrew the female slave possesses certain fixed rights. These are enumerated in Ex. xxi 8—11. They consist of two ways in which the slave can become free, by payment of a ransom and by non payment of a ransom; and of a regulation of the treatment of the slave who has been used as a wife.

Whenever the slave ceases to find favour in the eyes of her master, he can sell her. But if the slave is a Hebrew, he does not possess unlimited freedom in this respect. He is bound to sell her to her family. The use here, vs. 8, of the verb פדה, to redeem, is very clear. The girl returns to her family as the result of payment; either the father pays the ransom or a ransomer. This is emphasized very clearly in the second part of the 8th verse. In the events here discussed the master of the slave may not sell her to a strange family. In my opinion עם means here, as we often find, family, *gens*. The Targumim translate and explain עם נכרי with גבר אוחרן.

In the tenth and eleventh verses the second possibility of gaining her freedom is discussed. If after some time the master takes a second wife, the Hebrew slave who has been used as wife must continue to share the privileges of the wives. And as secondary wife she keeps her rights to food, clothing (shelter), and ענה, rights which are specially mentioned. ענה is a *hapax legomenon*. Neither etymology nor synonym gives an accurate translation of this word. Following up the ancient versions the usual translation is sexual intercourse, conjugal rights. The stem ענה, to mind, meddle with, is supposed here. The observation in Gesenius—Buhl's Dictionary, that in thus translating it we are rather deriving it from the stem ענה in the Pi., "forcing a marriage upon", is not quite clear. From the meaning "forcibly dishonoured" to "conjugal rights" is more than one step. Albert Schultens' conjectures on this passage, in his *Animadversiones philologicae et criticae ad varia loca Veteris Testamenti* 1709, are still fascinating. Schultens points to the Arabic stem عَوِنَ which means, to help; and on this ground he translates ענה by *auxilium*. And he adds that in this sense it is often used in Arabic to indicate at the same time conjugal duty. He refers to עזר כנגדו, Gen. ii 18 and 20. Schultens reads as the Onkelos' Targum עונתה, *plenum*.

If the master does not give the slave her full rights, no duty rests on her family to pay the ransom. This also holds good for the ransomer, so that she can return to her home without any payment being made.

We have seen thus how the Hebrew girl has to be treated when she is at the same time the wife of her master. She has also the right to a fixed favourable treatment when she has been given in marriage by him to his son. By this arrangement of her master she shares the rights of a daughter and in this case too strict account is taken of the fact that she is a Hebrew.

The translation and explanation of the 8th verse, that treats of the ransoming of the female slave, are more difficult than the above would lead to believe. The Masoretic text runs as follows

אם־רעה בעיני אדניה אשר־לא יעדה והפדה לעם נכריﬦלא־ימשל למכרה בבגדו־בה

Many scholars are of opinion that the denial לא before יעדה should be altered to לו, so the Greek and Aramaic translations, and they translate the parenthetic clause אשר־לו יעדה by "who has set her aside for himself". Others make a radical alteration by reading the verb ידע instead of the verb יעד, Budde in ZAW 1891, and many others after him. Still others find it necessary to leave out the negative too, Robertson Smith in ZAW 1892, and others after him.   We have not found any text-critical foundation for these alterations.

Scholars consequently argue over the original reading with the supposed meaning of the sentence as foundation.   At the end of the verse one uses to say that a moral judgement is pronounced on the behaviour of the master of the slave in the words בבגדו־בה. The above expression is causally translated, "since he has been unfaithful to her".   Here we have the starting point for various suppositions regarding the moral behaviour of the slaveholder which would be criticised in our text.   These suppositions are the base of the alterations in the text.   Such a starting point allows various views !

The liberation of the Hebrew male slave in the preceding pericope, however, does not depend on the moral behaviour of the master.   Besides the difficulty of deciding which criteria must be applied by the judging of this behaviour, it does not seem to me necessary that we should explain our text in this moral way. Our chapter judges neither the keeping of slaves, nor the taking of a slave as wife, nor the giving of her as wife to another member of the household.   And so far as I can see neither does it judge the case in which a master repudiates his slave wife.   It only decides how in such a case a slave who is a Hebrew girl must be treated.

If these presumptions are correct, it would be useful to restudy the above text.   The verb יעד means "to keep in doing something", "to appoint", "to assign", "to declare indissoluble".   2 Sam. xx 5 informs us that Amasa has not been successful in mobilizing Juda within the fixed time, וייחר מן־המועד אשר יעדו.   JHWH's sword, according to Jer. xlvii 7, does not rest but remains by the orders of him, aimed at, or in—cp. Numb. x 3 and 4, and Neh. vi 10—, the city Askelon and the coast.   So JHWH's rod remains in the city for the judgement, Mic. vi 9. Corresponding with this meaning the Nif. means "to show itself somewhere", "to appear in public", "to reveal", Ex. xxv 22, a.o. ; said of many, "to come together", Josh. xi 5, a.o.   And in the Hif. it means, "to make fixed regulations with regard to", Jer. xlix 19 = l 44 מי כמוני ומי יעידני," Who is like unto me and who makes fixed regulations with regard to me ?" ; and Job ix 19, where, as if to make it more clear, has been added למשפט. Ex. xxi 9 uses the same verb to express the arrangement of the master with regard to the slave destined as a wife for his son.

The first part of our verse can thus be paraphrased as follows : If she ceases to please her master, who therefore does not keep her, then he must see that she is ransomed.

The subordinate clause אשר־לא יעדה explains what the result is of the main verb. The master finds her no longer pleasing and so keeps her no longer. The displeasure is of such a nature that he keeps her no longer in his house. Both verbs are necessary to explain the situation. The master puts away his slave. But because she is a Hebrew, he cannot sell her to all and sundry, he can only cause her to be ransomed. He must see that she returns to her fathers house in payment of a ransom.

אם וג׳־והפדה, I render with : If ..., then ..., cp. vs. 3, If he is a married man, then goes his wife with him, אם־ויצאה; and vs. 11, And if he denies her ..., then she shall be free, ואם־ויצאה.

The second part of the verse gives us no new ideas on the subject but only stresses the first. The last words בבגדו־בה do not lead our thoughts to a new chapter, the moral behaviour of the master of the slave, but keep to the subject of our and the prece peri-cope, that of the liberation of the Hebrew slaves. The expression, in my opinion, has no causal meaning. ב before the Infinitive has, as usual, a temporary meaning. The verb בגד means, "to break a contract", "to dissolve", "not to keep in doing some-thing". Naturally the breaking of a contract is usually condemned. But the verb בגד itself has not always such a condemnatory mean-ing. In Judg. ix 23 it is 'elohim who sends a spirit of calamity, a "bad" spirit, to bring about a rupture. Perhaps in Hab. ii 5 we find the literal meaning, היין בוגד גבר יהיר ולא ינוה, "The wine makes the reckless man unsteady and he does not reach his goal". I think the word בגד, "dress", "mantle", the covering which is changeable and covering, is connected with the same stem. The meaning "to deceive" is closely connected with this.

The verb בגד expresses, in my opinion, in our text the same meaning as לא יעד, "to break the bond", "not to keep it up". A connection, a contract is broken. In our text the master breaks the contract with his female slave. No mention is here made about his right to do so. His right to do so is admitted without comment. What is fixed is what he must take care for, when he ends the contract in this way, especially when the girl is a Hebrew. For this reason I think the end of the 8th verse must be translated thus : when he breaks the contract with her, *id est* when he puts her away.

This second part of our verse codifies emphatically the right of the Hebrew female slave : the purchased girl remains under the *potestas* of her own father, the master was forbidden from selling her to a strange family.

Here follows a translation of our passage, on the base of the preceding remarks.

7 And if a man sells his daughter as a slave, she cannot be liberated as the male slaves can.

8 If she ceases to please to her master, who does not keep her, then he must see that she is ransomed.
To a strange family he may not sell her, when he breaks his contract with her.

9 And if he decides to marry her to his son, he shall deal with her after the manner of daughters.

10 If he takes a second wife, he may not diminish her food, her clothes and her conjugal rights (?).

11 And if he denies her these three, then she shall be free, without ransom, without payment.

April 1946

4
AN INSCRIPTION FROM ṢOᶜAR

The ruins of Ṣoᶜar are near the village of Ghor eṣ-Ṣāfī, south-south-east of the Dead Sea, at the foot of the mountains of Moab. The region differs from the other coastal areas of the Dead Sea only by its width, just like the plain north of the see. The plain stretches far into the south. It lies some 1150 feet below Mediterranean level. Stones and bumps filled with pitch stand out on the dull grey earth. But here and there one's attention is caught by bushes, sometimes of a bright green colour, which form a surprising contrast with their surroundings. There one finds freshwater springs that already in Antiquity lent attraction to both the shores of the Dead Sea and those of the Sea of Tiberias. I may mention only Herod's countryseat on the Moabite shore of the Dead Sea. Some sources produce hot water and are visited by people who want to be cured of their illnesses.

The presence of spring water and possibly also irrigation from the surrounding mountain country make it not unlikely that these regions were once more densely populated than they are nowadays. Tradition refers to city states; among these is Ṣoᶜar. According to Gen. xiii 10, before Yhwh had destroyed Sodom and Gomorra, the Jordan region was well watered, "like the garden of Yhwh, like the land of Egypt, in the direction of Ṣoᶜar." The king of Ṣoᶜar, then still called Belaᶜ, belongs to the alliance of five monarchs who go to war against the four kings of Gen. xiv. A battle in the plain, the Valley of Siddim near the Salt Sea, ends in their defeat. Through the plain (which is full of pitch) they flee into the mountains. In the narrative about the destruction of Sodom and Gomorra in Gen. xix, Ṣoᶜar, "The small one", occurs as the place where Lot seeks refuge but dares not stay after all. He goes further eastward, into the mountains of Moab. In the Books of Isaiah and Jeremiah, Ṣoᶜar is mentioned as a place in Moab (xv 5 and xlviii 34 respectively), and it serves to indicate the border of the land shown to Moses on Nebo (Deut. xxxiv 3).

In May 1953 I had the opportunity to travel in several regions near the Dead Sea; among those were parts of Moab. In the new National Museum in Amman[1], the then director of the Jordanian

---

[1] After Jerusalem (al-Quds) had become a border town for the kingdom of Jor-

Department of Antiquities, G. LANKASTER HARDING, showed me a stone with an inscription from Ṣoᶜar. HARDING also showed me a photograph of the stone, telling me that G.R. DRIVER would be publishing the text in the second volume of the *Annual of the Department of Antiquities*. A few weeks ago DRIVER's edition of the text was indeed published.[2] As HARDING permitted me to study the inscription at Amman, I am now able to compare my conclusions with DRIVER's. In the Israelite section of Jerusalem, about a month after my stay at Amman, I learnt that the Jewish archaelogist E.L. SUKENIK had edited the inscription together with two other ones in 1945.[3] Here follows a translation of the stone from Amman, which I shall use to state at what points I agree or disagree with other transcribers and translators. The stone with the inscription edited by COWLEY was discovered in 1925 by H.St.J.B. PHILBY. It was in the possession of inhabitants of Ghor es-Safi, who told him that it had been found among the ruins of Qasr al-Tuba. There is an elaborate report by W.F. ALBRIGHT in *BASOR* 14 (1924) about the expedition to Moab and the Dead Sea, which among other things drew scholarly attention to the inscription discussed here.

The stone from Amman, then, bearing the number J376, is 9.45 inches high by 7 inches wide and 1.9 inches thick. It is of a rather hard type of sandstone found locally. The inscription is outlined in red. Just like the other two mentioned above, it is an epitaph.

---

dan, Amman became its capital. The admirable enthusiasm with which in this young state people study the long past of its territory has resulted in the creation of a new museum besides the well-known Palestine Archaeological Museum in Jerusalem. It is conducted by a board of trustees of which the Director of the Department of Antiquities is a member. Ammon, Moab, and almost the whole of Old Testament Israel are part of Jordan.

[2] *Annual of the Department of Antiquities of Jordan* 2 (1953), pp. 64f.

[3] In the second instalment of *Kedem*, Jerusalem, 1945, a periodical (in Ivrit) which since then has ceased to appear. This instalment contains a number of other articles about these inscriptions, one of which will be quoted below. The *Annual* shows a photograph of two stones, as does *Kedem* (plate 6). A.E. COWLEY was the first to edit the text of one of the three stones (not the one discussed here), in *Pal. Expl. Fund Quarterly Statement* 1925, pp. 207–210. About this stone, see also S. DAICHES in the same periodical in 1926, pp. 31f. (The photographs which originally illustrated the article were taken by Dr H.J. Franken, Professor de Boer's travelling companion. They are replaced by a photograph recently taken by Dr G. van der Kooij. Editor's note).

Text	*Translation*
hdh npšh	1. This is the gravestone
dʾstr brth	2. of Esther, daughter
dᶜdyw dmytt	3. of 'Idyo, who died
byrḥ šbt	4. in the month of Sebat
dšth g dšmṭh	5. of the third year of the year-week
šnt tlt mʾ	6. the three hundredth-
mw šnyn lḥrbn	7. and forty-sixth year of the years since the destruction
byt mqdšh	8. of the Sanctuary.
šlwm šlwm	9. Peace, peace.
(?) *nwlh*	10. (?) dishonourable.

5. SUKENIK erroneously *šnt*; his commentary, however, has the correct reading. DRIVER instead of *dšmṭh*: *wšbᶜ(yn)*, on account of the dating problem. The reading *dšmṭh*, however, is certain and supported moreover by the parallel expression on the other two stones.
7. *mw* with CASSUTO, *Kedem* ii. SUKENIK and DRIVER read *mn*.
10. SUKENIK: *ʾᶜlt*; DRIVER: *slh*.
Attention may be drawn to the final letter *h* in *npšh*, *brth*, *šmṭh*, *mqdšh*, which here clearly indicates the *status emphaticus*. Cf. CIS, vol. II, Nr. 162 *npšh dy ḥmrt dy bnh lh ʾdynt bᶜlh*; the Greek text of this is Ὀδαιναθος Ἀννηλου ὠἰκοδόμησεν τὴν στήλην χαμράτῃ τῇ αὑτοῦ γυναικί. Nr. 4210:

npšh dnh dy ḥlʾ br
nbwzbd br kyly ḥbl
bšnt   548
byrḥ sywn ywm   18

RES 1265 *yhwdh br ʾbh*; RES 1868 *ʾbh*. LIDZBARSKI, *Ephem.* I, p. 205 spells the name with ʾaleph: *br ʾbʾ*. In *Ber. Rabba* again *ʾbh* x 8; xi 6; in both cases there is a variant reading *ʾbʾ*. Other examples from *Ber. Rabba*: *šqph*, xii 9; *rʾ ywdn nšyʾh* xii 10. See also JASTROW, *Dictionary of the Targumim*, s.v. *nšyyʾ*, var. *nšyyh*. From the texts recently found in Murabbaᶜat: line 2 of the contract *lyšwᶜ bn glgwlʾ* and in the letter *glglh*. The meaning "gravestone", "monument", of the word *næpæš* was already known, see e.g. B.D. EERDMANS, *The Religion of Israel*, Leiden, 1947, p. 311.
The reading of the last word is uncertain. It does not stick to the

regular line and may have been added later. Is it the term of abuse *dégénérée*? (*nwlh* = *nblh*.)

The inscription is dated in two ways. It mentions the month and the year of the group of seven years or week of years called *šᵉmiṭṭâ*, as well as the number of years that has passed since the destruction of the Second Temple. SUKENIK and DRIVER read the first word of the seventh line as *min*. The second date then becomes "the three-hundredth year of the years since the destruction of the Sanctuary". This creates the problem of a difference between the two indicated dates. According to Jewish chronology, the destruction of the Second Temple is to be dated in the year 68/69 of the Christian era. The "300th year since the destruction" would then be the year 368/69 AD. The first date mentions the third year of a week of years. Here the year 68/69 AD can serve as a point of reference, being a sabbatical year. Starting from that one would have to date the stone not in 368/69, but in 356/66, as calculated by DRIVER. This difference makes him suspicious of the first date. Although he admits to some uncertainties in his reading, he assumes that in line 5 one might read "and seventy" (*wšbᶜ[yn]*) instead of "of the week of years". To me this seems impossible, not only because the text offers better support for the reading *dšmṭh* note the *daleth* and the *teth*, both clearly visible even on the photograph), but also because of the existing parallels: the other two funerary inscriptions both have the reading *šᵉmiṭṭâ* in a twofold dating as well. Moreover the expression *min šᵉnin* is very odd, as is also pointed out by DRIVER.

The lines of the inscription all begin at the same distance from the outlining, except line 7. Before the letter *mem* there is space for another character. The letter after the *mem* does not have the usual form of the *nun*. I think, therefore, that the suggestion made by CAS-SUTO's gives the correct reading of the first word of line 7. He thinks that there was a *waw* before the *mem* and that one should read *wmw*, which is the indication of a number: "and 46". This removes the strange reading *min šᵉnin* and makes the two dates compatible with each other. It is the fiftieth week of years after the destruction of the Second Temple, and the third year of it, that is, 343 + 3 = 346 years, or 49 full Year-weeks, plus three years. So the dying day of Esther, Idyo's daughter, was in the month of Sebat of the year 414 – 15. According to the Mishnaic tractate Rosh Hashanah I i the beginning of a week of years is also the beginning of a Jewish year, in the month of Tishri. The years after the destruction start on the ninth of Ab. So Esther must have died around February 415. About Esther nothing further is known.[4] The way in which her father or husband dated her death gives rise to a few observations about the sabbatical year. The custom of dating from a far-reaching event is found in many ages and among many nations. I could refer to the dating found in Amos i 1: "two years before the earthquake", and to that of our own time: in "such-and-such a year after the War". For the Jewish people, the destruction of the Second Temple is a sharp disruption. It was the beginning of a national life that lacked a geographical centre and closed the era of Temple worship. It is not surprising that one should count the years starting from that year of disaster. The first date on the gravestone, counting by sabbatical years, suggests the observance of an instruction found in the Torah (Exod. xxiii 10f.; Lev. xxv 2 – 7). "For six years", says the Book of Exodus, "you may sow your land and gather its produce; but in the seventh year you must let it lie fallow [šmṭ] and leave it alone [nṭš]": the poor will profit from it and the beasts of the field will eat what they leave. The same rule holds for the cultivation of vineyards and the growing of olive trees. The Book of Leviticus calls this instruction a "sabbath of Yhwh", also a šabbat šabbātôn. Men and animals live on things that grow without the aid of human activity.

There are some data suggesting the observance of the sabbatical year in the period of the Second Temple. Thus in the first Book of Maccabees we read, "He came to terms with the people of Bethsura, who abandoned the town, not having the food to withstand a siege, as it was a sabbatical year when the land was left fallow." After the siege the king finds no food in the storerooms "because it was the seventh year" (vi 49). The Mishna and the Talmud also assume the observance of the sabbatical year. Witnesses are tested with the question: "In what week of years?" (cf. the weeks [of years] in Dan. ix 24f.) (Sanh. v 1). In Neh. x 32 (31) the šᵉmiṭṭâ is mentioned as a special obligation and linked with the instructions of Deut. xv 1 – 11: the prohibition on the collection of debts in the seventh year, which is the year of remission.

Leviticus gives great emphasis to the promised land, in which the obligation of the sabbatical year will hold. The rule that the šᵉmiṭṭâ obligation applies only to a limited area also occurs in the Mishnaic

---

[4] In connection with these discoveries L.H. VINCENT wrote an article entitled "Une colonie juive oubliée", *RB* 36 (1927), pp. 401 – 407.

tractate *Shebiᶜit* (= 'the seventh year') (vi 1). The definition of this area is even a factor in the spiritual leaders' emigration policy (*Yad.* iv 3 about Ammon and Moab). In the initial phase of the colonies of Jewish immigrants in Palestine at the end of the 19th century, the question of the observance of the instructions with regard to the sabbatical year was a source of argument. Orthodox leaders were even able to force the big financier of the first colonization, baron Edmond DE ROTHSCHILD, to forbid work in the sabbatical year. The rapid development of modern Jewish life in certain parts of the Palestine country, however, largely took place independently of orthodox believers, so that the problems related to the observance of these instructions are only felt in a very limited circle.

What can have been the meaning of an institution like the sabbatical year? TACITUS was probably beside the mark when, after mentioning the sabbath, he observed that idleness suited them so well that they also reserved the seventh year for it.[5] GISPEN[6], who wrote a thorough and carefully edited commentary on the Book of Leviticus, thinks that it corroborates the message of every sabbath, that is that all labour has only relative value. The purpose and crown of labour is rest, the sabbath of Yahweh. The main factor is not the steady stress of labour in the fields but Yahweh as the Giver of the land. Others, such as recently BEER[7], think of a combination of religious motives and practical experiences. One allows the soil a period of rest in order to maintain and possibly improve its fertility. By doing so, one secures the favour of the vegetation spirits at the same time.

It seems clear that in later times the urge to maintain the *šᵉmiṭṭâ* year springs from people's fidelity to the instructions of the divine Book and from the conviction that only a strict observance of those commandments is likely to bring about the day of liberation, rather than from an understanding of the meaning of *šᵉmiṭṭâ* itself.

---

[5] *Historiae* II 4, *dein blandiente inertia septimum quoque annum ignaviae datum*: "thereupon they also devoted the seventh year to sloth, as idleness suited them well." Not all of Tacitus' reports about the Jews can be trusted. In this observation one can also hear an Occidental's superficial judgement of Orientals. Cf. the opinions held by Israeli from the West about oriental Jews and about Arabs! About Tacitus and the Jews, see A.M.A. HOSPERS-JANSEN's dissertation *Tacitus en de Joden*, Utrecht, 1949.

[6] W.H. GISPEN, *Het Boek Leviticus*, COT, Kampen, 1950, pp. 349ff.

[7] G. BEER, *Exodus*, HAT, Tübingen, 1939, p. 119.

In his discussion of the sabbatical year, EERDMANS[8] is more concerned with chronological questions than with the religious meaning
of this custom. In discussing the *yobēl* year following in Lev. xxv, he
does attempt to offer an explanation. He perceives in the customs
belonging to the fiftieth year (the restitution of fields to their original
owners) the traces of originally common property left in an age that
saw the rise of private property.[9] In the line of this idea one might
see *šᵉmiṭṭâ* as an enduring memory of an earlier form of life in which
migration did not allow permanent cultivation of the land. *šᵉmiṭṭâ*
would then be a kind of agreement between an earlier age and the
more recent one of sedentary life. EERDMANS, who defended the antiquity of the agricultural instructions in the Torah, did not support
the theory that the Hebrews were once nomads. This may have been
the reason why he did not explain *šᵉmiṭṭâ* on the lines of his interpretation of the *yobēl* year or jubilee year.

My memories of the scenery of Judah and in particular those of
the areas near the Dead Sea where one discovered the gravestones
(whose dates clearly show that *šᵉmiṭṭâ* was a reality for the Jews living there) give rise to the suspicion that the custom of leaving fields
and orchyards unused may have had a religious meaning closely
related to the condition of the soil.

Before further explaining my suspicion, I should like to remind
the reader of a few Old Testament texts dealing with the curse of exile: Lev. xxvi 34, 35, 43 and 2 Chron. xxxvi 21. Towns will fall into
ruin, and fields will lie desolate. Chaos will have returned, as is expressed by the words "the land [. . .] shall enjoy its sabbaths."
Those who were able to describe the time of desolation and destruction in this way saw *šᵉmiṭṭâ*, the year in which the fields lay fallow,
as a manifestation of Chaos. In ancient Israel, too, the believer knew
his God as the conqueror of Chaos. His regulating power suppresses
the powers of heaven and the creatures of the earth. The heavenly
powers are curbed, thorns and thistles are burnt. Cultivation, made
possible with the aid of springs and collected rainwater, and the

---

[8] B.D. EERDMANS, *The Religion of Israel*, pp. 39, 89ff., 267. In id., *Alttestamentliche Studien III, Exodus*, Giessen, 1910, our passage is not referred to. The background of what EERDMANS writes in *The Religion of Israel* can be found in *Alttest. Stud.
IV, Leviticus*, Giessen, 1912.

[9] I may here mention in passing EERDMANS' subtle argument on the differences
between *šᵉmiṭṭâ*, the sabbatical year and the year of *dᵉrôr* (*Alttest. Stud.*, IV, p.
121ff.).

growth of vineyards and olive trees are signs of "*het leven uit de dood*"
(life out of death). Instinctively my mind turns to those spots in the
mainly arid land where cultivation is possible. The contrast of life
and death, the defeat of chaos—all this justifies the assumption that
the faithful experienced the life that grew out of death as an act of
their God. Their farming is the service of that life-spending God, to
whom therefore all agricultural laws are traced back. Perhaps one
may assume that a regular recall of chaos, a period in which they
probably travelled through the plain and the mountains with their
cattle, underlined the religious meaning of the cultivation of fields
and vineyards.

"*Het leven uit de dood.*" At these words it would be impossible for
us not to think of KRISTENSEN, who was part of the Leiden theological world for almost half a century. I should like to conclude this lecture by respectfully remembering him.[10]

---

[10] Lecture delivered on Leiden University foundation day, 1954.

5

"WHEN DAVID HAD TO FLEE FROM SAUL,
THE TYRANT"[1]

Als David moeste vluchten
Voor Saul den Tyran:
Soo heb ick moeten suchten
Met menich Edelman:
Maer Godt heeft hem verheven
Verlost uut alder noot
Een Coninckrijk ghegheven
In Israel seer groot.

(Just as David had to flee from Saul, the Tyrant, so I was made
to suffer, together with many a Nobleman: But God raised him,
delivered him from all distress, and granted him a Kingdom [which
was] very great in Israel.)[2]

A biblical scholar venturing into the field of national literature
and national history needs some form of justification. I have one.
"The image dominating the whole *Wilhelmus*: David-Orange,
brought with it the innumerable biblical and especially psalmistic
words in our national anthem," says the literary specialist LENSE-
LINK in a study on Marnix and the *Wilhelmus*.[3] The eighth stanza
refers to David and Saul and to a Kingdom in Israel and thus calls
for an analysis of the *Wilhelmus* from the point of view of the interpretation of the Old Testament and the research made into it. Not
that in their investigations men of letters and historians have failed
to pay attention to the function of the Bible in the anthem. I may
only refer to the fine dissertation by J.B. DREWES, in which by the
use of a considerable amount of reference material he shows to have

---

[1] Lecture given on the occasion of the 388th *dies natalis* of Leiden University.

[2] [*Translator's note*:] The Dutch national anthem consists of fifteen stanzas, each
beginning with a letter of the name of prince *Willem van Nassau*, commonly known
as William of Orange. After him the anthem is called the *Wilhelmus*. The stanzas
usually sung and therefore most familiar to the Dutch people are the first and the
sixth. The stanza reproduced here is the eighth; throughout the article, the Dutch
text has been quoted in full, short prose translations have been added by the
translator.

[3] S.J. LENSELINK, "Marnix en het Wilhelmus", *Tijdschrift voor Nederlandse Taal-
en Letterkunde* 67 (1950), p. 253.

taken seriously what F.K.H. KOSSMANN chose as his *Leitmotiv* in a well-known essay about the origins of the *Wilhelmus* written in 1933: "What inspired the poet and how he found the form that could make his heart sing, that is what we are trying to perceive."[4] Drewes has paid a great deal of attention to the biblical expressions used in the anthem, just as with the aid of convincing references he indicates the connection with the biblical-theological thought process of Calvin and others as a background of this national anthem. I should also like to mention G. BROM's study of 1946, *Het Wilhelmus en de Bijbel*[5], and LENSELINK's essay in the *Tijdschrift voor Nederlandse Taal- en Letterkunde* of 1950. It seems to me that we have reason to ask ourselves whether the analysis of biblical expressions and conceptions in the *Wilhelmus* should not refer to contemporary (biblical) exegesis as much as it does to the translations of the Bible known in that period. As soon as one starts doing this, questions arise with regard to the history of exegesis and the meaning of the texts in the period of their origin.

Van EYCK's attempt to define the anthem as a farewell song has evoked criticsm.[6] Yet it appears to me that the poet, comparing his Prince to the fleeing David, assumes that those for whom he writes his song have the *exiled* Nobleman in mind. The "farewell" label is connected with the dating of the song: *if* it was composed in the winter of 1568, after the withdrawal of the army towards the south, the dismissal of the mercenary troops owing to lack of money, the avoidance of creditors in German towns, *then* there is a lot to be said for the idea that the comfort and consolation the author wants to provide for the inhabitants of the Netherlands is imbued with the thought of parting. If those are right who place the song later, in 1570 or 1571, then its setting is not a parting, but the hope for the return of the Prince to the Netherlands. To my knowledge it has mainly been KOSSMANN who with respect to the contents of the song

---

[4] F.K.H. KOSSMANN, "Het ontstaan van het Wilhelmus", in: *Prins Willem van Oranje 1533–1933* (memorial volume), Haarlem, 1933, p. 363; J.B. DREWES, *Wilhelmus van Nassouwe. Een proeve van synchronische interpretatie*, Amsterdam, 1946 (dissertation Amsterdam 1945). This mainly literary study is also very important for historians and theologians occupying themselves with the sixteenth century.

[5] Gerard BROM, *Het Wilhelmus en de Bijbel*, Mededeelingen der Kon. Akademie van Wetenschappen, afd. letterkunde NR, vol. 9, Nr. 1 (1946).

[6] P.N. VAN EYCK, in the memorial volume *Wilhelmus van Nassouwe*, ed. P. GEYL, Middelburg, 1933, pp. 225–270. VAN EYCK's view is challenged with solid arguments in DREWES' dissertation.

drew attention to the propaganda writings issued by the Prince in 1568: the *Justificatie* ("Justification") of April, affirming the Prince's loyalty towards the King by accentuating the difference between the rights and liberties to which the King had pledged himself and the practices of Alva and the Brussels government; the *Verklaringhe* ("Declaration") of July 20th, in which, aided by allies, the Prince acts as ruler against Alva, representing the interests of the King, the German Empire, and the oppressed Dutch nation; and the *Waerschouwinghe* ("Admonition") of September ist, addressed to the Dutch, encouraging them to take part in the struggle for liberation. In a printed sermon, the Prince's chaplain, Adriaan Savaria, elaborated the same idea on a spiritual level, in order that the people might support the Prince in his venture by prayer and trust in God.[7]

In the opening part of the *Wilhelmus* one comes across the idea of return in the second stanza—*Dat ick sal wederkeeren in mijnen regiment* ("that I may regain the power of government"), in the third stanza—*Dat hy my cracht wil gheven dat ick u helpen mach* ("[pray God] that he may give me power to assist you"), and in the well-known sixth stanza: *Dat ick doch vroom mach blyven uw dienaer taller stondt, die Tyrannie verdryven die mij mijn hert doorwondt* ("that I may remain your faithful servant, and drive out the tyranny that wounds my heart"). All these words have the form of prayers, and all who have consciously experienced war and occupation will remember how people used to separate the line *die Tyrannie verdrijven* from that form and read their own belligerent feelings into it. It is, however, hardly possible to call the tone of the *Wilhelmus* belligerent, not even in the lines that refer to the Prince's return. VAN ECYK seems to be more right in calling the anthem a song of comfort and consolation.[8] The hope for return has developed into the longing for an honourable death on the field of battle and eternal life *als een getrouwe Helt* ("like a faithful Hero") (9th stanza). And the god-fearing poet exhorts his compatriots to resign themselves to God's will: *tsal hier haest zijn ghedaen* ("All will soon be over here") (end of the 14th stanza).

---

[7] KOSSMANN, *art. cit.*, p. 346.
[8] Cf. also KOSSMANN, *art. cit.*, p. 348: "De dichter van het Wilhelmus heeft deze (bedoeld zijn de drie publicaties van de Prins uit 1568) in een tijd zonder uitzicht, na de teleurstelling der eerste ondernemingen, tot eenheid gebracht en ze als troost gesteld in het licht van het geweten en van de bedoelingen van God." See also p. 364.

Following the *Verklaringhe* of July 1568, the last stanza defines the limits put to one's obedience to the authorities. Apparently some of the poet's compatriots saw the Prince's efforts to end Alva's rule as a form of rebellion. Their doubts concerning the right of resistance and perhaps also with regard to the Prince's intentions may have been fed by experiences of failure: the struggle against the King's agent did not seem to be blessed with luck. Rebellion is permitted when obedience to the authorities means disobedience to God.[9]

This brings us to another aspect of the *Wilhelmus*: its justification of the Prince's action. The poet tries to persuade his audience by comparing the Prince to a biblical figure who (in the tradition of the Jewish people that gave shape and meaning to the biblical narratives known and acknowledged by his compatriots as God's message) is the divinely elected, new King for whom the old one must stand down: David. Prince William's intentions are in agreement with the respect due to the anointed King, just as David spares the King's life when Saul (who is persecuting him) falls into his hands, because he is the Lord's anointed: *den Coninck van Hispaengien heb ick altyd gheeert* ("I have always honoured the King of Spain"). He is selfless, sacrifices his money and his property, his relatives and himself in the fight for the impoverished and oppressed people of the Netherlands, governed by God *als een goet Instrument*. The people for whom the *Wilhelmus* was written, read the Bible with a view to their own lives and futures.

The eighth stanza (*Als David moeste vluchten voor Saul, den Tyran*) underlines both the apologetic and the comforting character of the song. Neither the end of the year 1568, in which Alva had shown himself to be an abler strategist and politician than William, nor 1570 with its renewed preparations for war, fit a conception in which the Prince is seen as a substitute for King Philip. In comparing William to David, the poet is not anticipating a Kingdom of the Netherlands under William of Nassau, nor the Spanish Empire with the Prince as King instead of Philip. The *Wilhelmus* only refers to a return of the Prince to a high office, his *regiment* in the Netherlands.

---

[9] In "De dichter van het Wilhelmus" (*De Nieuwe Taalgids* 1939), pp. 241ff) W.J.C. BUITENDIJK draws attention to the emphasis that is put on the Prince as sovereign, who as such had a right to resist the King's tyrannical representative. In the same essay he tentatively mentions Adriaan Savaria as the poet who wrote the *Wilhelmus*. This suggestion is abandoned in his *Nederlandse Strijdzangen uit de 16e en eerste helft der 17e eeuw*, Zwolle, 1954, p. 17.

Nor does the *Acte van Verlatinghe* ("Act of Abjuration") of 1571, which abandons the fiction of unswerving loyalty to the King, refer to a king: it only speaks of a *Hoofd en Herder der Ondersaten* ("Head and Shepherd of the Subjects"). The description of the latter's duties will serve as the introduction to a new age two centuries later, when the form of government of the United States of (North) America is established and the *ancien régime* comes to a definite end.

It seems easy to read the comparison to David fleeing from Saul as a continuation of the few lines referring to the hope for return. This interpretation, however, cannot be maintained if in addition to the argument that there is no question of King William's taking King Philip's place, the purport of the preceding stanzas is also kept in mind. The misfortunes that befell the Prince must not be explained quasi-piously by saying that success is indicative of the assent of Providence and defeat of its disapproval and punishment. On the contrary, the poet seems to say, the way in which the Prince bears his adversities proves that he is a god-fearing man fighting for a noble cause and humbly beseeching his God to be so good as to employ him in his service. In my opinion, the eighth stanza should be understood in connection with the seventh. The Prince prays that he may be protected from attacks by his persecutors:

> *Van al die my beswaren*
> *End myn Vervolghers zijn,*
> *Mijn Godt wilt doch bewaren*
> *Den trouwen dienaer dyn*
> *Dat sy my niet verrasschen*
> *In haren boosen moet*
> *Haer handen niet en wasschen*
> *In myn onschuldich bloet.*

(From all those who oppress and persecute me, my God, protect thy faithful servant; that, evil as their hearts are, they may not attack me by surprise and may not wash their hands in my innocent blood.)

I read this verse as an introduction to the comparison made to David, persecuted by Saul and his servants. The "evil heart" may be an allusion to the "evil spirit" that filled Saul when he came to see the once valued officer and courtier as his rival. If I am right in this, all emphasis in the eighth stanza falls on the position of the persecuted Nobleman in flight. According to the encouraging message of the text, however, there is redemption from all distress, just as the outlawed David is given a "Kingdom in Israel". If the poet does not expect his princely refugee to be raised to the royal office instead of the persecuting tyrant, what, then, is the redemption he hopes for? It must have been a redemption that can be compared to an elevation by God and to a royal position in Israel. In my opinion, to interpret the second part of the eighth stanza one must refer to the next stanza of the anthem, just as for the first part we referred to the preceding stanza.

> *Nae tsuer sal ick ontfanghen*
> *Van Godt myn Heer dat soet*
> *Daer na so doet verlanghen*
> *Myn Vorstelick ghemoet . . .*

("After bitter experiences I shall receive of God, my Lord, the sweetness for which my Princely heart is craving . . .")

These lines are closely connected with the comparison to David's elevation to the kingship in Israel. After the persecution and its threats, after bitter misery comes the sweet happiness granted by God.

What this means is explicitly said in the second part of the ninth stanza: the princely, faithful hero receives from God the privilege not to be killed in an assault on his life, but to die with honour in the field and thereafter acquire an eternal Kingdom:

> *Dat is dat ick mach sterven*
> *Met eeren in dat Velt*
> *Een eeuwich Ryck verwerven*
> *Als een ghetrouwe Helt.*

("That is: that I may die with honour in the Field, and acquire an eternal Kingdom like a faithful Hero.")

If with this interpretation I am on the right track, then *Een Coninckryck in Israel seer groot* was for the poet the image of eternity, of the Kingdom of God, into which the Prince will be received on account of his noble resistance to the oppressor of the people with whose fate he sympathized. Already in the Old Testament itself, David's kingship is called "eternal". In 2 Sam. vii 16 we read "et fidelis erit domus tua et regnum tuum usque in aeternum ante faciem tuam . . .'''. The faithful who lived after 586 BCE—the year in which the Davidic dynasty vanished forever—came to believe in a return, a restoration. They began to read the texts about David's Kingdom as a promise. *Psalms of Solomon* xvii contains a prayer for fulfilment of the old biblical text. Mark xi 10 is a blessing about the coming Kingdom of David:

εὐλογημένη ἡ ἐρχομένη βασιλεία τοῦ πατρὸς ἡμων Δαυίδ. At the time of origin of our national anthem the texts about David's eternal kingdom were also explained as the promise of a blessed hereafter, *post mortem*. This is found for instance in the *Notationes* or (biblical) "annotations" (on 2 Sam. vii 16) by the Jesuit Emanuel Sà, published in Antwerp in the late sixteenth century.[10] With respect to the wishes for a long life addressed to the king in the Psalter, where Hebrew idiom speaks of "length of days for ever and ever", Gilbertus GENEBRARDUS' explanation has "ad vitam immortalem". This French archbishop published his commentaries in Paris from 1575 onwards.[11]

For the poet, David's kingdom may therefore well have been the eternal Kingdom of God, the hereafter, which took a large place in the lives and minds of the faithful as the fulfilment of the promises in the Word of God.

In the eighth stanza there is another word that might be explained from the way people read the Bible in the period in which the anthem was written. The poet confers upon King Saul the epithet "the Tyrant". What was meant by this word in his days, becomes clear from a passage in the *Acte van Verlatinghe* ("Act of Abjuration") referred to above, in which the States-General endorsed William's *Apologie* ("Apology"), in which the Prince defended himself against Philip's edict of 1580 that had declared him an outlaw. One may call both the Prince's *Apology* and the text issued by the States official confirmations of the *Wilhelmus*. Both, however, emphasize and show a greater belief in the favourable outcome of a rebellion against the Spanish rule. In the Act of Abjuration we read, "Thus it is known to every one that a Ruler of the Nation is appointed by God to be Head of his subjects, to preserve and protect them from all injustice,

---

[10] See M. POLUS. *Synopsis criticorum aliorumque Sacrae Scipturae interpretum et commentatorum*, Frankfurt am Main, 1694. Besides Emauel Sà one could mention Johannes Stephanus MENOCHIUS, whose *Explicationes* were published in 1630.

[11] His *Psalmi Davidis vulgata editione* . . . were published in Paris in 1577.

disturbance, and violence, like a Shepherd protecting his Sheep: And that the Subjects are not created by God for the Prince's needs, to be subject to him in all that he commands, be it godly or ungodly, right or wrong, and serve him as slaves; [but] that the Prince [is created] for the sake of his Subjects, without whom he cannot be a Prince, to rule them with justice and fairness, to defend and love them, just as a Father acts towards his Children, and a Shepherd towards his Sheep, who would give his body and his life to protect them."[12] Tyrant and Prince are clearly opposed here. In the eleventh stanza of the *Wilhelmus* the bold tyrant who has entrenched himself near Maastricht and is avoiding battle is the duke of Alva. The tyrant in the also anonymous Beggars' song of 1572 at the introduction of the "Tenth Penny" is clearly Alva as well:[13]

Helpt nu u self, so helpt u Godt
uut der tyrannen band en slot
benauwde Nederlanden . . .

Vernielt den tyran, tis meer dan tyd
met al syn tyrannisten.

("Help yourselves, then God will deliver you from the tyrants' fetters an locks, O oppressed Netherlands . . . Destroy the tyrant, it is high time, and all the likes of him".)

But Alva is the executor of the King's orders. Saul, the Tyrant, may therefore surely be seen as a reference to the Spanish King. The refugee is afraid of being attacked on Philip's orders even in Germany. In the *Wilhelmus*, tyrant and tyranny have the negative meanings of oppressor and oppression, in which the subjects have no rights but are at the mercy of the ruler's arbitrary power.

---

[12] "Alsoo een yegelick kennelick is, dat een Prince van de Lande van Gode ghesteldt is Hooft over syne Ondersaten, om deselve te bewaren ende beschermen van alle ongelyck, overlast ende gheweldt, gelyck een herder tot bewarenisse van syn Schapen: Ende dat d'Ondersaten niet en syn van Gode gheschapen tot behoef van den Prince, om hem in alles wat hy beveelt, weder het goddelick oft ongoddelick, recht ofte onrecht is, onderdanich te wesen, ende als slaeven te dienen; maer den Prince om d'Ondersaten wille, sonder dewelcke hy gheen Prince en is, om deselve met recht ende redenen te regeeren, voor te staen ende lief te hebben als een Vader syne Kinderen, ende een Herder syne Schapen, die syn lyff ende leven settet om deselve te bewaren."

[13] Text in BUITENDIJK's edition referred to in n. 3, with explanatory notes.

Before asking your attention for the interpretations given in the commentaries, I should like to say something about the biblical text as it has come down to us. For the biblical scholar, the most interesting question is whether Saul deserves to be designed as a Tyrant. This designation is not found in the Hebrew text of the Bible, nor in that of the earliest translations. The narratives in the first Book of Samuel were edited by Judaic, pro-Davidic "redactors". The anti-monarchical passages may contain memories of opposition to hereditary leadership: their transmission clearly shows traces of their origins in prophetic-priestly circles.[14] Yet every reader must be struck by the fact that they often refer sympathetically to Saul. He is called *bāḥûr* (*electus*) and *ṭôb* (*bonus*): flawless and vigorous, and is in no way excelled by any of the Israelites.[15] His stature agreed with his character: "From his shoulders upward he was taller than any of the people". Pedersen aptly characterizes him: "Saul is the single-minded chief".[16] When the youthful David, who came to court from the South, the popular commander of the royal troops, having become part of the royal family by his marriage to Saul's daughter, clearly becomes Saul's rival and Crown Prince Jonathan chooses David's side, the King is filled with an evil spirit towards David. His spirit is angry and evil: such is the description by the victorious party, given from David's point of view. Saul is now portrayed unfavourably. He is called a "fool", someone who does not obey God's commands.[17] From being successful he turns into a man who always fails. The later theological "explanation" of this is that Saul is rejected and that David inherits his blessings.

Nevertheless several, obviously persistent popular stories show that it was Saul to whom the people remained loyal until his death. His kingship is characterized by his battles with the Philistines, who for a long time were able to maintain their power in the whole of Palestine and as far as the Transjordan region. David's tribal terri-

---

[14] One can find a good characterization of the nature of the data in A.C. WELCH's fine study *Kings and Prophets of Israel*, London, 1952, published posthumously byWELCH's pupil and successor N.E. Porteous. It must be called uncertain whether Samuel did really crown Saul. See recently I.L. SEELIGMANN, "Hebräische Erzählung und biblische Geschichtsschreibung", *ThZ* 18 (1962), p. 313, with bibliographical notes.

[15] 1 Sam. ix 2.

[16] Johs. PEDERSEN, *Israel, its Life and Culture*, vols. I/II, Copenhagen-London, 1926, p. 189.

[17] 1 Sam. xiii 13ff.

tory in the South, which was directly controlled by the coastal state of Philistea, did not play a significant part in Saul's wars. The narratives about David's taking refuge with one of the Philistine rulers rather seem to suggest that Judah was a rather weak point in Saul's realm.

In the series of narratives illustrating David's courage, ability, cleverness and religion, Saul is the persecutor, the one who is after David's life, but never the despot, the tyrant and oppressor who exploits the people or treats it capriciously. And nowhere is David the champion of this people. David becomes a gang leader (1 Sam. xxii 1f.); in the mountains of Judah, which are an ideal place to hide, his relatives join him, together with all those who had not been able to hold their own in everyday life, such as people harrassed by creditors, approximately 400 men in all. If in those days the rule from the *Book of the Covenant* found in Ex xxii 24 (25) was kept, there must have been non-Israelites among them.[18]

It was the Lord of Israel who killed Saul, says the later Chronicler (1 Chron. x 14), summing up the reasons for it: Saul had been unfaithful to the Lord, ignored his command, and consulted the spirit of a dead man rather than seeking guidance of the Lord. We hear nothing about his government; in the Chronicler's view, he was condemned solely because he had failed in his duty towards Israel's Lord.

Looking at the whole of the data about Saul's kingship, we can find no reason to call him a tyrant as opposed to David. Both he and David (the latter even more than the former) show features of an oriental ruler, who can decide about life and death of his subjects without having to justify himself.

The word τύραννος refers to the autocrat, who has acquired absolute power in a free republic. It also has the more general meaning of ruler, monarch.[19] In its verbal, nominal and adjectival forms, it

---

[18] In MENOCHIUS' interpretation, quoted in POLUS, *Synopsis* (see n. 10), 1 Sam. xxii 1f. become: "hi omnes rebus novis studebant." Ps. xxxiv 12 (11) is sometimes also associated with this Samuel passage. The text "Come, O sons, listen to me, I will teach you the fear of the LORD", etc., is supposed to refer to David, who teaches fairness and justice to those who seek refuge with him. Pietro Martire VERMIGLI also quoted in POLUS, *Synopsis*, observes: "Jure satellites habet a deo rex designatus."

[19] In his *Annotata ad Vetus Testamentum*, Paris, 1644, Hugo GROTIUS quotes EURIPIDES: Εἶδος ἄξιον τυραννίδος. Here the word is used in a favourable sense and serves to illustrate 1 Sam. ix 2, the laudatory description of Saul.

is used in the Septuagint, but not in the narratives about Israel's kings. The Greek translators of the Old Testament use it to denote the rulers of the earth, of foreign kingdoms, or "rulers" in general. As a borrowing from Greek, the word is known in Aramaic and Syriac. In the translations it is sometimes parallel to forms of the stem *šlṭ*, from which the word sultan derives. The Greek translators also use the word in a few texts from the earlier period of Israel's existence, in the Books of Judges, Joshua and Samuel[20], where it is the translation of Hebrew *serānîm* (*pl.t.*), "monarchs", which only denotes the Philistine rulers, and refers to foreign rulers again.

We shall now consider the earliest known interpretations of the biblical narratives.[21] The narratives in Rabbinic literature are not only meant to clarify the biblical text in places that require some explanation, but also to adjust texts that are a likely cause of conflict with established opinion, with orthodoxy, to the needs of national and religious life, of the narrator's present. These narrative comments are called *midrashim*. They originate in an analysis of the appreciation of the biblical text grown in the course of Jewish tradition. Thus the Midrash on the narratives about Saul and David starts from the interpretation that is already apparent in the final editing of the Old Testament material and in Chronicles: Saul is the man who is rejected by Israel's God; David is the one who is chosen to be king of God's people.

One can understand that in this way even the darker pages from David's book of life are given a "deeper" meaning that can be judged positively. The Midrash evaluates David's clever deception of the Philistine king Akish, when he simulated madness, in the following manner: by his simulation David discovers that even madness has a place in God's universal plan. His sin with Bathsheba was committed only to show the power of penitence. Thus there are many narratives about or induced by the vicissitudes of David's life. Their main purpose is to underline his piety and justice.

How does Saul appear in rabbinic tradition? On the one hand one finds consistent rejection: a person's ruin is a punishment, and punishment points to guilt—such is the dogma of Job's friends, of

---

[20] Judg. iii 3 and elsewhere; Josh. xii 3; 1 Sam. v 8.

[21] See e.g. M.W. MONTGOMERY, *s.v.* David, in *The Jewish Encyclopedia* and J.Z. LAUTERBERG, *s.v.* Saul, ibid. R. EDELMAN's *Subject Concordance to the Babylonian Talmud*, Copenhagen, lists the texts in *Babli* in which Saul is mentioned.

orthodox theology. 1 Sam. ix 2 praises Saul's excellent qualities, but is nonetheless explained unfavourably in a *midrash*: Saul was excellent only with regard to his appearance. He became king on account of the merits of his grandfather, who had provided street lanterns for when people went to the house of study at night, to study the "sacred writings" with a view to their own times and futures.

It is a remarkable and agreeable fact that there are also midrashim about Saul that will not hear a word said against him. The old biblical material preserved in the Book of Samuel in spite of the revisions *post eventum* in David's favour also kept haunting and clearly fascinated the minds of the rabbinic interpreters, apparently notwithstanding their orthodoxy. This did no harm to David, however. David and theology stay out of it, and whenever David's shortcomings are mentioned, it is said that David's great blessing, his good fortune, is obvious from the fact that he has been forgiven so much.

From the narratives that refer positively to Saul it is evident that one availed oneself of the opportunity to use any biblical text that might give the people courage. Frequently the midrashim reflect the distress of the age, the threat to national existence under foreign domination, the time in which the close association of faith and nationalism characteristic of Jewish faith and life developed. Saul is honoured as the Hebrew hero who saved the people of Jabesh-Gilead from the power of the Ammonites, who defeated the Amalekites, fought against the powerful Philistines all his life and would rather die than fall into their hands alive. His sparing the cattle after the victory over Amalek (1 Sam. xv)—which by the editors of the biblical text that has come down to us is seen as disobedience to God's command and is for them the theological explanation of his ruin—is thought well of by the midrash: it is his gentleness for which he has to pay with his crown. Saul spares the young people and the cattle because they are innocent and ought not to die on account of the sins of their elders. Of course these narratives are aware of the fact that his sparing king Agag is counted against him as a sin, but they call it his only sin. They recognize the tragedy of Saul's life and call it his misfortune that he was not forgiven this sin, while David, who sinned many times, was always pardoned. Nowhere in the rabbinic data does Saul, the rejected king, Saul, Israel's redeemer and hero, become Saul, the tyrant.

In *1 Henoch* lxxxix 42ff. Israel's enemies are referred to as dogs, foxes and bears devouring the sheep, that is, the people; Saul is called the ram raised up by the Lord. The dogs are the Philistines, the foxes the Ammonites, the wild boars the Edomites. The ram Saul attacks them successfully. The sheep whose eyes are opened (i.e. Samuel the seer) sees Saul, until that ram "forsook his way and began to walk on wicked ways."[22] CHARLES's translation assumes a longer text that with respect to those wicked ways says that the ram started butting and kicking at the sheep and behaving itself unseemly. Sent by the Lord, the seer then goes to another lamb, which he raises to the position of ram and leader of the sheep instead of Saul. This is David, the new "bell-wether".

Here we have the thought that Saul is rejected because he has supposedly used his royal power against his own people. To my knowledge, this thought does not occur anywhere else. In the New Testament and in the so-called Qumrân texts known thus far, there is no mention of Saul.

In his narration of the data from the Book of Samuel, Josephus pays particular attention to Samuel and his warnings against the (oriental form of) kingship.[23] In his *Antiquities* VI v 224 we read, "You are debasing your God, to raise a man to the throne, who will use the power you grant him to treat you as cattle, according to his passions and pleasure"—a word spoken by the prophet before the lot is cast which will appoint Saul to be king. Josephus concludes this chapter of his work with the sentence "Thus in accordance with Samuel's prophecies, Saul's life came to an end because he had broken God's command on account of the Amalekites, had killed the High Priest Ahimelech together with all the priestly family, and had burnt the city that God had granted them as their dwelling-place" (VI xviii 256). Josephus does not use the epitheton tyrant with reference to Saul. He does mention, however, the tyranny of the neighbour kings, from which Samuel is said to have delivered the people (*ibid.* VI v 224).

So far the earliest known interpretation of the biblical texts about Saul. It does not seem likely that the poet of the *Wilhelmus* should have indirectly borrowed his designation of Saul as a tyrant from

---

[22] For the text and its uncertainties see R.H. CHARLES, *The Apocrypha and Pseudepigraphia*, Vol. II, Oxford 1913, p. 254.
[23] [*Translator's note:*] The translation of the quotations from Josephus is based on the Dutch version by W. SÉWEL used by the author, which in its turn is based on the French translation by D'ANDILLY, published in Amsterdam in 1732.

1 Henoch. The metaphor of the people as sheep used by the writer of *1 Henoch* uses the widespread element of the ruler as shepherd. Our national anthem does not use *Henoch*'s metaphor of the prince as ram. It is, however, possible that some of the commentaries contemporary with the *Wilhelmus* itself lie at the root of the designation of Saul as a tyrant. About the difficult text "he reigned .. two years" (1 Sam. xiii 1), Cornelius à LAPIDE (VAN DER STEEN), a Belgian who entered the Jesuit order in 1592, observes, "scilicet in bonitate et innocentia sua. Postea regium ejus imperium abiit in tyrannidem."[24]

His fellow brother Franciscus DE MENDOZA[25] qualifies Saul's government as *tyrannicus*. With Franciscus JUNIUS, we get even closer to the *Wilhelmus*, both historically and theologically. JUNIUS was one of Calvin's pupils in Geneva in 1562; he became a reformed preacher in Antwerp in 1565, in the Palatinate in 1567, chaplain to the Prince in 1568, and after a professorship in Neustadt and Heidelberg a Leiden professor from 1592 until his death in 1602. In his Latin version of the Old Testament[26], the term *tyrannice* occurs in the annotation on 1 Sam. xiii 1. JUNIUS' co-religionist Johannes PISCATOR (1546–1625) commented this text in the same sense. In connection with Ps. lix 6 (5) ("Thou LORD ... Awake to punish al the nations"), PISCATOR—who in his comments on the Psalms likes to observe that the enemies and persecutors mentioned in many psalms are to be connected with Saul and his circle—writes, "(omnes gentes): Saulem cum ministris tyrannidis suae".[27] It is

---

[24] The *Biografisch Woordenboek* (VAN DER AA, vol. XI, 1865, p. 167) does not think highly of Van der Steen's work: "Deze commentariën hebben grove gebreken. De stijl is duister, niet beschaafd, en het ontbrak den schrijver aan de noodige kennis der Oosterse talen." His commentaries on the Books of Ruth and 1 Samuel appeared in 1642.

[25] MENDOZA's work on the Bible started appearing in 1622.

[26] *Testamenti Veteris Biblia Sacra, sive Libri Canonici ..., Latini recens ex Hebraeo facti, brevibusque Scholiis illustrati ab I. Tremellio et F. Junio ...*, 5 vols., Frankfurt, 1575–1579, reprinted many times.

[27] PISCATOR (1546–1625) was a professor at Heidelberg, Neustadt; a rector at Moers; and a professor again at Herborn. His *Commentarii* on the books of the Old Testament started appearing in 1601. He associates the following texts from the Book of Psalms with Saul: ix 1f. (heading + v. 1); xiii 3 (2), 5 (4); xvii 13; xxv 1 (heading); lix 4 (3), 6 (5). I have mentioned only those texts which are explained differently by others. Simeon DE MUIS, whose *Commentarius* on the Psalms appeared in Paris in 1630, also likes to connect Saul with the persecutors and enemies in the Book of Psalms.

likely that this interpretation of the biblical text about Saul was influenced by contemporary experiences of tyranny.

> *Als David moeste vluchten*
> *Voor Saul den Tyran:*
> *Soo heb ick moeten suchten*
> *Met menich Edelman . . .*

Als—soo ("just as . . . so"). This stanza is an example of an illustrative, non-normative way of using the Bible. The poet is not concerned with exegesis, nor with the preaching of the biblical text as normative. His mind is fully occupied with his own age and his own faith, in which the Prince—brave, selfless, noble, religious, true till death—is his ideal. He is familiar with the Old Testament and apparently justified in assuming that his readers know the Old Testament narratives and their traditional interpretations and appreciate them as the word of God intended for them, too. Thus he can use the idealized figure of David as an image of his idealized Prince.[28] It seems to me that there are reasons to ask both literary scholars and historians to include the following considerations in their researches into our national anthem:

1. As part of the whole of the song, the eighth stanza of the *Wilhelmus* becomes clearer when it is read as the direct sequel to the seventh stanza (which prays for protection from attacks) and in connection with the ninth stanza, which prays for an honourable soldier's death and the Kingdom of Heaven;

2. The designation of Saul as a Tyrant is indicative of the poet's close relationship with contemporary experience, as according to the evidence of the Old Testament text and the earliest use of the Bible it had not been used with reference to Saul's style of government before;

3. By calling Saul "the Tyrant" in his metaphor, the poet shows knowledge of the sixteenth-century interpretations of the Samuel narratives; he may even have influenced these. At the end of my excursion into the field of national literature and history I will not make the mistake, so aptly described by DREWES, of another guess

---

[28] About "the mythical national anthem" in connection with "the mythical Orange", see J.W. BERKELBACH VAN DER SPRENKEL, *Oranje en de vestiging van de Nederlandse Staat*, Amsterdam, 1946, ch. VIII, pp.214–218.

at the name of the poet of the *Wilhelmus* without having conclusive evidence.[29] Yet it appears to me that there is sufficient reason to call van Eyck's conjecture that the poet was a man of humble origins[30] an unlikely one.

---

[29] *Op. cit.*, pp. 35ff.
[30] *Art. cit.*, pp. 262f.

6

A LOST BIBLICAL TEXT

(In an introductory passage the autor discusses the problems related to theological education and the importance of the biblical languages in the study of theology. He recommends their retention in the curriculum. One of his arguments is "that Protestant theologians will not leave the knowledge of theology to an elite and that there is no better remedy for ecclesiastical domination than the knowledge of grammar. SALMASIUS' adage "Omnis discordia theologorum oritur ex ignorantia grammaticae" is still worth reflecting, even if "discordia" is not the exclusive monopoly of theologians. Finally he advocates greater coherence in the teaching of theology without any lowering of academic standards.)

Now I ought to be able to demonstrate from my own field that this coherence really exists and that the obligatory study of the languages in which the Bible has been transmitted to us is important for all theologians and not only for the specialists of a specific subject. I shall try to do this and, both with a view to the study of the subjects I have to teach and to the whole of theological education, should like readers to inform me of their opinions about the examples given below and if possible also about the ideas expressed above.

I am going to put a text before you which in the first centuries of the Church was used in communities where people spoke either Greek or Latin, but fell out of use later. It can no longer be found in our translations of the Bible. I came across it in a rather prosaic manner. While working on the critical apparatus of the new edition of the Hebrew Bible by the Württemberger Bibelanstalt I came upon an addition to a biblical text in the Greek version which also occurs in a number of Old Latin manuscripts. However, one can also get to this text in another way. In 1905 MAGISTRETTI published an old church book entitled *Manuale Ambrosianum, Psalterium et Kalendiarium,* in Milan. Among other things, it includes the Song of Hannah (see 1 Sam. ii) (pp. 56ff.; 166ff.). But here it does not start with the familiar words "My heart exults in the LORD", nor with the early Christian recension to be found in Luke i 46, "My soul magnifies the Lord". In the old church book the beginning of the psalm runs as follows: "Confirmatum est cor meum in Domino". This opening is also known from the Septuagint. It may be remarked in passing that an examination of the term found in the Hebrew text ("to exult") shows that the expression known to us is a Hebraism and should be rendered as "to be proud of", "to glory in". The first verse of this song has four verbs, which are used as synonyms. The exalted or raised horn is equivalent to "priding oneself on"; the opening of the mouth is equivalent to "mocking"; "to rejoice" might be rendered with more colour as "to revive". The sense is that of revival after a situation of stress, of breathing easier after one has been saved. The translation found in the Septuagint, which also occurs in the Old Latin versions and is confirmed by the Syriac translation, has been explained as the rendering of another Hebrew verb: ꜥṣm instead of ꜥlṣ. This does not seem necessary. It is altogether possible that "to have been strengthened" and its active form "to be strong" (thus the Syriac translation and the paraphrase in the Aramaic version) provide a correct, explanatory rendering of the Hebrew text that has been handed down to us. If this is true, the beginning of the Magnificat in Luke i does not offer a different text but only a subtle variation.

In the tenth verse of the text of the hymn found in the *Manuale Ambrosianum*, we find an addition that may be called remarkable. It also occurs in the Greek text. The subject of the song is the same both in the Hebrew recension known to us and in that of the translations: "quia non in virtute sua potens est vir"—"it is not by strength that a mortal prevails." The church book here adds:

> Non glorietur sapiens in sapientia sua
> neque glorietur potens in virtute sua
> neque glorietur dives in divitiis suis
> sed in hoc glorietur, qui gloriatur,
> scire et intelligere dominum
> facere iudicium et iustitiam super terram.

The same text can be found in the writings of St. Augustine, with minor variants. The Church Father quotes the song in *De civitate Dei* xvii 4.[1] His quotation shows the following variants with respect to the text in the *Manuale Ambrosianum*: in the first line of the addition he reads *in sapientia* instead of *sapiens*; *in prudentia* instead of *prudens*; in the second line *in potentia* instead of *in virtute*; in the fifth line Augustine has the same verbs in a different order; in the last line he reads *in medio terrae* instead of *super terram*.

The longer text of the Song of Hannah is also found, with some

---

[1] Migne, P.L., 86, Paris, 1850, pp. 739f. (= Corpus Christianorum XIV 2, Turnholti, 1955, pp. 555f.).

variants, in *Liturgia Mozarabica*. In the fragmentary remains of the Old Latin text of the Bible, which will in due course be published by the Vetus Latina Institute of the Benedictine monastery at Beuron (Hohenzollern), the addition is found several times, both in the oldest remains preserved and in later recensions. For the critical apparatus of the fourth edition of the *Biblia Hebraica ed. Kittel* of the *Libri Samuelis* the earliest manuscripts of the Old Latin text were also taken into account. At 1 Sam. ii 10, this apparatus, which the student of theology learns to decipher, will probably say: G L[115.93.94] + plur vb .... But there is something else. The earliest communities who spoke and sang Greek and Latin knew and used the longer text of the psalm as the biblical text and recognized the expression of their faith in it. Additions as such are not uncommon. In the traditional Hebrew text of the Bible, too, one meets this phenomenon more than once. As long as there is no *textus receptus*, no text is seen as "holy", that is, not subject to alteration, it develops along with its users. What functions in life, is subject to change. The traces of changes, which may vary widely, are often indicative of the living faith of the people who use the text.

The addition to our text does not sound strange in the ears of someone who is familiar with the Bible. It is an old custom, though somewhat fallen into disuse, that worshippers follow the reader in their own copies of the Bible. This custom reminds one of the synagogal use prescribing that the reading of the Law should be performed by several members of the community at the same time. This implies a certain check, a form of protection of the community, which might be harmed if the Law were to be garbled in reading. The warning not to add to or take away anything from the text known from Deuteronomy iv and from the conclusion of the New Testament Apocalypse already occurs in the letters and contracts of the Ancient Near East. For our text the reader and those who read with him would only have to turn to Jeremiah to feel at home again. Vv. 22ff. of Jer. ix run as follows:

> These are the words of the LORD:
> Let not the wise boast of their wisdom,
> nor the valiant of their valour;
> let not the wealthy boast of their wealth;
> but if anyone must boast, let him boast of this:
> that he understands and acknowledge me
> [*haśkel w^{e}yādo^{ac} ^{ɔ}ôtî* (scire et nosse me)].

For I am the LORD, I show unfailing love,
I do justice and right on the earth;
for in these I take pleasure.
This is the word of the LORD.

In the text of Jeremiah, the people in whom God delights (cf. Luke ii 14) are those who boast of their knowing and acknowledging that it is the Lord who realizes love, justice and righteousness (or: privilege, the right conferred by the Lord) on earth.

What strikes one here? The addition to the text of 1 Sam. ii 10 in the Greek and Old Latin Bibles and church books and religious treatises probably originated in the text of Jeremiah ix, but did not leave this text unchanged. One may allow for the possibility that those Christians who spoke Greek and Latin were familiar with a different text from the one that has been handed down to us in the Book of Jeremiah, even though this does not seem likely. The Greek version of Jeremiah ix does not differ from the text as we know it. The difference between the text in Jeremiah and the addition in the Greek and Old Latin versions can be summarized as follows: in the tradition of Jeremiah the Lord remains the subject of all actions, in the enlarged text of the Greek and Latin communities the believer has taken over this rôle. Should anyone wish to boast, let him boast of his knowledge of God (theology), of his being in harmony with God's will, his acting in agreement with Gods commands. All this should become visible in sound judgement and just deeds *in medio terrae*, in real life. If in the case of the Old Latin text one could still think of the possibility that the last line (*facere iudicium et iustitiam*) refers to God's actions, in conformity with the unambiguous text of Jeremiah ix, the Greek reading (on which the Old Latin version depends) leaves no room for doubt here. It starts the last line with the conjunction *kai*, putting the verb *poiein* on the same level as the verbs of the preceding line.[2] The critical apparatus of the new Kittel Bible

---

[2] Some witnesses of the Old Latin text also have the reading *et*, as appears from the quotations brought together by the *Vetus Latina* Institute at Beuron. *Ps. Aug.* spec. 22 (ed. Weihrich, 1887) has the reading *sed glorietur qui gloriatur scire et intellegere dominum et facere iustitiam et iustificationem, iudicium in medio terrae*. Eucherius I, l. 1 (Migne, PL 50, 1865) has: *et facere iudicium et iustitiam in medio terrae*; Clemens ad Cor. 13 (ed. G. MORIN): *sed qui gloriatur, in Domino glorietur, in quaerendo et faciendo aequitates et iusticias eius*; Hier. Zach. 2 (Migne, PL 25, 1884, p. 1498B): *et facere misericordiam et iudicium*; Prim. (882B): *et facere iudicium et iustitiam*. See also the author's "Confirmatum est cor meum. The Old Latin Text of the Song of Hannah", *OTS* 13 (1963), pp. 173–142.

should therefore run as follows: ... + *plur vb partim ex Jer. 9,22f.*
One has here an example of the religious life and theology of the early Christian communities who knew and used the Bible in its Greek
and/or Latin forms. In an almost Northern Dutch, down-to-earth
manner, the knowledge of God is related to the duties of life. Some
knowledge of the biblical languages is needed to get in touch with
this lost biblical text through study. But so are the skill of using the
critical apparatus of an edition of the Bible and a mind trained to
understand the history of the biblical text as the history of faith. A
bit of church history comes into it as well, and I would not be sur-
prised if it inspired theologians with a talent for dogmatics to study
their favourite theological subject. It certainly contains material that
can be reworked, that might be elaborated into a sermon. This lost
biblical text can illustrate the faith granted to us, and we may thus
use it in trying to arouse, purify, and reinforce the faith of others.
Faith is a gift, but the finding of illustrations requires the effort of
pursuing the study of theology. In my opinion, this cannot be done
properly without a knowledge of the biblical languages.

7

A SYRO-HEXAPLAR TEXT OF THE SONG
OF HANNAH: 1 SAMUEL II. 1–10

I

SINCE Ceriani's photolithographic edition of MS. C. 313 Inf., Bibl. Ambros., Milan, 1874, and de Lagarde's edition of six manuscript fragments from the British Museum and one from Paris, *Bibliothecae syriacae . . . quae ad philologiam sacram pertinent*, Göttingen, 1892, some more Syro-hexaplar texts have been published. C. C. Torrey published as variants to de Lagarde's edition of the Syriac apocrypha quotations from Esdras i (iii), to be found in a catena commentary from the ninth century, B.M. Add. 12.168, and fragments of the book of Nehemiah, *A.J.S.L.* xxiii, 1906–7, pp. 65–74. J. Gwynn brought out the same text of Nehemiah together with the fragments of 1 and 2 Chronicles, to be found in the same manuscript, B.M. Add. 12.168, and fragments of the books Genesis, Joshua, Proverbs, and Ecclesiastes, MS. B.M. Add. 7145, London, 1909. M. H. Gottstein published a fragment from the University Library at Cambridge, Or. 929, Deut. xxxii. 8–15, *Muséon*, lxvii, 1954, pp. 291–6. Fragments of the book of Psalms were published by Mme V. V. Pigoulewskaja in *Palestinskij Sbornik*, 1 (63), 1954, pp. 59–60. This Psalm manuscript is from the collection of A. Noroff (cf. *Bibliothèque de M. Abraham de Noroff* 1, Saint-Pétersbourg, 1868, at present in Publičnaja Biblioteka S.S.S.R. im. V. I. Lenina, Moscow; cf. A. Každan, 'Grečeskie rukopisi biblioteki im. V. I. Lenina', in *Voprosy istorii*, x, 1946, pp. 107 f.). A. Rahlfs mentions this manuscript as Norov 74 in his *Verzeichnis der griechischen Handschriften des Alten Testaments* (Göttingen, 1914), p. 141. These fragments of the book of Psalms have the same text as codex Ambr. C. 313 Inf. Finally, Gottstein published Syro-hexaplar texts from the British Museum, B.M. Add. 14.485, Add. 14.486, and Add. 17.195, *Biblica*, xxxvii, 1956, pp. 162–83.[1]

[1] Cf. the discussion and further study in *Biblica*, xxxvi, 1955, pp. 227 f., by G. Mercati, who asks the important question, what relation do the Bible text and the text of the Odes bear to one another, and in *Biblica*, xl, 1959, pp. 199–209, by H. Schneider, who treats the texts of the Odes Exod. xv, Deut. xxxii, Ps. cli, and Dan. iii. 52–88, the song of the three holy children.

II

The Syro-hexaplar text of the song of Hannah published here became known to me during the collection of Bible manuscripts on microfilm for the preparation of a critical edition of the Old Testament Peshiṭta.[1] The text is part of a manuscript from the patriarchal library at Mosul, Bibl. Patr. 1112. This manuscript is not mentioned in A. Scher, 'Notice sur les manuscrits syriaques conservés dans la Bibliothèque du patriarchat Chaldéen de Mossoul', *Rev. d. Biblioth.* xvii, 1907, pp. 237–60, but it belongs to the manuscripts saved from Diarbekir; cf. J. Vosté, 'Notes sur les manuscrits syriaques de Diarbekir . . .', *Muséon*, l, 1937, p. 345 : Cod. 2.

Mosul Patr. Chald. 1112 consists of two parts. Fols. 1a–127b are parchment, twelfth century. They consist of 13 quires of 10 fols. each, but the first and the last folio of quire ܐ and fol. 8 of quire ܝ are missing. The second part, fols. 128a–140b, is paper, probably fourteenth to sixteenth century.

The manuscript contains the Psalms, fols. 1a–130a, and seven Odes. The lacunae are: Ps. i. 1–5, xii. 3–xiv. 1, and xxxix. 13–xl. 12. Fols. 128a–130a, from a later hand, contain Ps. cxlvi. 8–cli. The text of the seven Odes is found on fols. 130a–140a. The Odes are:

> The song of Moses, Exod. xv, fols. 130a–131a;
> The second song of Moses, Deut. xxxii, fols. 131a–134b;
> A song of Isaiah, Isa. xxvi. 9–19, fols. 134b–135b;
> The song of Hannah, 1 Sam. ii. 1–10, fols. 135b–136a;
> The psalm of Habakkuk, Hab. iii, fols. 136a–137b;
> The psalm of Jonah, Jonah ii. 2–9, fol. 137b;
> The song of the three holy children, Dan. iii. 52–88, fols. 138a–140a.

Fol. 140b has a colophon which is unreadable except the initial words.

III

Mosul Patr. Chald. 1112, fol. 135b.

ܢܚܒ ܐܬܠܡܐܢ ܐܠܣܐܘ ܐܠܕܟ,   1   (1)

ܐ܊ܠ܊ܘܟܠܚ ܐܝܨ ܠܐܡܨܐܕܠ܊ . ܐܒܚܡܕ   2

[1] I owe Mgr Dr. R. Bidawid, Bishop of Amadiyah, Iraq, a debt of gratitude for his good offices in the acquisition of microfilms from the patriarchal library at Mosul. Our Syro-hexaplar text is unique. Even if Masius' manuscript were preserved, we should not have the S.H. text of 1 Sam. ii. 1–10; cf. Rahlfs on the missing parts in Masius, in de Lagarde, *Bibliothecae syriacae . . .*, p. 32h.

Fol. 136a.

  9 (10a)

  11 (10b)

  14 (10c)

IV

Ishodad of Merw's commentary has one S.H. quotation from the song of Hannah: ܚܡܪܐ ܠܟܗ ܠܐ ܠܐ ܡܪܐ .ܘܠܣ B.M. Or. 4524, fol. 120a, line 23, 1 Sam. ii. 5.[1]

Ishodad continues with the still enigmatic ܚܙܒܐ ܠܟܗܐܘ ܚܕܬܐ. His 'Hebrew' reading is the Peshiṭta version, ܡܚܕܐ being a different spelling for ܡܚܕܐ also found elsewhere.[2]

This reading ܠܐ ܠܐܡܚܠܟ، ܠܗܘ ܪܗ in verse 3, which is neither Peshiṭta nor S.H., is remarkable.

In Bar Hebraeus' *Auṣar Rāzē*[3] occur three quotations from S.H.: *ad* verse 3: ܒ ܡܓܠܐ ܘ܆ ܐܠܗܐ، ܐܡܒܟܐ ܐܗܝܠܐ ܗܢܡܐ ܗܢܡܐ ܘܡܓܗܝ ܘܥܠܟ، ܘܠܟܗ، without variants; *ad* verse 5: ܒ ܠ/ ܐܠܟܪ؛, with the following variants: 1 manuscript *praem.* ܘ; 17 manuscripts read the plural ܐܠܟܪܪܐ. And it seems possible to suppose this plural reading too in the basic text of Sprengling–Graham's edition. And *ad* verse 5: ܣܠܒܐ، ܠܟܐܡܚ ܠܟܗ., without variants.

Bar Hebraeus' quotations do not coincide entirely with Ishodad's quotations.

In September 1961 I had an opportunity of seeing in the Vatican Library at Rome two more Syro-hexaplaric readings of the song of Hannah. Bar Hebraeus' three quotations mentioned above occur too in Vat. sir. 489, in the margin of fol. 304a. A remarkable text of the song of Hannah is to be found in Barberiniani orientali 2, fols. 119b–201a, being one column of the manuscript which consists, for the greater part, of five columns—Armenian, Arabic, Coptic, Syriac, and Ethiopic versions. I hope to deal with this text elsewhere. A description of Vat. sir. 489 and Barb. or. 2 is to be found in *List of Old Testament Peshiṭta Manuscripts* (edited by the Peshiṭta Institute of Leiden University, Leiden, 1961), p. 67, and in *Vet. Test.* xii, 1962, p. 128.

Finally, in the Syriac translation of 1 and 2 Clement[4] occurs a quotation (which in the Greek original text is indicated as Jer. ix. 23 f.) of

---

[1] B.M. Or. 4524 is a manuscript from the seventeenth or eighteenth century; cf. G. Margoliouth, *Descriptive List of Syriac and Karshuni MSS. in the British Museum acquired since 1873* (London, 1899), pp. 45 f. It is the only known manuscript besides Syr. 10 of the Greek patriarchate in Jerusalem, dated A.D. 1380. My thanks are due to Dr. J. B. Segal, who kindly copied the passage on fol. 120a for me.

[2] Cf. Payne Smith, *Thes. Syr.* 4036.

[3] Edited by M. Sprengling–W. C. Graham, *Bar Hebraeus' Scholia on the Old Testament*, Part I (Chicago, 1931), p. 302.

[4] 1 Clement xiii. 1, cf. R. L. Bensly, *The Epistles of S. Clement to the Corinthians* (Cambridge, 1899), p. ܟܣ. I owe this quotation to Mr. W. Baars, who has helped me in many ways.

1 Sam. ii. 10; in choice of words it recalls the S.H. text of 1 Sam. ii. 10: ܠܐ ܢܫܬܒܗܪ ܚܟܝܡܐ ܒܚܟܡܬܗ: ܐܦ ܠܐ ܚܝܠܬܢܐ ܒܚܝܠܗ. ܐܦ ܠܐ ܥܬܝܪܐ ܒܥܘܬܪܗ. ܐܠܐ ܗܘ ܕܡܫܬܒܗܪ ܒܗܢܐ ܢܫܬܒܗܪ. ܠܡܣܬܟܠܘ ܘܠܡܕܥ ܕܝܢܐ ܘܙܕܝܩܘܬܐ.

V

The S.H. text suggests some observations.

Fol. 135b. *Line 1*

ܐܫܬܪܪ] In Ps. xxxiii. 6 S.H. is ܫܡܝܐ ܐܫܬܪܪܘ, a rendering of *οἱ οὐρανοὶ ἐστερεώθησαν*. A figurative use of the verb is made in Rom. i. 12 P. (= Peshiṭta): ... ܪܘܚ ܕܒܗ ܬܫܬܪܪܘܢ

Line 3

ܐܬܦܬܝ] This form is in Jer. li. 58 S.H., a rendering of *ἐπλατύνθη*. The same verb renders *πλατύνω*, figur., in Ps. cxviii (cxix) 32 S.H.

Line 4

ܐܬܒܣܡܬ] The Ethpa. of ܒܣܡ is the usual rendering of *εὐφραίνομαι*.

Line 7

ܠܡܫܬܒܗܪܘܢ] ܢܫܬܒܗܪ is 4 times the rendering of *καυχάσθω* in Jer. ix. 23 f. (22 f.) S.H.

Line 8

ܒܝܬܝܪܘܬܐ] *εἰς ὑπεροχήν*. This expression occurs in the Bible only here. But once, in Jer. lii. 22 S.H., *ὑπεροχή*, with its literal meaning, is rendered by ܪܒܘܬܐ. Cf. too Rom. xiii. 1 P. ܫܘܠܛܢܐ ܕܪܒܘܬܐ < *ἐξουσίαι ὑπερέχουσαι*.

Line 9

ܡܪܘܪܒܘܬܐ (ܡܠܐ)] A hitherto unknown formation in Syriac, a rendering of the *hapax legomenon μεγαλορρημοσύνη*. The verb *μεγαλορρημονεῖν* is rendered by ܪܘܪܒ ܡܠܐ in the S.H. texts Pss. xxxiv (xxxv) 26, xxxvii (xxxviii) 16, liv (lv) 12, and Ezek. xxxv. 13. Cf. too the rendering of *μεγαλορρήμων* by ܡܠܪܘܪܒܢܐ, e.g. in Ps. xi (xii) 4 S.H.

Line 11

ܐܘܡܢ̈ܐ] A rendering of *ἐπιτηδεύματα*, Judges ii. 19; Ps. ix. 11 S.H.

Line 12

ܐܬܡܚܠ] Ethpa. Cf. Ps. xvii (xviii) 36 S.H., a rendering of *ἀσθενεῖν*, metaphorically.

ܐܬܚܣܢܘ] A rendering of *περιζωννύναι*, cf., for example, Ps. xvii (xviii) 32 S.H.

Line 13

ܐܬܒܨܪܘ] A rendering of ἐλαττοῦν, cf. Ps. xxxiii (xxxiv) 10 S.H.

Line 17

ܡܚܝܐ] Aph. of ܚܝܐ, a rendering of ζωογονεῖν in Exod. i. 17, 18, 22; Judges viii. 19; 3 Kings xxi (xx) 31; 4 Kings vii. 4, all S.H.

Fol. 136a. *Line 1*

ܡܡܣܟܢ] A rendering of πτωχίζειν, *hap. leg.* in LXX.

ܡܡܟܟ] In S.H. the usual rendering of ταπεινοῦν, cf., for example, Judges xvi. 5.

Line 2

ܡܪܡܪܡ] A rendering of ἀνυψοῦν, cf., for example, Ps. cxii (cxiii) 7 S.H.

ܡܣܟܢܐ] A rendering of πένης, e.g. in Exod. xxiii. 3 S.H.

Line 3

ܚܫܝܟܐ] The usual but not exclusive rendering of πτωχός in S.H., cf., for example, Job xxii. 8; Jer. v. 4.

Line 4

ܚܣܝ̈ܢܐ] Not the usual rendering of δυνάστης, which is rendered by ܫܠ̈ܝܛܢܐ, e.g. Judges v. 9 S.H.: ܫܠ̈ܝܛܢܐ ܕܥܡܐ. Our ܚܣܝܢܐ is used in Ps. lxxi (lxxii) 12 S.H.: ܦܪܩ ܠܚܫܝܟܐ ܡܢ ܚܣܝܢܐ < ἐρύσατο πτωχὸν ἐκ . . . δυνάστου.

Line 7

ܕܠܗ] Possibly an error; read ܕܠܐ.

ܫܠܝܛܘܬܐ] The usual rendering of ἰσχύς in S.H.

Line 8

ܒܥܠ ܕܝܢܐ] The rendering of ἀντίδικος in S.H., Hos. v. 11; Prov. xviii. 17; Jer. l. 34.

Line 9

ܒܪܝܫܐ] The rendering of φρόνιμος in, for example, 3 Kings v. 7 (21) S.H.

Line 12

ܕܠܡܣܬܟܠܘ] The rendering of συνίειν, e.g. in Ps. lii (liii) 2 S.H.: the same construction with ܠ: ܠܡܚܙܐ ܐܢ ܐܝܬ ܕܡܣܬܟܠ ܐܘ ܕܒܥܐ ܠܐܠܗܐ.

Line 15

ܠܫܡܝܐ] Without *s*ᵉ*yāmē*.

ܪ̈ܫܝܗ] A rendering of ἄκρα, e.g. in Isa. xli. 5 S.H.: the same construction with ܐܪܥܐ γῆς: ܪ̈ܫܝܗ ܕܐܪܥܐ.

VI

A comparison of the Greek text, edited by Brooke–McLean, Cambridge, 1927, with our S.H. text from Mosul gives the following results:

Verse 1

μου 2°] ܣܡܝ؟ — *cum* M.T.

ἐπὶ ἐχθροὺς τό στόμα μου] ܩܘܡܐ ܣܡܝ؟ ܠܠ ܕܠܠܬ݂ܚܕܠ = στομα μου
επ εχθρους μου *cum* Aabnopxc₂e₂𝔄𝔅𝕮𝕴ˢ Or-lat Chr.[1]

εὐφράνθην] *praem.* ܣܠܓ = οτι *cum* Ap[b].

Verse 2

ὅτι] *om. cum* A.

δίκαιος — σοῦ] ܣܡܝ؟ ܠܠܐ ܝܘ ܠܡܐ؟؟ ܠܝܡܠܕ ܘ. ܥܠܚ؟ ܣܘܗ؟ ܗܘ = πλην σου και
ουκ εστιν δικαιος ως ο θεος ημων *cum* A.

Verse 3

ὑψηλά] *add.* ܠ݂ܐܘܢܝ ܁܈ = εις υπεροχην *cum* AMa-hmoswxzc₂e₂𝕾ʲ.[2]

μὴ 3°] ܠܐܘ؟ may be a rendering of και μη *cum* bqtzc₂e₂ or of μηδε
cum MNac-hm-psv-ya₂b₂𝕴ˢOr-lat⅓. Cf. Ps. i. 5 μηδε (S.H. : ουδε).

γνώσεως] ܠ݂ܐܣܝ؟ = γνωσεων *cum* AMNa-no*p-b₂𝔄𝕾-ap-Barh𝕾ʲ Or-
lat½ Cyp.

Verse 5

καὶ ἀσθενοῦντες παρῆκαν γῆν] ˅ ܠ݂ܐܕ؟؟ ÷ ܩܘܡܚ؟ . ܥܠܕܝܒ؟ ؟ܩܒܘܠ؟ ܘܐܘܩ = οι
πεινωντες (*cum* AMNa-hm-e₂𝔄𝔅𝕮𝕴𝕾ʲ Or-lat) derelinquerunt ÷ terram
(*cum* Or-lat).

Verse 8

καὶ 1°] *om. cum* —; cf. M.T.

λαῶν] ܠ݂ܐܚܩܕ؟:— *cum* M.T. Cf. om. in 𝔏ᴮ (inter potentibus).

δικαίου] ܠ݂ܐܡ؟؟ = δικαιων *cum* Aqtyz*a₂𝔄𝔅𝕮𝕮𝕴ᵇˢ𝕾ʲ.

Verse 10a

καὶ 1° — αὐτοῦ 2°] *om. cum* p𝔏ᵉ.

Verse 10b

συνίειν] *praem.* ؟ ܠ݂ܘܗܒ = εν τω *cum* a-fiᵃm-pswxzc₂e₂𝕾ʲ (vid) Thdt.

Verse 10c

— after ܠ݂ܚܝܒ?

VII

S. R. Driver observed in his *Notes on the Hebrew Text . . . of the Books
of Samuel* that the Alexandrian manuscript exhibits a text which has

[1] Cf. Berlin MS. Or. Oct. 1019, edited by M. Black, *A Christian Palestinian Syriac
Horologion* (Cambridge, 1954), pp. 164 ff. and 24 f.   [2] Ibid., pp. 165 and 25.

been systematically corrected so as to agree more closely with the Hebrew.[1] How did they correct the Greek manuscript? F. C. Burkitt stated: 'In all four books of Kings and in some other parts A has been conformed to the Hexaplar text. . . . In fact A is often little more than a transcript of the fourth column of the Hexapla, but without the critical signs by which Origen's additions were marked off from the rest.'[2] H. B. Swete, quoting Burkitt's words in his *Introduction to the Old Testament in Greek*, continues: 'In other words, adaptation to the Hebrew has been effected not by direct use of the official Hebrew text, but through the medium of Origen's work.'[3]

The S.H. text published here seems to prove the correctness of the thesis that the Alexandrian manuscript is based on the Hexapla. Similarity with A is striking. Only in two cases S.H. does not follow A: verse 3 $αυτων$ A and verse 8 $καθισαι$ $αυτον$ A. Origen's influence is obvious too in the second part of the variant reading in verse 5. And the use of Origen's *sigla* points in the same direction.

Striking similarity in a rather short passage, however, is not sufficient to form a general rule. In the S.H. texts of 1 and 2 Samuel published by Gottstein in *Biblica*, xxxvii, only one case occurs where S.H. + A vary from the other manuscripts: 2 Sam. xxiii. 13 ܝܘܡܣܐ // A $κασωαρ$. The same fragments, on the other hand, have many cases of unique A readings without support in S.H., e.g. 1 Sam. vii. 6, 11, xx. 12, 16, 19, 20, 22, 41; 2 Sam. vii. 1, xxi. 5, xxiii. 16. It remains remarkable that in all these cases A differs from M.T.

It seems very probable that G. Mercati's important questions, *Biblica*, xxxvi, do find an answer in our S.H. text. The text appears to be quoted from a Bible manuscript and not from a manuscript of the Odes. It is striking that the S.H. text in a number of cases follows the Bible text of the Alexandrian manuscript and not the text of Odes to be found in the same codex: verse 2 $οτι$; verse 2 $πλην$ $σου$ $κτλ$.; verse 8 $δικαιων$. A conclusive answer, however, is made difficult by the fact that fols. 135b and 136a do not belong to the original Psalter manuscript and may have been copied from a Bible manuscript.

---

[1] 2nd edn., Oxford, 1913, p. xlvii.
[2] *Fragments of the Books of Kings according to the Translation of Aquila* (Cambridge, 1897), p. 19.
[3] 2nd edn., Cambridge, 1914, p. 489.

The handing down of this text in which a second name, Jedidja, is given to Solomon, poses certain questions for the translator. Is the text a direct continuation of the end of verse 24: And Jhwh loved him? In this case then Jhwh is also the subject of the verb with which verse 25 begins. Or does something new begin in verse 25, the education of the child which by the grace of Jhwh remains alive, entrusted to the prophet Nathan? In this case David, the father, is the subject of the first verb. There is also much difference of opinion concerning the subject of the second verb in the verse. Does Nathan give the second name to the child or does David do so? Then there is the difficult term וישלח ביד whereby commentators either want to add an object, or to delete ביד or to transpose it with נתן to the second part of the sentence. The end of the verse also produces difficulties. If we take the *atnach* into consideration, the second part of the sentence is abnormally short and not a true part of a sentence at all. This is the reason that one comes across additions in translations or an assumed alteration in the reading, by which the meaning of the *atnach* is obliterated.

Some of these questions have already been posed by earlier translators as we can see from some of their readings. The Syriac translations is: (verse 24 end) 'and the Lord loved the child (verse 25) whereupon he (David) sent for Nathan the prophet and he (Nathan) named the child Jedidja because the Lord loved him'. The Vulgate repeats the end of the verse more extensively: 'eo quod diligeret eum Dominus'.[1] Further, certain mss of the Vulgate have given the first verb an object: 'misitque *eum* in manu Nathan prophetae'. This reading occurs in Λ^{H_1} (Madrid, Acad. de la Hist., 2, xii cent.), Ψ (Rome, Vatic. Libr., vat. lat. 10510, 10511, 12958, xii cent.), Ω^S (Paris, Bibl. Nation., lat. 15467, xiii cent.), Ω^M (Paris, Bibl. Mazarin 5, xiv cent.).[2] These are all late mss which does not make the conjecture very attractive.

In M. Polus' Synopsis Criticorum[3] there are to be found various

---

[1] Ehrlich, *Randglossen* 1910, suggests the reading באהבת instead of בעבור in connection with this Latin rendering.
[2] Comp. Biblia Sacra iuxta latinam vulgatam versionem. Liber Samuhelis. Romae 1944.
[3] Volume I, Frankfort 1694, column 1444.

opinions which could also be met with in modern translations and explanations. 'Misit Dominus per Nathan. – Aliqui ad Davidem referunt: quod Salomonem Nathani educandum miserit; ut alios liberos sacerdotibus erudiendos tradidit; unde *Cohanim* dicti suprà in calce 8. cap. – Nathan renunciavit Davidi eum fore Deo amabilem; ideò per eum Rex manadatum misit ad Bethshabe, ut vocaretur Jedidiah. *Vocavit,* nempe David, ex se et sua sponte.'

R. Kittel in his Biblia Hebraica, 3rd edition, indicates the proposal to read וַיְשַׁלְּמוֹ instead of וישלח. We saw little or no value can be placed on the argument, cf. V^MSS (+ eum). In his translation (in Kautzsch-Bertholet) he procedes from the mentioned conjecture, translating: 'Und er übergab (ihn)', thus linking up with the already old suggestion: 'nämlich zur Erziehung'. However, in his translation Kittel does rightly note that this reading is uncertain and that the reading of the Massoretic text is not impossible. W. Nowack, in his commentary, Göttingen 1902, the Zürcher Bibel and H. Th. Obbink in the 2nd edition of his translation, 1934, all choose to change the Hebrew text. This change rests on a suggestion made by Wellhausen. In his *Der Text der Bücher Samuelis,* Göttingen 1871, Wellhausen agrees with a suggestion made by O. Thenius,[1] to read וישלחו, but adds here that it can be argued both here and in 2 Sam 18:2 that 'in der in der Dialekten üblicher Bedeutung' השלים could be taken as the original reading. K. Budde, commentary 1902, and some others already mentioned followed this suggestion. It has no support from the history of the text or from the ancient versions. S. R. Driver[2] rejects it, as it has to be supported by a very late stage of the Hebrew language. Driver maintains the Hebrew text but considers it better to let the sentence begin with the last words of verse 24: And the Lord loved him. Many commentators have followed him in this. The subject of וישלח is then, however, the Lord. This is so, among others, in the translations of A. Schulz (commentary, Münster in Westfalen, 1920; the Revised Version; Buber-Rosenzweig; H. P. Smith (commentary, Edinburgh 1912); J. de Groot (commentary, Groningen 1935); A. van den Born (Canisius' translation 1938; commentary 1956); Fryske translation, 1946; Dutch Bible Society translation 1951; the Revised Standard Version; E. Dhorme (Pleïade, 1956); R. de Vaux (Bible de Jérusalem, 1956,

---

[1] Thenius, commentary Leipsic 1842, 2nd ed. 1864 (3rd ed. Lohr 1898), believes he can find support for his reading in 2 Sam 18:2.

[2] *Notes on the Hebrew text and the topography of the Books of Samuel,* Oxford 2nd ed. 1913, p.293.

2nd ed. 1961); C.J.Goslinga (commentary, Kampen 1956); H.W. Hertzberg (commentary 1956, 3rd ed. 1965). The Dutch Authorised Version (the so-called Statenvertaling) and the Leiden translation also took Jhwh as the subject of the verb וישלח. The latter, dating from 1899, even added Jhwh to make things clearer.

In these translations various answers have been given to the question: who is the subject of the second verb? In some translations it remains uncertain. Several translators, however, take Nathan to be the subject: the Leiden translation; the Revised Version; the Zürcher Bibel; Kittel; Buber; Schulz; de Groot; van den Born; Goslinga; Hertzberg; de Vaux. Others have chosen David: Klostermann;[1] Caspari;[2] Dhorme. Yet again others take Jhwh as the subject: Smith; the Fryske translation; the Dutch Bible Society translation.

The words בעבור יהוה 'because of Jhwh' have been changed to בדבר יהוה 'suivant la parole de Yahvé' (de Vaux) or 'by the word of Yahweh' (Smith). Others follow the fuller text of the Syriac and Vulgate translations, thus the Confraternity Version, New York 1964. M.S.Segal omits the *atnach* (in his commentary, Jerusalem Isr., 1956). Kittel, Biblia Hebraica 3rd ed., supposes that the Hebrew reading בדבר, 'by command of' has been the 'Vorlage' of some ancient versions. This concerns the Lucian recension of the Septuagint, certain Hebrew mss, the Vetus Latina ℒ[94.93] (quod est interpretatum) in verbo (Domini), and Theodotion's translation ἐν λόγῳ. However it must be said to be uncertain whether these versions indicate a different tradition to that reflected in the Hebrew text of the rabbi's. Besides meaning 'because' בעבור also means 'by order of', comp. Karatepe II 6.11f, III 11.

If one considers the use of שלח without an object and followed by a verbal form, the imperf. consecutive or lamed plus the infinitive, it turns out that, like the Greek ἀποστελλειν, it is far from rare. וישלח without an object and followed by a verbal form which carries the main thought of the sentence, is to be found in: Gen 31:4; 41:8, 14; Numb 16:12; Josh 24:9; 1 Sam 16:20, 22; 22:11; 25:39; 2 Sam 3:15; 6:6; 9:5; 11:3, 18, 27; 14:2; 1 Kings 2:36, 42; 5:16, 22; 7:13; 18:20; 20:17; 2 Kings 5:8; 6:9; 1 Chron 19:5; 2 Chron 2:2; 25:17, 18; 34:29

---

[1] A.Klostermann, commentary Nordlingen 1887, transposes verse 25 to follow verse 23. No-one has followed his change of the name Jedidja to Jedinja, which he considered to be the name of the dead child.
[2] W.Caspari, commentary Leipsic 1926, reads וישאל 'und er stellte durch Natan die Anfrage (bei Gott) und gab ihm mit Jahwes Genehmigung den Namen Jedidja'.

Our text 2 Sam 12:25 is not an exception. The use of וישלח in such sentences can be called adverbial. The unmentioned object is usually the subject of the following and main verb. The main verb of the sentence is marked by וישלח as a causative: 'now he sent and he took' = 'now he sent (a servant) and he took' = 'he caused him to take'. In a few cases the causative form is used for the second and main verb of the sentence: 2 Sam 10:16; 1 Kings 1:53; Esth 5:10. In each of these places the same ideas could have been expressed with the Qal of the verb, by which the object of the Hiphil form would have become the subject.

By the recognition of the idiom in which is expressed that he who is the subject of וישלח causes somebody or some people to do something, not all the difficulties of 2 Sam 12:25 are solved. Hertzberg believes that ביד is left over from a second reading. He supposes the reading וישלח את־נתן וג׳ next to an alternative reading ויקרא ביד נתן וג׳. The traditional text would then contain the somewhat unfortunate combination of these two readings, helped on by 2 Sam 11:14 וישלח ביד אוריה. Others take the first part of the verse as the end of a sentence: That Jhwh loved this son He did know the king through the prophet Nathan. Thus, albeit in different ways, de Vaux; Dhorme; van den Born; the Revised Standard Version.

Hertzberg's solution as well as the attempt to make an independant sentence of the first part of verse 25 breaks the connection between וישלח and the following verb ויקרא. We shall have a better chance of staying on the right track if we assume that the above mentioned combination of two verbs is valid for our verse too. Schulz has already demonstrated this to be so in 1 Kings 2:25 where וישלח occurs followed by ביד. Besides this, 2 Chron 36:15 can also be mentioned, although in this verse the continuation is different. 1 Kings 2:25 runs: 'Then king Solomon caused him to be struck down so that he died by Benaja, Jehojada's son.' 2 Chron 36:15 may be rendered by: 'Jhwh, the god of their fathers, persistently showed compassion to them by his messengers, verily compassion towards his people and towards his dwelling place'.

Both Benaja (1 Kings 2:25) and the messengers, or prophets (2 Chron 36:15) are carrying out the order of he who is the subject of וישלח. The verb is in such a close relationship with the following main verb of the sentence that the phrase ביד וג׳ which belongs to the carrying out of the expressed will or order can be placed in front, after וישלח and before the main verb.

If the syntax of the verse is made clearer by this, the translation should read: '(And Jhwh loved him) and did call him Jedidja by means of Nathan the prophet.'

However, we have not yet translated the last two words בעבור יהוה. We saw that they can mean: by order of Jhwh. If in translating one wishes to lay stress on the fact that Nathan gave the second name to David's son, even though it was done by order of Jhwh, then the remark can be a repetition – albeit rather unnecessary – of the beginning of the verse. De Groot was aware of this somewhat excessive use of בעבור יהוה and sought in these words for another reason for the name Jedidja. He translated: 'because (in this the name) Jhwh (is found)'. In his commentary he does not give any explanation concerning this significant attempt to solve the problem.

It seems possible to me that these two last words of our verse are secondary and that the placing of the *atnach* as well as the addition to the words in the Syriac and Vulgate translation, inspired by the end of verse 24, indicate the secondary character. The words could have been added in order to emphasise and do away with any misunderstandings that Jhwh's preference for Solomon was not invented by Nathan. That is why here too Nathan is called *the prophet*, a qualification which before then was not made. 2 Sam 12:25 belongs to those verses which contain a certain theological evaluation of history which later became predominate.

9

ומרחוק יריח מלחמה—JOB 39: 25

The war-horse possesses superhuman strength, velocity, and courage. His qualities are described in the poetry of Job 39: 19–25. The last part of the strophe reads like this in the usual translation

> and he smells the battle from afar,
> the thunder of the captains, and the shouting.

The Greek and the Syriac versions each have a reading which differs from the rabbinical text preserved in our Hebrew bible. Instead of the last line, 'the thunder of the captains, and the shouting' the Greek version reads '(and) with a bound (—at a leap—) and a cry (he goes out)'. It has been supposed that the translator misread the Hebrew word רעם, overlooking its first character. The Syriac rendering of these last words of the line runs as follows: 'and he is shaking (terrifying) the captains with his neighing.' These renderings may of course go back to Hebrew readings not preserved, but to me it seems more probable that the translators have tried to avoid, each in his own way, the difficult connection of the verbal form יריח with, as well as מלחמה, two other objects: the thunder of captains and shouting, battle-cry. The Greek as well as the Syriac translation render the verb by 'he smells (the battle)'.

The line 'and he—the war-horse—smells the battle from afar' contains also another difficulty. All hooved animals have a well-developed sense of smell and the horse is no exception. With his nose he sniffs and he snorts. 'His proud snorting is terrible', runs a possible translation of verse 20 b. But smelling something at a long distance is no peculiarity of the horse. It is because of this difficulty that commentators have supposed the Hiph'il of the verb ריח had a metaphorical sense. Arnoldus Boot interpreted it in this way, and, in his *Animadversiones sacrae ad textum hebraicum Veteris Testamenti* (London, 1644), refers for the metaphorical sense of the verb to Martinus Borrhaus's commentary of 1555, Valentinus Schindlerus's lexicon of 1612, and Johannes Mariana's scholia of 1620. In liber III, caput xi, paragraph 4 of Boot's work we read that הריח means 'sentire, persentiscere: quomodo etiam sumitur Jud. 16: 9 et Esa. 11: 3'. In Samuel Bochartus's *De scripturae animalibus* (Utrecht, 1692), one finds a more detailed discussion of the supposed metaphorical sense of the verb. In part I, liber ii, col. 151 the following observations are to be found: '"Et pugnam eminus praesagit". Sagire enim (inquit Tullius lib. 1 De Divinit.) sentire acutè est, Cicero in Epist. ad Atticum: odorari quid futurum sit. Itaque: pugnam odoratur, id est futurum praesagit.' Bochart refers further to Kimchi who brings forward the verbal form ירגיש, a form occurring in the Targum Jon. of Exod. 2: 3 with the meaning: to feel the scent of, trace, track. He continues with:

Nempe *odorem* pro sensu in genere *Hebraei* passim usurpant; ut cum de arbore dicitur Job 14: 9—ex odore aquae germinat, *odor* ibi pro *sensu.* Ita Jud. 16: 9 ut frangitur filum stupeum—cum odoratum est ignem, id est sensus ignis. Et Esa 11: 3, ubi de Christo,—et odoratus ejus erit in timore Domini. Odoratus, id est, sensus, judicium. Proinde sequitur, Non secundum aspectum oculorum judicabit, etc. Eo igitur sensu dici potuit equus *praelium odorari,* id est, sentire, vel praesentiscere.

In recent lexica, translations and commentaries a figurative sense has been ascribed to the noun ריח in some places. But the verbal form, which occurs in Job 39: 25, is rendered by to smell, to absorb the smell of.[1] As far as I know Tur-Sinai is the only recent commentator to question the exactness of the usual translation.[2] 'To smell from a great distance', he says, 'does not

---

[1] Suffice it to mention: 'to smell, perceive odour'—*BDB*; RV; RSV; W. B. Stevenson, *Schweich Lectures 1943* (London, 1947). 'riechen, wittern' —Gesenius–Buhl; G. Fohrer, *Kommentar* (*KAT*, XVI, Gütersloh, 1963). '(das Wehen eines luftförmigen Stoffs) spüren, riechen'—*KBL.* 'flairer'— E. Dhorme, *Le Livre de Job* (Paris, 1926), *Pléiade* (1956); C. Larcher, *La Bible de Jérusalem* (Paris, 1956); S. Terrien, *Commentaire* (Neuchâtel, 1963). In Syriac the rendering of the Aph'el of ריח by *praesentiscere* is given—Payne Smith, *Thesaurus Syriacus*, referring to Ephraim, ed. Romana 272 C: the devil and his hosts scented out the coming of our Lord, *praesenserunt*. Brockelmann gives in his lexicon the following meanings of the Aph'el: 1. odoratus est (meton. de igni); 2. flavit; 3. praesagavit, Job 39: 25.

[2] N. H. Tur-Sinai, *The Book of Job, a new commentary* (Jerusalem, 1957), pp. 548 and 551.

fit the horse at all.' But he did not try to solve the problem by supposing a metaphorical sense for the verb הריח. He suggests that Job 39: 20–5 is a description of a bird of prey and not of a war-horse. Verse 19 does, of course, refer to a horse, but remains in Tur-Sinai's translation an isolated line of a strophe of which the remainder has perished. Other scholars have supposed that after verse 19 one line has been lost. A serious objection to Tur-Sinai's opinion would seem to be that he does not mention any texts from ancient sources which actually refer to the sense of smell as a peculiar quality of birds of prey. Do birds of prey smell from afar? The poet of Job 39 stresses the visual faculty of the bird of prey: 'From thence [from his place high in the mountains]', he says in verse 29 of chapter 39, 'he spies out a prey, his eyes pierce to the farthest distance.' It is not his sense of smell that has impressed the poet.

Dhorme, although translating 'And from afar he sniffs the smell of battle', suggests a more or less figurative sense for the verb by referring to the sense of the noun ריח in Job 14: 9 and Judg. 16: 9 in his explanation.[1] A tree cut down, a stump, flourishes anew מריח מים, 'at the scent of water', is Dhorme's translation of Job 14: 9. This rendering is close to the Vulgate which reads: 'ad odorem aquae', explained by Jacobus Tirinus (Antwerp, 1632), with 'ad tactum. Est catachresis, et enallage sensuum'. This analogical application of the noun ריח can be found in several translations and commentaries. Dhorme calls it 'an admirable image suggesting as it does the approach, the slightest contact'. He refers to Judg. 16: 9, rendering the expression בהריחו אש by 'as soon as it smells the fire'.

The rendering of מריח by 'at the scent of' seems to me open to discussion. The meaning of the preposition מן is 'out of', 'from', 'through'—very rarely is a meaning more or less similar to 'at' suitable. A more serious objection is in my opinion that the noun ריח everywhere has the meaning *smell given out*. 'Your anointed oils are fragrant', 'my nard gave forth its perfume', we read in the Song of Sol. 1: 3 and 12. The word also occurs with a similar concrete meaning in 2: 13; 4: 10, 11 (*bis*); 7: 9

[1] Dhorme, *Livre de Job*. English translation by Harold Knight, *A Commentary on the Book of Job* (London, 1967).

and 14 of the same Book. Hos. 14: 7 is very close to Song of Sol. 4: 11, 'and his fragrance like Lebanon', the scent given out by the cedars of Lebanon, an expression which is paralleled by 'the scent of your garments', i.e. the smell given out by your clothes. The smell of garments also occurs in Gen. 27: 27, next to the smell of the field and the smell of Isaac's son—three times in one verse the same expression, the smell given out. In Jer. 48: 11 Moab is compared to wine, wine that has not been emptied from vessel to vessel, 'so his flavour remains in him and his bouquet (ריח) is not changed'. Also instructive is Dan. 3: 27, a text referred to by Bochart, where we are told of Shadrach, Meshach, and Abednego coming out from the fire, that 'no smell of fire had come upon them', which stands for 'they did not even smell of fire'.

There remains Judg. 16: 9, quoted by Dhorme to support his rendering of Job 14: 9, 'at the scent of water'. Dhorme explains both Job 14: 9 and Judg. 16: 9 as an 'image'. I doubt whether it is right to render the Niph'al of נתק by 'se rompre'. Elsewhere the Niph'al means: be snapped, be torn apart, be drawn away. Cords of tents are torn loose, Isa. 33: 20 and Jer. 10: 20. 'A threefold cord is not quickly broken', Eccles. 4: 12. Dalman rightly remarks upon the inflammability of flax, quoting Isa. 1: 31. But his rendering of Judg. 16: 9 seems to me inaccurate: 'Werg—dessen Faden schon in der Nähe des Feuers auseinandergeht.'[1] The Revised Version translates the text with: 'as a string of tow is broken when it toucheth [note, Heb. *smelleth*] the fire.' Vincent, in *La Bible de Jérusalem*, which was published in 1956, the same year as Dhorme's translation appeared in *La Bibliothèque de la Pléiade*, also uses 'se rompre', cf. RSV: 'as a string of tow snaps when it touches the fire.' I suppose that the translations quoted have been influenced by the assumption that the expression is an image. I shall leave out of consideration whether expressions like 'to smell water' and 'to smell fire' are likely images for 'le plus léger contact'. Nor will I stress the inveracity of figurative language in which a root or stump, and a string of tow are endowed with a sense of smell. But it is, in my opinion, a serious objection to the assumption of meta-

[1] G. Dalman, *Arbeit und Sitte in Palästina*, v (Gütersloh, 1937), 28.

phorical language if the sentences are comprehensible without such an assumption. In Judg. 16: 9 it is said that Samson snapped the bowstrings, as a string of tow is snapped when it smells of fire. It is not the string of tow that smells but the flax-worker smells the string of tow. He may be using a flame to snap the string. When the string smells of fire he is able to snap it. Or, if a string of tow gets into touch with fire so that it smells of fire, one is obliged to tear it loose. Samson was able to snap the seven fresh bowstrings as if they were no more than a string of tow that smells of fire. The same simile occurs in Judg. 15: 14: '...and the ropes which were on his arms became as flax that has caught fire...' This supports my rendering of Judg. 16: 9.

The Hiph'il of the verb ריח has the meaning: 'to give out a smell', a meaning in full agreement with the clear sense of the noun ריח. And in Job 14: 9 the roots or stump of the supposed dead tree bud and flourish anew as a result of the smell of water. The opinion that water, unlike fire, has no scent has been advanced by Tur-Sinai[1] but seems to me untenable. Tur-Sinai did not realize that the text deals with water in contact with roots in the earth. The author of the passage in the Book of Job is alluding to the life-giving power of water. The scent of water can be compared with the scent of oil and perfume. Anointment and perfuming are evidence of power and life. The scent of water performs a similar task for the supposedly dead tree.[2]

The usual rendering of the Hiph'il of ריח by 'to smell, to perceive odour', and its explanation as feeling presentiments, do not receive support from the noun ריח whose unmistakable meaning is fragrance, perfume, stench—smell given out. Judg. 16: 9 can be translated and explained in accordance with this meaning of ריח. We may therefore be justified in doubting the

---

[1] *The Book of Job, a new commentary*, p. 235.

[2] P. Reymond, who has published an important monograph on water in the Old Testament—*L'eau, sa vie, et sa signification dans l'Ancien Testament* (*VTS*, VI, 1958)—did not give full attention to Job 14: 9. His observation, made on page 6 of his work, 'l'arbre dont parle Job 14: 9, sentant de loin l'eau du ruisseau, y envoie ses racines et retrouve vie', is an inexact paraphrase of the Hebrew text. As for the relation of anointment and life I may refer to my paper 'Vive le roi!', *VT*, v (1955), 225–31. Compare also Rivkah Harris's article in the *Journal of Cuneiform Studies*, IX (New Haven, 1955), 92 f.

correctness of the renderings and explanations usually given. And so in spite of the ancient versions and traditional and modern views it seems desirable to reconsider the meaning of a few passages.

The verbal form הריחו also occurs in Isa. 11: 3. A metaphorical interpretation, 'odoratus, id est, sensus, judicium', is given in Bochartus's work, as we have seen. The Greek and Latin translators may have altered or misread the Hebrew, probably reading והניחו, cf. Ezek. 24: 13 in the LXX, ἐμπλήσω. But their use of the term 'the spirit (of the fear of the Lord)' indicates their familiarity with the reading in Hebrew: הריח derived from the root רוח. The Peshiṭta version reads: 'and he shall be illustrious, or, shine forth (in the fear of the Lord)', using the verb dnḥ, a verb that is also known in Aramaic, and that corresponds to זרח in Hebrew. The author of this version may have read וזרחו, literally 'and his shining', instead of והריחו.

The non-figurative meaning 'to smell' has been kept by some commentators. Ibn Ezra stresses the reliability of perception by the sense of smell as contrasted with ear and eye. Calvin underlines the sharpness of perception by rendering 'et sagacem illum reddet in timore Domini'. Piscator (1546–1625) and others, like Bochartus, stress the power of judgement because of the next sentence in Isaiah, 'he shall not judge by what his eyes see', etc. Hugo Grotius derives his translation and explanation of the sentence from the meaning of the Qal of רוח, 'to relieve', 1 Sam. 16: 23 and Job 32: 20. His rendering runs as follows: 'Et consolari ipsius (id est, solatium).'[1]

Dillmann, whose commentaries excel in accuracy and brevity, ascribes to the verb 'to smell' in our passage the sense not of 'to perceive' but a satisfied stay, dwell upon (ב), 'das befriedigte Verweilen des Sinnes am'. His explanation of 'sein Riechen' is: 'sein Wohlgefallen', his delight.[2] This rendering, 'his delight', is found in most of the recent translations.

Many reject the authenticity of Isa. 11: 3a and consider the

---

[1] *Annotata ad Vetus Testamentum*, II (Paris, 1544), 21

[2] A. Dillmann, *Der Prophet Jesaja* (Leipzig, 1890), p. 118. Cf. J. Barth, *Etymologische Studien zum Semitischen insbesondere zum hebräischen Lexicon* (Leipzig, 1893), p. 65, who quotes Amos 5: 21 and Isa. 11: 3, translating 'Wohlgefallen haben', and bringing forward some parallels in Arabic.

line to be due to dittography. One of the supporters of this view is Duhm who has pointed out the problems with his characteristic clarity. In his well-known commentary on the Book of Isaiah we read on verse 3 a:[1] ' " und sein Riechen ist an die Furcht Gottes" eine Variante mit sinnlosem Text. Wenn noch das verb. fin. stände,[2] dass wenigstens die Konstruktion erträglich wäre! Und wie riecht denn die Gottesfurcht? Diejenigen, die V. 3 a festhalten, müssten es wissen, aber sie sagen es nicht.' To assume a figurative sense for the verb 'to smell' is an attempt to get away from the real problem so clearly stated by Duhm. Skinner, who himself uses the rendering 'his delight', rightly observes that the expression is very awkward.[3]

Should we be tempted to deviate from the literal sense of הריח to get an understandable sentence? The explanation of הריחו in Judg. 16: 9 given above and the statement that scent/smell does not mean 'odour perceived by', but 'odour given out', may give us freedom to leave the beaten track. The Hiph'il of ריח possibly has an intransitive sense (also?), similar to נתן ריח, used in Song of Sol. 1: 12. Such a meaning, 'to give forth scent, perfume', should make it possible to render Isa. 11: 3 a by: 'and his giving forth scent (is done) with the fear of the Lord.' הריח ב is used with the same meaning in Exod. 30: 38, as will be shown below.

Scent given forth is a manifestation of the power of life. I do not defend the authenticity of verse 3 a in its context. The line may be a gloss. If so it is a gloss in accordance with the trend of the passage. The qualities of the new prince—his inspiration, his wisdom, his piety—can also be called the manifestation of his observance of the Lord's will. To be gifted with the spirit of the Lord means to shine and to smell like a priest in the Lord's sanctuary who is anointed with oil and fragrance. In his observance of the will of the Lord the new prince gives evidence of his power.

[1] B. Duhm, *Das Buch Jesaia* (Göttingen, 1914), p. 82.
[2] G. Fohrer translates as if the Hebrew text reads a *verbum finitum*: [Er riecht nach Gottesfurcht], without an explanatory note, *Zürcher Bibelkommentar* (1960), p. 150.
[3] J. Skinner, *The Book of the Prophet Isaiah, chapters 1–39* (Cambridge, 1930), p. 105.

In Exod. 30 two instructions are given, one for the compounding of a special kind of anointing oil, for the anointing of the implements of the sanctuary and for the anointing of the priests, verses 22–30; and the other for a special kind of incense, perfume, for the sanctuary, 'where I shall meet with you', verses 34–6. Anointing oil as well as incense fabricated according to these instructions is called most holy. Both sets of instructions are followed by prohibitions on the use and compounding of the anointing oil and incense for profane purposes, verses 31–3 and verses 37–8.

In verse 38 we find: 'Whoever makes any like it לְהָרִיחַ בָּהּ shall be cut off from his people.' The words לְהָרִיחַ בָּהּ have been rendered in the LXX by ὥστε ὀσφραίνεσθαι ἐν αὐτῷ, cf. the Peshiṭta version *lmrḥw bh*. The rendering of the Vulgate is more explicative. It runs: 'ut odore illius perfruatur.' Recent translations follow either the Greek rendering or that of the Vulgate.[1] In these renderings the fact that the purpose of compounding perfume is not 'to smell *thereto*' but to give forth scent *with* that perfume is overlooked. The purpose of both anointing and perfuming is to manifest oneself as healthy and full of power and life. The anointed implements of the sanctuary and the anointed priests are filled with divine life and glory through the holy anointing oil. The purpose of the holy perfume—the incense—is the same. It fills the place where the deity meets his believers with divine strength and grace. To shine with the anointing oil and be perfumed with the holy incense are the benefit and the privilege of the sphere of God, his sanctuary and his priests. Appropriation of these privileges is sacrilege. Such profanation should be punished by death. This penalty is also needed to

[1] 'to smell thereto', RV; 'pour en humer l'odeur', *La Bible de Jérusalem* (1956, 2nd ed. 1958): B. Couroyer; 'pour le respirer', Dhorme, *Pléiade* (1956); more neutral is the rendering given in the RSV: 'to use as perfume', to be found also in the English edition of M. Noth's commentary on *Exodus* (London, 1962). Evidently in the line of the rendering of the Vulgate is Noth's German text: 'um seinen Geruch zu geniessen' (*ATD*, v, Göttingen, 1959); 'um seinem Geruche zu ergötzen', H. Holzinger, *Kautzsch-Bertholet* (Tübingen, 1922); 'um sich an seinem Geruch zu erfreuen', G. Beer–K. Galling, *Kommentar* (Tübingen, 1939). Compare also D. Lys, '*Rûach*', *Le souffle dans l'Ancien Testament* (Paris, 1962), p. 20: 'pour en sentir l'odeur, c'est-à-dire pour s'en régaler par l'odeur.'

secure the people against the after-effects of the sacrilegious acts performed by a member of the people. 'Whoever makes any like it to perfume with shall be cut off from his people.'

The conception of divine smell and its correlation to sacrifice will be dealt with at a later date. I shall therefore be considering here neither texts like Lev. 26:31 and Amos 5:21—both of which use the term הריח ב—nor the other places where the deity himself is the subject of the verbal form הריח, nor the expression רֵיחַ נְחוֹחַ. I shall confine myself here to passages of a more or less profane character, but I will not conceal my opinion that the meaning of the verbal form הריח proposed here has far-reaching consequences for the meaning of sacrifice.

In Gen. 27:27 the subject of the verbs changes without any indication in the Hebrew text, a rather frequent phenomenon in the Hebrew literature. The usual rendering of the beginning of Gen. 27:27 runs as follows: 'And he (Jacob) came near, and kissed him (Isaac); and he (Isaac) smelled the smell of his (Jacob's) garments, and blessed him, and said...' The ancient versions have the same interpretation. Any possible uncertainty is excluded in the reading of the Vulgate: 'Accessit, et osculatus est eum. Statimque ut sensit vestimentorum illius fragrantiam, benedicens illi, ait...' In recent translations one finds other small additions to exclude uncertainty about the subject of the verbs, as appears from the following quotations: 'Da trat er hinzu und küszte ihn; er aber roch den Geruch seiner Kleider; da segnete er ihm und sprach...'[1]; 'Il s'avança et le baisa. Isaac sentit l'odeur de ses habits et le bénit. Il dit...' (Dhorme, 1956); 'Il s'approcha et embrassa son père, qui respira l'odeur de ses vêtements. Il le bénit ainsi:...' (De Vaux, 1956); 'As he went up and kissed him, [Isaac] sniffed the smell of his clothes. Then, at last, he blessed him, saying...' (Speiser, 1964). Translating is interpretation.

The rendering of וירח by 'and he smelled', 'perceived the odour', ascribing a transitive sense to the verb, makes good

---

[1] H. Gunkel, *Genesis* (3rd ed. Göttingen, 1910), p. 312. His observation—which is beside the point—on 'Rassen- und Nationalgerüche' made B. Jacob so angry that the latter forgot to translate verse 27a in his commentary, *Das erste Buch der Tora, Genesis* (Berlin, 1934), p. 566.

sense. If we make Jacob instead of Isaac subject of וירח, ascribing an intransitive sense[1] to the verb, we also get a meaning that fits in with the course of events in the passage: 'And he (Jacob) came near, and kissed him; and he gave forth the scent of his clothes. After that he (Isaac) blessed him, and said...' The words 'and he gave forth the scent of his clothes' can be rendered less literally by: 'and his clothes gave forth their smell.'

In conclusion I come back to the text from the Book of Job. There is no doubt that the horse described in the strophe Job 39: 19–25 is a war-horse. Horse means war-horse everywhere in the Old Testament. For the authors of the Old Testament texts the horse was a new weapon that changed the manner in which war was waged. We may compare the appearance of horses in the theatre of war with tanks or bombers in our days. A tank, or a bomber, makes us think of war. Just so a horse in ancient times. Even from a distance he recalls war and its features, the thunder of captains and battle-cries.

If we assume that הריח has an intransitive meaning we are rid of the difficulties in the rendering of Job 39: 25 that are mentioned at the beginning of this study. We do not need to take refuge in the supposition of meanings that sometimes lead far away from the direct sense of the verb and the noun that is at the root of it. The horse gives forth the scent of war. The horse gives out a penetrating smell. His appearance, even seen from afar, recalls a battle-field, and the air beaten with shouts.

I hope to have brought forward here sufficient arguments to suggest the possibility of a new translation of the final lines of the strophe on the war-horse:

and even from afar he recalls war,
thunder of captains, and battle-cry.

[1] P. Haupt has suggested that we should distinguish *verba voluntaria* and *verba involuntaria* instead of the usual transitive and intransitive verbs, *American Oriental Society Proceedings* (Boston and New Haven, 1894), p. ci. F. R. Blake, who wrote a detailed article on the so-called intransitive verbs in the *JAOS*, xxiv (1903), 145–204, does not mention the texts dealt with here. He mentions in his list of intransitive verbs that indicate states or conditions, under no. 352 רוח: Job 32: 20, become wide, pleasant.

10

EIN NEUGEFUNDENES FRAGMENT DES
SYRISCH-RÖMISCHEN RECHTSBUCHES

Das sog. 'syrisch-römische Rechtsbuch' [1] ist nicht nur eine Quelle von größter Wichtigkeit für unser Wissen vom bürgerlichen und kirchlichen Recht bei den syrischen Christen, sondern auch vom antiken Recht im allgemeinen [2]. Unsere Kenntnis von diesem Text beruht vor allem auf einer einzigen, aus dem sechsten Jahrhundert datierenden [3] syrischen Handschrift, die als Add. MS. 14.528,

---

[1] Vgl. A. BAUMSTARK, *Geschichte der syrischen Literatur* (Bonn 1922), S. 83 und I. ORTIZ DE URBINA, *Patrologia Syriaca* (Romae 1958), S. 225.

[2] Man vgl. z.B. die zahlreichen Studien, die C. A. NALLINO diesem Werk gewidmet hat. Diese Studien sind gesammelt in NALLINO's *Raccolta di scritti editi e inediti* (a cura di Maria NALLINO), Vol. IV: Diritto Musulmanno, Diritti orientali cristiani (Roma 1942). Vgl. noch W. SELB, *Zur Bedeutung des syrisch-römischen Rechtsbuches* [Münchener Beiträge zur Papyrusforschung und antiken Rechtsgeschichte. 49] (München 1964).

[3] Über diese Datierung kann für jeden, der etwas von syrischer Palaeographie versteht (man vgl. nur die Photos bei diesem Artikel), kein Zweifel bestehen. NALLINO's Versuche (*o.c.*, S. 548-550), die er auf Argumente stützt, die lediglich dem Inhalt des Syrisch-römischen Rechtsbuches entnommen sind, die Handschrift ins 8. oder 9. Jahrhundert zu datieren, entbehren allen Wirklichkeitssinn. Seine Behauptung (*o.c.*, S. 548), daß W. WRIGHT (vgl. die folgende Anmerkung) die von ihm beschriebenen Handschriften gewöhnlich zu früh datiert, muß man als ein Argument 'pour besoin de la cause' betrachten, wovon der Beweis nicht leicht zu liefern sein wird; wer sich mit den syrischen Handschriften des Britischen Museums beschäftigt, wird gerade immer wieder getroffen durch die Richtigkeit von W. WRIGHTS Datierungen, wenn auf Grund einer anderen Quelle hierauf neues Licht geworfen wird! Man staunt darüber, daß weder NALLINO noch andere ihre Aufmerksamkeit dem Text (auf fol. 152a-191b) geschenkt haben, der in Add. MS 14.528 dem Syr.-röm. Rechtsbuch unmittelbar vorhergeht und damit, wie aus der Lagezählung hervorgeht (anders als fol. 1-151, die nur durch Zufall mit fol. 152-228 zusammengebunden sind), von Anfang an eine Einheit gebildet hat. Das auf diesen Folioblättern vorkommende - einzigartige - syrische *capitulare lectionum* (ܩܪܝܢܐ ܩܦܠܐܘܢ) repräsentiert das älteste syrische System von Bibelperikopen, das am Ende des 7./Anfang des

f. 152-228 im Britischen Museum [1] aufbewahrt wird. Es ist der Aufmerksamkeit der beiden Herausgeber dieses Textes, des vielseitigen J. P. N. LAND [2] und K. G. BRUNS und E. SACHAU [3] wie auch aller anderen [4], die sich mit der Handschrift beschäftigt haben, entgangen, daß darin außer einer Anzahl kleiner Lücken (durch Risse und Löcher im Pergament) auch ein größerer Schaden festzustellen ist, und zwar dadurch, daß nach fol. 212 ein ganzes Blatt ausgefallen ist [5]. Diesem Versäumnis der Herausgeber, das verständlich ist, weil in der Beschreibung der Handschrift [6] — wie es sonst in dem Katalog gebräuchlich ist — das Fehlen dieses Blattes nicht erwähnt wird [7], kann man leicht auf die Spur kommen, wenn man auf die Struktur der Lagen und weiter auf die *running titles* in der Mitte und am Ende der Lagen der Handschrift achtet. In dem Teil der Londoner Handschrift, der uns hier beschäftigt (nämlich fol. 192-228), ist der Beginn jeweils neuer Lagen durch Numerierung kenntlich gemacht auf fol. 194a und 204a, doch nicht auf fol. 214a und 224a, wie man erwarten würde, und auch nicht

---

8. Jahrhunderts von einem anderen ersetzt wurde (was für einen Sinn sollte es dann überhaupt noch gehabt haben, diesen vor allem auf die liturgische Praxis gerichteten Text noch im 8. oder 9. Jahrhundert zu kopieren?). Man vgl. F. C. BURKITTS grundlegende Studie *The early Syriac Lectionary System* in den Proceedings of the British Academy X (= 1921-1923), S. 301-338 (und separat). BURKITT weist auch daraufhin (*o.c.*, S. 305), daß dieser Text für das Personalpronomen 1. Plur. noch einmal (in einem Zitat aus Hebr. iii 6) die Form ܐܢܚܢܢ statt ܚܢܢ verwendet, eine archaische Schreibweise, die man nach dem 6. Jahrhundert kaum noch erwarten würde.

[1] Vgl. W. WRIGHT, *Catalogue of the Syriac Manuscripts in the British Museum acquired since the year 1838* (London 1870-1872), S. 176-177.

[2] J. P. N. LAND, *Anecdota Syriaca*, vol. I (Leiden 1862), S. 30-64 (Text), 123-155 (Übersetzung), 184-198 (Anmerkungen); vgl. noch *Anecdota Syriaca*, Vol. II (Leiden 1868), S. 19-20 und 24-25.

[3] K. G. BRUNS und E. SACHAU, *Syrisch-römisches Rechtsbuch aus dem fünften Jahrhundert*. Leipzig 1880 (abgekürzt als BRUNS/SACHAU, SrR).

[4] z.B. NALLINO, *o.c.*, S. 548-550. Auch W. SELB, *o.c.*, S. 100 oben, 130[7], ist sich hierüber kaum im klaren gewesen.

[5] BRUNS/SACHAU, SrR, S. 22, Fußnote 4 (und völlig unbegreiflich ebenda S. 265 der zweiten Seitenzählung) sprechen wohl von einer „Lücke", aber sie machten sich offensichtlich nicht bewußt, daß ein Schaden gerade auf dem Übergang von einem Folio zum anderen umfangreicher sein muß als die Paar Zeilen, die sie scheinbar als verloren ansahen.

[6] Vgl. WRIGHT, *o.c.*, S. 176.

[7] LANDS Edition, die vor der Ausgabe des Katalogs liegt, ist in diesem Punkte leicht zu entschuldigen.

auf fol. 213a und 223a, weil von diesen Folioblättern das untere Stück (wo die Lagebezeichnungen sich meistens befinden) verloren gegangen ist. Hier können uns die *running titles* helfen; man findet sie, in der *Mitte* einer Lage, auf fol. 198b, 208b, 217b (!) und, am *Ende* einer Lage, auf fol. 193b, 203b und 222b (!). Hieraus ergibt sich, daß zwischen fol. 208b und 217b ein Blatt (= das eigentliche fol. 213), das — als letztes der Lage [1] — auf der Rückseite einen *running title* haben muß, verloren gegangen ist [2].

Das Department of Egyptian Art des Metropolitan Museum of Art in New York besitzt nun seit 1921 [3] eine Anzahl Blätter von syrischen Handschriften [4], die aus dem Kloster Dair as-Suryan in der Nitrischen Wüste stammen, d.h. aus dem gleichen Kloster, wo auch Add. MS 14.528 herkommt [5]. Hierunter befinden sich verschiedene Bruchstücke, die sich als zu Handschriften gehörig identifizieren lassen, die sich nun im Britischen Museum befinden, aber ebenfalls aus Dair as-Suryan stammen. Eines dieser Bruchstücke Nr. 21.148.18 [6], das auf der Rückseite den *running title* ·�ܐ ܟܘܬܒܐ ·ܿ· hat, d.h. identisch mit dem in Add. MS 14.528 üblichen Titel, ist (wie sich auch aus der Tatsache ergibt, daß der Text des Stückes nach vorn wie nach hinten lückenlos an den Text der Londoner Handschrift anschließt) das Blatt, das in der Londoner Handschrift nach fol. 212 fehlt.

Dies ist der Text, den wir hier in Photographie und in Transkription (wobei die kleinen Lücken meist an Hand der Parallelen ange-

---

[1] Das äußerste Bifolium einer Lage ist am verletztbarsten und daher zuerst Beschädigungen ausgesetzt.

[2] Add. MS 14.528 ist, wie W. BAARS im Britischen Museum feststellte, seit den Tagen von WRIGHT aufs neue gebunden. Hierbei hat man die Lücke nach fol. 212 bemerkt und durch einen losen Leinenstreifen zwischen den heutigen fol. 212 und 213 angedeutet.

[3] Vgl. H. G. EVELYN WHITE, *The Monasteries of the Wâdi 'n Natrûn* (New York 1932), S. 457 und vgl. *ebend.* Bd III (1933), S. 177.

[4] Vgl. J. T. CLEMON, *A Checklist of Syriac manuscripts in the United States and Canada* in Orientalia Christiana Periodica XXXII (Roma 1966), S. 491-493; doch es sei darauf hingewiesen, daß CLEMONS Nr. 265-268 keine syrische, sondern koptische Texte, daß die Nr. 269-271 arabische Texte und daß Nr. 272 Bruckstücke eines gedruckten Buches enthalten.

[5] Vgl. WRIGHT, *o. c.*, S. xiii.

[6] Vgl. CLEMON, *o.c.*, S. 493, Nr. 281.

füllt sind) publizieren [1], zu dem wir eine (vorläufige) Übersetzung hinzufügen.

Der hier publizierte Text hat (was beim Ergänzen der Lücken und für die Übersetzung wichtig ist) nicht wenig Parallelen mit der schon bekannten syrischen (oder davon abhängigen) Rechtsliteratur. Hierzu läßt sich das folgende bemerken:

Recto, Z. 1-9 (= der Schluß von § 91 in BRUNS/SACHAUS Einteilung des syrisch-römischen Rechtsbuches) findet seine nächste Parallele in § 56 der zweiten sog. römischen Rezension [2] dieses Werkes. Vgl. noch § 45 der sog. pariser Rezension [3]; § 32 der ersten römischen Rezension [4] und § 91 der dritten römischen Rezension [5].

Recto, Z. 9-24^{ult} (= ex hypothesin § 92 des Londoner Textes) hat seine beste Parallele in § 133 der zweiten römischen Rezension [6], in § 129 der armenischen Übersetzung [7] und § 130 der arabischen Übersetzung [8] des syrisch-römischen Rechtsbuches. Man vgl. noch § 48 der ersten römischen Rezension [9] und § 92 der dritten römischen Rezension [10] [11].

Verso, Z. 1-23^{ult} (= Beginn von dem, was § 93 [12] in der Londoner Handschrift sein muß) hat als nächste Parallele § 51 der zweiten römischen Rezension [13]. Man vergleiche noch § 93 der dritten römi-

---

[1] ○ bezeichnet Buchstaben, die schwer beschädigt sind, aber über deren Lesung kein Zweifel bestehen kann.

[2] Vgl. E. SACHAU, *Syrische Rechtsbücher*. Erster Band: *Leges Constantini Theodosii Leonis*. Berlin 1907. (abgekürzt als SACHAU, SR), S. 86, 88 (Text); S. 87, 89 (Übersetzung).

[3] Vgl. BRUNS/SACHAU, SrR, S. 54 (Text); S. 60-61 der zweiten Seitenzählung (Übersetzung).

[4] Vgl. SACHAU, SR, S. 16, 18 (Text); S. 17, 19 (Übersetzung).

[5] Vgl. SACHAU, SR, S. 168 (Text), S. 169 (Übersetzung).

[6] Vgl. SACHAU, SR, S. 120, 122 (Text); S. 121, 123 (Übersetzung).

[7] Vgl. BRUNS/SACHAU, SrR, S. 134 (Text); S. 145 der zweiten Seitenzählung (Übersetzung).

[8] Vgl. BRUNS/SACHAU, SrR, S. 94 (Text); S. 114 der zweiten Seitenzählung (Übersetzung).

[9] Vgl. SACHAU, SR, S. 24 (Text); S. 25 (Übersetzung).

[10] Vgl. SACHAU, SR, S. 168 (Text); S. 169 (Übersetzung).

[11] Dieser Teil fehlt in der sog. pariser Rezension.

[12] Vgl. SACHAU, SR, S. 207 wo auf Grund der dritten römischen Rezension (= ein Auszug eines Textes, der dem in Add. MS 14.528 ganz ähnlich ist) die richtige Paragraphennummerierung schon postuliert wird.

[13] Vgl. SACHAU, SR, S. 80 (Text); S. 81 (Übersetzung).

schen Rezension [1], § 31 der ersten römischen Rezension [2] und § 40 der pariser Rezension [3]. Der Text der Verso-Seite des New Yorker-Stückes findet weiterhin noch eine Parallele in den Fragmenten einer erst vor kurzem bekannt gewordenen [4] alten (*saec.* VIII) Handschrift der zweiten römischen Rezension.

Speciminis causa folgen hier die Varianten dieser Handschrift (= V) [5] und des bisher bekannten Textes der zweiten römischen Rezension, die auf einer Handschrift (Borg. sir. 81 = B) aus der zweiten Hälfte des vorigen Jahrhunderts beruht, im Vergleich mit dem Text des Stückes in New York [6].

Z. *1* ܘܗܢ] + ܕܐܝܠ ܕܠܗܘ ܝܢ ܕܗ V: + ܗܘ ܝܢ ܕ B | ܘܕܝܢܗܝ] *pr* ܕ V | *2* ܕܠܗܘ ܕܐܝܠ ܕܐܒܘܗܝܘ] *om* V | ܕܠܗܘ ܐܝܠ] ∾ B | ܕܗܝܕܝܢ] *pr* ܘܒܩܪܗ ܡܥ ܡ VB(ܕܩܘܗ): *om sey* B | *4* ܕܒܩܡܥ.] ܕܩܘܡܥܗ VB | ܕܗܘܢ] ܗܘܘܢ V | *5* ܕܗ] ܕܗܝܡ V | ܕܐܝܡܝܢ] + ,ܗ V | *6* ܕܠܒܘܕ] ܐܝܒܠ V | *7* ܘܠܝ] *om* ܘ V | ܕܩܝܒ] *pr* ܕ B | *8* ܕܠ ܐܝܟ/ ܐܟܘܕ B | ܕܠܩ] *om sey*(*ut vid*) V | *9* ܐ] *om* B | *10* ܘܠܡܗܝ] *c. sey* V | ܕܐܝܗܒ] + ܗܘܒܘ ܘܐ VB | *11* ܘܢܗܝ] *om sey* V | *12* ܕܩܘܗ] ܕܠܗܩ ܘܐ ܕܝܢܗ ܘܠܩ ܘܐܬܗܪ.ܕܠܗܐ.ܕܝܗ ܐ VB (ܕܝܗ.ܢ) | ܕܩܘܗܝ] *om sey* VB | ܕܩܘܗܝ] *pr* ܗܒ ܕܐܝܬ B: ܕܩܘܗܝ ܠܗ ܕܐܝܬ V | *13* ܐܝܢܐ] ܕܩܝ VB | ܕܐܒܘܗܝ] ܕܐܒܘܗ V | ܘܗܝܐ] *c. sey* B | ܕܩܘܗܝܠ] *pr* ܕ B: *om* V | *14* ܗܘܗ] ܠܘ B | [ܗܕ.]ܕܩܘܗܝܠ] ܕܩܘܗܝܠ VB | *15* ܕܠܝܗ] ܗܕ V: *om* B | *17* ܘܗܝܕܝܢ] *om* VB | *18* ܘܗܒܘܕ] ܕܩܘܗܝܕ B | ܕܠܩܬܢ] *pr* ܘܩܒܠ ܕܢܬ VB: + ܕܠܩ ܗܒܘ V: +

---

[1] Vgl. SACHAU, SR, S. 168 (Text); S. 169 (Übersetzung).

[2] Vgl. SACHAU, SR, S. 16 (Text); S. 17 (Übersetzung).

[3] Vgl. BRUNS/SACHAU, SrR, S. 51, 52 (Text); S. 58 der zweiten Seitenzählung (Übersetzung). Verso, Z. 21-23 bilden den Anfang des § 41a in der pariser Rezension.

[4] Vat. sir. 560A, fol. 28a-31b; vgl. A. VAN LANTSCHOOT, *Inventaire des manuscrits syriaques des fonds Vatican* (490 [*sic* statt 460]-631), *Barberini oriental et Neofiti* [Studi e Testi 243], (Città del Vaticano 1965), S. 79-80.

[5] Verso, Z. 1-23 des New Yorker Bruchstückes korrespondiert mit fol. 28a, Kol. 2, Z. 11 - fol. 28b, Kol. 1, Z. 17 in Vat. sir. 560A.

[6] Die Kollation folgt den Regeln, die formuliert sind in: *The Old Testament in Syriac according to the Peshiṭta version.* Sample edition (Leiden 1966): General Preface.

 B | *19* VB |
VB | *20*] totaliter aliter | *21*
VB | B | V | B |
] om B: + V | *22* VB |]
 VB | *23* V

New York, Metr. Museum of Art: Dept. of Egypt. Antiquities

21.148.18

recto   1.

New York, Metr. Mus. of Art: Dept. of Egypt. Antiquities 21.148.18 *recto*

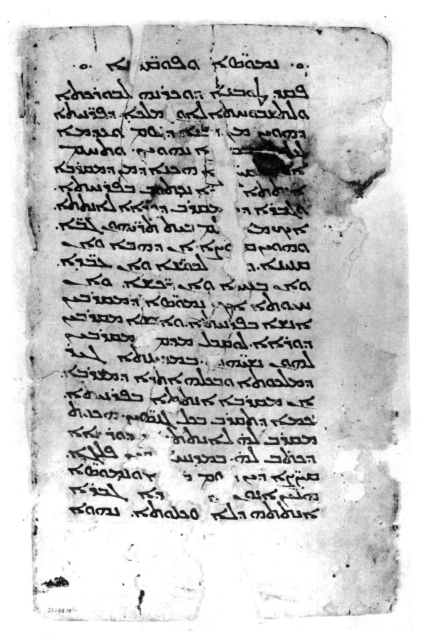

New York, Metr. Mus. of Art: Dept. of Egypt. Antiquities 21.148.18 *verso*

New York, Metr. Museum of Art: Dept. of Egypt. Antiquities
21.148.18

verso

L. 14 † †] Text

Übersetzung

recto

. . . .] dessen Familie, wird ihr überlassen.
Wenn er <*sc.* ein Mann> aber das Mädchen nur aus der Ferne hat
werben lassen durch Vermittlung seiner Eltern oder von anderen,
dem Mädchen aber nicht ein Brautgemach zuteil geworden ist (5)
und der Bräutigam sie nach der Verlobung weder gesehen noch ge-
küsst hat, (dann) bekommt er, wenn sie stirbt, alles was er oder
seine Eltern ihr gegeben haben von ihren Verwandten zurück,
ausgenommen Essen und Trinken.

(§ 92)

Wenn (10) jemand einen Knaben oder Mädchen, ein Kind des
Ehebruchs oder Armenkind, dessen Angehörige unbekannt sind,
von der Kirche oder aus dem Balneum annimmt, es mit Milch auf-
zieht und auch weiterhin ernährt (und) das Gesetz (15) wird be-
fragt, ob er oder sie Sklave oder frei ist, nachdem sie <*sc.* Knabe
und Mädchen> mündig geworden sind, so befehlt es <*sc.* das
Gesetz>:
Maßgebend ist der Wille desjenigen, der sie erzogen hat. Nachdem
sie mündig geworden sind, sind sie frei wenn er sie als (seine eigenen) Kinder erzogen hat. Aber wenn (20) er sie als Sklaven erzogen
hat, sind sie Sklaven. Und wenn er sie als Sklaven belassen hat und
er stirbt, dann bleiben sie Sklaven. Wenn er sie aber wie Freie
erzogen hat und er stirbt, bleiben sie frei.

verso

(§ 93)

Befohlen hat der glückselige König Leo, dessen Andenken zu Segen
und Preis gereiche: daß die φερναί von der Zeit seines Erlasses ab
bis in Ewigkeit in schriftlichem Vertrag niedergelegt werden. Und
er hat (5) den schriftlichen Vertrag folgendermaßen bestimmt:
Was die Frau dem Manne gewährt, schreibt er auf als φερνή. Der
Mann aber gewährt der Frau eine δωρεά, wie sie zwischen beiden
Parteien übereingekommen ist. So gibt es schriftliche Verträge
sei es über Gold, oder (10) über Besitztümer, oder über Kleider,

oder über Sklaven, oder über Vieh, oder über Reittiere, oder über
(sonstigen) Viehbestand. (Es richtet sich) nach den (lokalen) Ge-
setzen, was man als φερνή gewährt oder was man als δωρεά gewährt,
(letztere) entsprechend dem, was (15) ihre Weiber ihnen gewähren.
Denn in der Hauptstadt des Reiches und im ganzen Westen (gilt),
daß, wenn die Frau eine φερνή gewährt, so viel sie auch gewährt,
welcher Art die Sache auch ist, er <sc. der Mann> der Frau eben-
soviel gewährt als δωρεά, (20) die er ihr schriftlich festsetzt. Im
Osten <sc. des Reiches> aber (beträgt sie) nur die Hälfte.
Die Vertragsbestimmungen, die der König aufgestellt hat, und die
(dazu gehörigen) Gesetze sind folgende:
Wenn ein Mann seine Frau ohne ein Vergehen (ihrerseits) entläßt,
soll er [. . . . . .

11

IN SEARCH OF THE MEANING OF PSALM LI 6 (4)*

For the bibliography on this psalm, the reader may refer to a Columbia University dissertation containing a list of more than 670 titles: E.R. DALGLISH, *Psalm Fifty-One in the Light of Ancient Near Eastern Paternism.*[1] I have often consulted DALGLISH's book, but I know only some of the studies he mentions. In this paper, I shall mention a few works published after 1962 (the year in which DALGLISH's book appeared), and also a few that even he overlooked. DALGLISH's book, however, does not restrict itself to bibliographical information. His evaluation of the studies he consulted and his extensive comparisons with extra-biblical texts, which offer a deeper insight into the kind of literature that this psalm belongs to, have rightly been praised.[2] Every new study of a text that has been examined so often can easily get bogged down in the opinions voiced by earlier scholars.

DALGLISH's own explanation of the psalm contains few original judgments. Is this because his approach of the text is marked too much by the study of other scholars' results? I took the risk of following a more personal line. Naturally I consulted DALGLISH and others afterwards—discovering that I had done once more what others had done better before me, and that I had missed certain aspects of the subject. But a few points remained which I, for one, should like to put forward.

The Masoretic vocalization of Ps. li 6 does not seem to be the only possible one. This encourages one to examine the history of the transmission of this text. KITTEL's *Biblia Hebraica* prints the text with notes collected by F. BUHL in 1930. With regard to the word *bdbrk*, BUHL agrees with the reading *bdbryk* found in a number of Hebrew MSS[3] and assumed in the Septuagint, in Symmachus' translation, in the Vulgate and in St. Paul's reference to the verse in Rom. iii

---

* The verse numbers in brackets are those used in English translations of the Bible and have been added by the translator.

[1] Leiden, 1962.

[2] G.R. CASTELLINO, the author of the excellent commentary *Libro dei Salmi*, Turin/Rome 1955, wrote an appreciative review of DALGLISH's study in *VT* 15/1 (1965), pp. 116–120. In this review one can find corrections and additions with regard to the relevant extra-biblical texts.

[3] DALGLISH, *op. cit.*, p. 66. See H. BARDTKE in BHS (1969): mit Mss G σ' *bidbārǽkā*.

4. But according to a number of manuscripts, *bšptk*, too, can be a plural. On the basis of the Greek reading ἐν τῷ κρίνεσθαί σε (LXX: one MS + the Coptic Psalter read με instead of σε[4]; St. Paul) and the reading of the Vulgate *cum iudicaris*, it has also been suggested that *bšptk* is a contracted form of the infinitive niph'al.[5] Furthermore, the two verbal forms *tṣdq* and *tzkh* can be read as pi'el. This was already noticed in an early stage of the history of the text, as will be seen below.

It is clear that the transmission of the text displays different interpretations. The question arises whether the Greek text or the Syriac or Aramaic ones have preserved an earlier Hebrew reading, be it in translation, than the rabbinical tradition, the so-called Masoretic text.

The Aramaic translation in particular diverges from the rabbinical reading of the Hebrew text. The Targum has, "Before you, you only, have I sinned, and what you consider wrong I have done in order that you may declare me innocent in your pronouncement, and declare me pure when you pass sentence."[6] The verbs in the second part of v. 6 are taken to be transitive, and the subject of the first part of the verse is added as their object: *tzky yty* and *tbwr yty*. The Midrash, however, is based on the Masoretic vocalization. It has (I quote W.G. BRAUDE's recent translation[7]): "*For Thee, Thee only, have I sinned ... That Thou mayest be justified when Thou speakest.* To whom may David be likened? To a man who broke a limb, and came to a physician. The physician marveled and said: 'How great is thy break! I am much distressed on thy account.' The man with the broken limb said: 'Art thou distressed on my account? Was not my limb broken for thy sake, since the fee is to be thine?' Just so David said to the Holy One, blessed is He: *For Thee, Thee only, have I sinned*: Shouldst thou receive me, then if Thou sayest to transgressors 'Wherefore have ye not repented?' all transgressors will submit to Thee, for all of them will behold me, and I shall surely bear witness, that Thou receivest the penitent." BILLERBECK adduces more

---

[4] *Psalmi cum Odis*, ed. A. RAHLFS, 2nd edition, Göttingen, 1967, p. 163.

[5] DALGLISH, *op. cit.*, refers to F.M. MOZLEY, *The Psalter of the Church*, Cambridge, 1905. Cf. BARDTKE, BHS: G pass = *bišša'* (*bᵉhišša'*).

[6] I have used the edition by P. DE LAGARDE, Leipzig, 1873. On p. 111 of his book, DALGLISH reproduces the translation by STRACK-BILLERBECK, *Kommentar zum Neuen Testament aus Talmud und Midrasch*, vol. 3, pp. 133ff.

[7] *The Midrash on Psalms*, translated by W.G. BRAUDE (Yale Judaica Series 13), New Haven, 1959.

examples of a similar purport from rabbinical literature.[8] When I
checked if there were other texts in which God is the subject of the
verbs ṣdq and zkh in qal, the result was negative. However, one cannot conclude much from such a negative result. There is too little
Hebrew left from the period with which the Hebrew material deals
to argue conclusively about frequencies of occurence. Still, I do believe that some weight may be given to the meaning of the piˁel of
these two verbs. In Jer. iii, the sins of Judah (called the "faithless
one") are emphasized by a comparison: the people of the North (Israel), who are known to have deviated from God and to have been
punished accordingly, are compared with Judah and justified. According to Jer. iii 11, Israel emerges as innocent (ṣiddᵉqâ napšâ) in
the Lord's judgment, as opposed to Judah. The same usage of the
word is found in Ez. xvi 51f. There Jerusalem is compared with
Samaria. Samaria—its fate is known by all—has not committed half
the sins of which Jerusalem is guilty. In a lawsuit Samaria would
emerge as innocent in comparison with Jerusalem.[9] Job xxxii 2 also
has the verb in the meaning "to justify oneself" (ṣaddᵉqô napšô). And
in Job xxxiii 32 it means "to put in the right" (ṣaddeqækkā).[10] In the
Aḥiqar story, the paˁel of the Aramaic verb ṣdq occurs with the same
meaning (l. 140). In J. Hoftijzer's translation, this line runs: "Il a
pris parti contre moi comme témoin malveillant (litt. a été pour
moi), qui donc me considérera comme juste (innocent)?"[11] Post-
biblical Hebrew, too, understands the piˁel in the sense of "to regard someone as justified, to defend". This usage also points towards a court of law.[12]

    zkh, piˁel, means "to keep pure": one's heart Ps. lxxiii 13; Prov.

---

[8] Strack-Billerbeck, op. cit., pp. 135ff.

[9] Cf. W. Zimmerli, Ezechiel, BKAT XIII/1, Neukirchen-Vluyn, 1958, p. 367.

[10] An English translation of Dhorme's commentary, Paris, 1926, appeared in
London in 1967. In his annotations to the texts he observes, "Le piˁel de ṣdq dans
le sens de 'donner raison'; cf. le qal au v. 12 et l'hifˁil dans xxvii, 5" (ad xxxiii 32).
He translates xxxii 2 as "il se justifiait devant Elohim". S. Terrien, commentary,
Neuchatel 1963, translates xxxii 2 as "parce qu'il avait justifié sa vie contre Dieu",
remarking that it is also possible to translate "plus que Dieu" or "devant Dieu".

[11] Jean-Hoftijzer, Dictionnaire des inscriptions sémitiques de l'ouest (DISO),
Leiden, 1965, p. 243. The text can be found in A. Cowley, Aramaic Papyri of the
Fifth Century B.C., Oxford, 1923, p.217. Cowley's translation ("And who then has
justified me?"), which can also be found in ANET, third edition, 1969, p. 429, by
H.L. Ginsberg, seems less correct than the one given by Hoftijzer

[12] See e.g. M. Jastrow, A Dictionary of the Targumim etc., London-New York,
1903.

xx 9; one's way of life Ps. cxix 9; "to consider right" cj. Mic. vi 11 (*ha⁾ᵉzakkǣ*): "Shall I declare innocent (the man who does business) with false scales and fraudulent weights?"[13] The Targum uses the pa⁽el of the verb with the meaning "to acquit, to leave unpunished". In post-biblical Hebrew, the pi⁾el means "to acquit, to grant a privilege or a divine favour; to convert to righteousness, to make pure". The Aramaic form can also mean "to control a discussion, to conquer". It is from this meaning that the Greek νικᾶν should be explained. All these meanings point to the context of a judicial sentence. It seems more natural to equate the person defended and acquitted with the first person poet of this penitential psalm, who is begging for forgiveness and appeals to God's mercy from the very first line of his song, than with the deity. Both *bdbrk* and *bšptk* fit in with the image of a court of justice. By (*bet instrumentalis* seems to be intended) his word (the Syriac version seems to be the least artificial) and by his decision (his judicial act) God can acquit the penitent.

If I am on the right track here, I should be able to explain the interpretation expressed both in the Masoretic reading and in translations as early as the Septuagint. I shall try to do this by considering the historicization of the penitential psalm found in the heading. Penitential psalms frequently occur both in the Old Testament and in other religious texts preserved from the Ancient Near East. DAL-GLISH's book offers numerous examples. Ps. li does not contain any indication that the narrator of the story of 2 Sam. 11f. is also the poet of this song. It would be useful to examine whether there are any traces that might help to date this kind of historicization. Here I shall only remark that it must have taken place before the Septuagint version of the Book of Psalms was made. It presupposes a divine judgement preceding the penitential psalm. Before Nathan pronounces Yhwh's condemnation, David shows no feelings of remorse in the story of 2 Samuel.

The house of David will always be at war, will never have

---

[13] A. DEISSLER, *La Sainte Bible*, 8, Paris. 1964, p. 347, translates this text as follows: "Dois-je *acquitter* pour des balances criminelles/ et une bourse de poids truqués?" At this he notes that "zkh au piel, semble être employé ici au sens absolu, sans régime direct." If the reading suggested here is correct, then Ps. li 6 with its absolute use of pi⁽el would have a parallel. Cf. also D. HILL, *Greek Words and Hebrew Meanings: Studies in the Semantics of Soteriological Terms*, Cambridge, 1967, p. 105.

peace—says the scathing judgement of 2 Sam. xii 10. The penitential psalm itself does not refer to specific events. In it one does
penance and asks for acquittal—as is common in this kind of littera-
ture, which uses more or less general terms and shows a preference
for synonyms. Its historicization presumably resulted in an interpretation of *bdbrk* and *bšptk* in v. 6b that went together with a change
in the vocalization of the two verbs *ṣdq* and *zkh*.

This does not answer all the problems. The idea of Davidic
authorship of the psalm is being increasingly abandoned. In DAL-
GLISH's book one can find references to those who still defend the
correctness of its heading. For a better understanding of the 6th
verse, let me quote the rabbinical dictum *nulla creatura iudicat regem,
sed deus benedictus* cited by Hugo GROTIUS in his *Annotata ad Vetus
Testamentum*.[14] This brings me to the question of the meaning of the
beginning of v. 6: "Against you, you only, have I sinned."

In recent years, various studies have been devoted to the idea of
sin in the Old Testament, such as: G. QUELL's article in *ThWNT*,
vol. I (1933), pp. 267–288, which contains valuable surveys of
terms and translations, although its explanation of Ps. li 6 ("Ich
habe gesündigt um der Ehre Gottes willen", p. 278) may be dis-
puted, see below; Th. C.VRIEZEN's article in RGG³ (1962), which
is very compact and rich in content, but does not refer to the text
under discussion; St. PORÚBČAN, *Sin in the Old Testament: A Soteriological Study*, Rome, 1963[15]; R. KNIERIM, *Die Hauptbegriffe für Sünde im
Alten Testament*, Gütersloh, 1965, the sequel to his Heidelberg dissertation of 1957. Furthermore we can find definitions of the idea of sin
in books describing the history of Israel's religion or dealing with
"the" theology of the Old Testament. From the latter category I
should like to mention L. KÖHLER's *Theologie des Alten Testaments*, in
which the various words for 'sin" are also briefly and clearly defined.[16] He translates the verb *ḥṭ*' used in Ps. li 6 by "verfehlen".
The two texts he cites here are very illuminating: "Du durchgehst
deine Flur und vermissest nichts Hiob 5: 24; wer mich findet, findet
Leben, wer mich verfehlt, schädigt sich selber Prov. 8: 35s". On the
whole it is remarkable that this category of studies often contains a

---

[14] Paris, 1644. Tomus I, pp. 461ff.
[15] R. KNIERIM reviewed PORÚBČAN's work extensively in an article called "The
Problem of an Old Testament Hamartiology", in *VT* 16/3 (1966), pp. 366–385.
[16] 4th impression, Tübingen, 1966, pp. 158ff.

discussion of Ps. li 7, while v. 6 is scarcely or not at all referred to.[17]

The declaration "I have gone wrong, I have failed" is continued in the words "I have done what is evil in your eyes." Because man acts wrongly and fails to reach his goal, his God is offended, and the same applies to the community as a whole. Offending God is a disaster for mankind. A new correlation arises between faults and disasters. There is a long list of texts in which people acknowledge that they are wrong. Besides Ps. 51 there are 51 texts in which the verb $ḥṭ^{\circ}$ is used. In a number of these it refers to the acknowledgement of an offence against a human person (Gen. xx 9 (question); xliii 9; xliv 32; Num. xii 11; Judg. xi 27; 1 Sam. xxiv 12 (denial); xxvi 21; 2 Sam. xix 21; 1 Kings xviii 9; 2 Kings xviii 14; Jer. xxxvii 18). In all these cases the acknowledgement is related to the consequences of the offence. The confession of guilt or the question what has been done wrong arises out of these consequences (sickness, persecution, the threat of war, the danger of death, imprisonment). Most of these texts, however, contain the acknowledgement of an offence against the deity ($ḥṭ^{\circ}$ l . . .).[18] When Pharaoh sees the consequences of his refusal to let the people go, he acknowledges himself to be guilty towards Yhwh (Ex. ix 27; x 16). This acknowledgement does not only concern himself but also his people. Moreover, it is Yhwh, the Lord himself who "hardened the heart of Pharaoh" (Ex. ix 12, 35; x 20). "To be guilty" cannot be the exact meaning of $ḥṭ^{\circ}$, the disastrous consequences being included in the meaning of the verb; "to fail" seems to be a better rendering. When the Israelites groan under the power exercised by their enemies, they interpret their fate in the acknowledgement "We have failed" (Judg. x 10, 15; 1 Sam. vii 6; xii 10). When David, encouraged by Yhwh, has allowed a census which then leads to disaster, the king acknowledges that he has made a mistake (2 Sam. xxiv 10, 17). There are further examples in Jer. xvi 10; Isa. xlii 24; Ps. xli 5 (4); Lam. v 16. One should take particular notice of instances in which more than one verb is used (2 Sam. xxiv 17; 1 Kings viii 47; Ps. cvi 6; Dan. ix 5, 15).

Before dealing with a special aspect of Ps. li 6 and parallels, I want to discuss briefly two passages from this series of texts. In Jer. ii 35,

---

[17] KÖHLER, *op. cit.*, mentions the verse under discussion on p. 169. He concurs with C.STEUERNAGEL (*Festschrift* Sellin 1926), who sees the psalm as a collective song of penitence.

[18] Here it may suffice to refer the reader to a concordance.

the people conclude from a favourable turn of events that they have not failed. However, the prophet foresees that a treaty with Egypt will not ward off disaster, and he prophesies the Lords' judgement. The second text is Mic. vii 9, which can be translated as follows:

Yhwh's anger I shall bear—surely I have failed him—,
until he pleads my cause and gives me justice:
he will make me go out into the light,
I shall see his justice.

In all probability, the pericope Mic. vii 7 – 13 stems from the post-exilic period: the walls of Jerusalem have not yet been rebuilt. The speaker, who is probably also speaking for his fellow sufferers, is in a bad situation. He sits in darkness (v. 8) and lacks the conditions in which his life can develop. He has enemies, and is waiting for the moment when his God will administer justice, in the conviction that the divine sentence will rehabilitate him and put his enemies to shame. On the day of judgement, Yhwh will no longer keep away from him. Now his enemy mocks him saying, "Where is Yhwh your God?" (v. 10). The translation of the first line ("Surely I have failed him", or: "For I have sinned against him") does not express the fact that the believer expects salvation from the divine sentence. "To bear Yhwh's anger" and "to have fallen" (v. 8; probably a reference to the lament of Amos v. 2) are both expressions pointing to the fate of exile and the loss of independence. The term $ht^{\circ}ty$ l^e means both "I have failed [him]" and "I miss [him]" or "I am separated from him". Our language cannot express both guilt and fate in one term. $ht^{\circ}ty$ and $ht^{\circ}nw$ do occur in absolute use, but are generally followed by l^e: "with respect to" Elohim or, more often, Yhwh. Apart from Ps. li 6, there are only two texts (if I am correct) in which "with respect to (God)" stands in front of the verb rather than after it. In Jer. xiv the prophet opens with a lament about a disastrous drought, which is a superb example of lyrical poetry. After this song, he goes on to say,[19]

---

[19] It is also possible to consider vv. 7–9 as a complaint of the people, with which the prophet does not agree. See W. RUDOLPH's commentary (2nd edition, Tübingen, 1958), pp. 90ff. From v. 11 (Yhwh's prohibition against praying for the people) I conclude that Jeremiah had already done so. In that case he may also have formulated the people's complaint. For more about Jeremiah, see the present writer's *De voorbede in het Oude Testament*, Leiden, 1943, pp. 88ff., 143, 148ff.

Though our sins testify against us,
yet take action, Yhwh, for your own name's sake.
Our disloyalties indeed are many;
we have sinned against you.

The drought, affecting the lives of both man and beast, is interpreted as the result of disloyalty. The prophet's intercession does not
use any arguments taken from the people and their critical situation,
but instead makes an appeal to Yhwh's mighty acts: has not this god
associated his name with that of the people (v. 7)? Is he not their
saviour in times of distress, one whom one may rely with reason (v.
8), is he not the heart of national life, and aren't the people called
by his name (v. 9)? Now, however, he is like a stranger in the land,
like a traveller who is only staying for a night and will continue his
journey (v. 8). With this the fate of both country and people seems
to have been decided: they will be destroyed. The prophet's passionate prayer ends in a cry: "Do not forsake us!"

The second text in which "with respect to our God Yhwh" comes
before the verb ("we have failed") is Jer. iii 25. This is the last line
of a confession of sins.[20] The worship of another god than Yhwh
has affected the people's strength. Through bitter experiences they
have come to acknowledge that salvation can only be expected from
Yhwh (v. 23). The bed (which is the centre of the house, the place
of intimacy, a sign of dignity and also of prestige, because one is able
to offer one's guests a bed) has been defiled: it is a spot of which one
feels ashamed, which has become a "scandal". The blanket (protection and warmth) has become a cause of mockery. The core of life
is affected, because "We have failed (with respect to) our god
Yhwh." The separation from Yhwh (Isa. lix 2) means guilt and
ruin, sin and disaster at the same time.

When the Psalmist says that he has failed (with respect to) his god,
he finds himself in a position where he needs to be saved and healed
(Ps. xli 5 (4); li 6 (4)). He prays that what has been lost may be restored to him. $ht^?$ does not mean to sin or act badly and profit by it,
but to act badly and also to become the victim of one's acts. This
verb assumes the presence of the deity, who guarantees people's wel-
fare. To forsake God results in misery and disaster. If God is the
starting-point of the confession that one is wrong or has failed, then

---

[20] For the text and the possibility of additions, see RUDOLPH, *op. cit.*, p. 26.

the penitent stresses his being dependent on him. Ps. 51 does not mention the penitent's faults, but it does refer to the consequences of these. There is no enjoyment of life, the penitent feels broken, the opposite of "whole", i.e. healthy (v. 10 (8)). His inner nature is aching for purity and steadfastness (v. 12 (10)). He feels oppressed by bloodguiltiness (v. 16 (14)), and may be threatened by a vendetta. In this condition he begs for mercy, and asks to be cleansed from his rebellion, his misconduct, his iniquities.

The verse under discussion does not only say, "Against you", but reinforces these words by adding *lᵉbaddᵉkā, seorsum*. VAN DER PLOEG takes this to mean "Against you, the Only One, ...", noting, "Literally it says, 'Against you alone', which means "Against you, who are alone, i.e. the Only One. Cf. Neh. ix 6.''[21] With JOUON[22] I prefer the meaning *à part*. *lbd* differentiates: it refers to a separation from a group. The other(s) fade away, and all attention is fixed on the one *à part*. The adverb here serves to underline a *specific* quality of the person spoken to or about. I think this is true of all instances occurring in the psalms (lxxi 16; lxxxiii 19 (18); lxxxvi 10; cxxxvi 4; cxlviii 13) and also in Neh. ix 6. This would mean that the basic meaning of Ps. li 6 (4) is: "In acknowledging that I have failed with respect to you, I think of you in your specific quality." What quality is this? The answer to this question must come from vv. 3–5 (1–3). The penitent addresses his god as the faithful one, who is rich in mercy and can graciously forgive misdeeds, failings, and rebellions. He continually experiences the consequences of these deeds and failings (v. 5 (3)), and it is in this situation that he says, "With respect to you, you especially, have I failed and acted wrongfully ..." You especially: i.e (with respect to) the god to whose forgiving nature this song of lament makes a passionate appeal. These words are the first of the verse and dominate its content.

What is the meaning of the word *lmᶜn*, with which the verse continues? The dictionary of BROWN-DRIVER-BRIGGS shows no doubts: *lmᶜn* always means *in order that*, never merely *so that*. But others believe that in a number of texts a consecutive meaning of this con-

---

[21] J. VAN DER PLOEG, *De Psalmen*, Roermond-Maaseik, 1963. In his commentary, however, he sticks to the traditional rendering "Against you, you only" (id., *Psalmen, Deel I, Psalm 1–75*, Roermond, 1972, pp. 314 and 319.

[22] P. Joüon, *Grammaire de l'hébreu biblique*, Rome ²1947, p. 269.

junction (i.e. "so that") is quite possible. In DALGLISH's book the various meanings are listed on pp. 109–111. DALGLISH himself prefers the final meaning of the conjunction. Following OLSHAUSEN (1853) and KITTEL (commentary 1929), however, he tries to avoid the blasphemous thought that sin should serve to bring God's justice to light, by making v. 6b (4b) continue v. 5 (3). M. BUBER does the same by making v. 6a (4a) a parenthesis (*Das Buch der Preisungen*, Berlin, 1936), and J.A. GRISPINO puts v. 6a (4a) between quotation marks to achieve the same result (*Confraternity of Christian Doctrine Translation of the Bible*, New York, 1965). D. MICHEL adopts F. NÖTSCHER's translation (Echter Bibel, Würzburg, 1953)[23]:

> Gegen dich allein habe ich gesündigt
> und getan, was dir mißfällt,
> so daß du recht hast mit deinem Urteil
> und unanfechtbar bist in deinem Gericht.

He defends this consecutive translation of *lm⁽n* by saying that it is the only one that makes sense. According to him, the instances from the Book of Psalms show that there is no clear division between final and consecutive sentences after *lm⁽n*. When read as final sentences, the texts listed by him[24] all fit their contexts. The pious are saved in order that they may praise the god who has saved them; the fathers receive the command to teach their children the law in order that the next generation may know the law; humiliation ensures that the law is learnt; the reign of the righteous does not last forever, for fear that they may resort to injustice. If the Masoretic reading of Ps. cxxx 4 is correct, this verse, too, does not exclude a final meaning: "For with you is forgiveness [the disposition and strength to forgive], in order that you may be feared [treated with respect]."

Some texts from outside the Book of Psalms are also quoted to

---

[23] D. Michel, *Tempora und Satzstellung in den Psalmen* (diss.), Bonn, 1960, pp. 173ff.

[24] D. Michel, *op. cit.*, *loc. cit.*. In this connection, I should like to refer to the quotation of Ps. li 6 in Rom. iii 4, on which M.A. KLOPFENSTEIN (*Die Lüge nach dem Alten Testament*, Zürich, 1964, p. 422, n. 874) remarks, "Röm 3,4 interpretiert Ps. 116,11 zunächst nach Ps. 51,6, sodann im Sinn der paulinischen Rechtfertigungslehre um. Die erste Uminterpretation ergibt: Lügner = Sünder; das Sündersein steht unter einer höheren Notwendigkeit, wie das *l⁽ma⁽an* (= *damit* Gott recht behalte, vs. 6b) anzeigt. Die zweite Uminterpretation ergibt: Die Rechtfertigungslehre des Paulus setzt die Sündhaftigkeit aller Menschen als Urteilsspruch Gottes voraus; die höhere Notwendigkeit wird durch das imperativische γινέσθω ausgedrückt."

confirm a consecutive meaning of *lm⁽n* (Ex. xi 9; Deut. xxix 18; Isa. xliv 9; Hos. viii 4). In Ex. xi 9, however, a final interpretation seems to be required: the heart of Pharaoh is hardened and therefore it is said to Moses that "He will not listen to you (in order) that my miracles may be multiplied in the land of Egypt." In the case of Deut. xxix 18, one may have doubts. I believe that it is safest to assume a final meaning here, too. In his commentary, A. BERTHOLET observed, "Was Folge seines frevelhaften Verhaltens wäre, wird als seine Absicht eingeführt (lm⁽n), um seine Schuld noch schärfer hervorzuheben" (Freiburg i.B, 1899, p. 90). Isa. xliv 9 may be an allusion to Isa. xli 18ff. The plain becomes fertile in order that this people may know and see that the strength of its god Yhwh becomes visible in this way (xli 18 – 20). The worshippers of idols of xliv 9 are not allowed to see or know anything—in order that they may be put to shame. The believer expects that this will happen, but he does not state that this is so. For in that case, the worshippers themselves would already have concluded that their gods were of no help. Hos. viii 4 deals with images of the deity. The meaning of the two last words of this vers (*lm⁽n ykrt*) is still unclear to me.

On the basis of this, it seems almost certain to me that we should translate *lm⁽n* by *in order that*. The special position of *lk*, reinforced by *lm⁽n*, forbids us to alter the sequence of the lines of this song of penitence, or to treat part of it as a parenthesis or put it between quotation marks. We have also seen that the interpretation of the first words of Ps. li 6 (4) can help us to avoid the obscure sense given to it in Jewish and early Christian thought in connection with the meaning of sin in a dogmatic system departing from the idea of divine omnipotence. Our investigations result in the suggestion that the translation of this verse might run as follows:

> With respect to you, you especially,
> have I failed and acted wrongfully,
> in order that you may acquit me by your word,
> by your sentence declare me innocent.

The penitent appeals to his god, knowing that his judgement can turn his guilt and fate into forgiveness and happiness.

In Ps. 51, the penitent's neighbour plays no part. It is possible that his desperate plight is caused by other people, who, rightly or wrongly, have a blood feud with him (v. 16 (14)), or by sickness, war, exil, or hunger, or by his neglect of the worship demanded by his god: the psalm gives no information about this. The penitent's mother, mentioned in v. 7 (5), cannot be reproached with his guilt and fate, nor can she be seen as his accomplice. His conception and birth serve to rule out any suggestion that anyone besides himself may be concerned. One may compare this with Jer. i 5, xv 10, and xx 14a, in which a similar memory of birth is used as a figure of speech to indicate the inevitability of the situation. The text discussed in this paper uses terms (like acquittal and sentence) which point to the setting of a lawsuit. Nowhere, however, does this appear to be a lawsuit between human parties, in which moral guilt plays a part. The poet does not appeal to God in order to be acquitted in a quarrel he has with his fellow people, in which he might influence the judge's sentence by pleading guilty. God is invoked because the poet experiences, and experiences painfully, that the foundations of his life are affected. And he assumes that this shows that he has lost god and will therefore be destroyed. He has failed (we are not told how, and we are not even sure whether the penitent himself knows this), and he appeals to god's power to grant mercy as his only chance of salvation. The impersonal form and the popularity of this form of the song of penitence indicate that the faithful considered their lives to be essentially dependent on their god (cf. v. 8 (6)). The fact that, although prayer has often remained unanswered, this appeal has not been silenced, makes me assume that for the believer, the twofold unity of justice and mercy is part of the secret of life.

12

Some Remarks Concerning and Suggested by Jeremiah 43:1-7

The seven verses which are the subject of this contribution belong to a fairly long piece of prose which deals with the conquest of Jerusalem and what happened directly afterward. Neither the translation nor the explanation of these verses is made more difficult by uncertainties concerning the historical background of the text. The Hebrew text of this part of the Old Testament shows very little irregularity and indicates a period in which a very great deal of the Old Testament obtained the form in which material from earlier periods had been reedited. Since no truly ancient witness to the text is preserved, a precise dating remains a guess. The oldest witnesses of the first translations are uniform to a great degree.

Yet an attempt to translate this passage faces all sorts of difficulties. Because a comparison of the old and modern translations does not bring all the difficulties to light, I have given my own translation; one in which an explanation is added in those places where it is different from the usual and generally similar translations. Finally, a few opinions about the editing of this passage follow, wherein differentiation is made between literature which describes events and literature which has at its kernel oracles concerning these events.

I

AN ATTEMPT AT TRANSLATION

Jer. 43:1-7 (1) When Jeremiah had completely transmitted the message from their God YHWH, with which their God YHWH had sent him to them, to them all—the whole message—(2) Hoshaiah's son Azariah and Kareah's son Johanan, and everyone, excitedly talking, said to Jeremiah: "Thou art an impostor. Our God YHWH has not sent you to say: Thou shalt not enter Egypt to remain there. (3) It is Neriah's son Baruch who has set you against us to deliver us to the Babylonians, who will take us to Babel in exile, which ends in death."

(4) And Kareah's son Johanan and all the commanders of the forces and all those—they did not obey YHWH's command to remain in the region of Judah.

(5) And Kareah's son Johanan and all the commanders of the forces took all the remnant of Judah, those returned from all the nations whither they had been driven to remain in the region of Judah, (6) men, women, and children, the court, and all those who by the aid of the head of the bodyguard, Nebuzaradan, had found shelter with Ahikam's son, Saphan's son Gedaliah—and the prophet Jeremiah and Neriah's son Baruch. (7) They now went into the region of Egypt—for they did not obey YHWH's command—and came to (*or* in) Tahpanhes.

II

SOME EXPLANATIONS

In this translation the word עַם ("people") occurring in vss. 1 and 4 is not used. The expression כל־הָעָם is rendered by "them all," for the author of this part was not thinking of the whole population of the area of Judah. The assembly, for whom YHWH's command is intended, are those who are planning to leave for Egypt and, owing to the development of affairs after the murder of Gedaliah, have gathered together in a place somewhere near Bethlehem. In vss. 4-5 this is made more explicit. The group consists of commanders and their gangs, among whom Johanan is the leading figure, and those who had remained at Mizpah under Gedaliah, insofar as they had survived at the time of Gedaliah's murder. A third group of those to whom the prophet directs YHWH's message are those who had been able to return from exile to join up with Gedaliah.

Not everyone became an exile with the arrival of the Babylonians. In Jer. 40:7-8 we have a summary of those who were left in the land. The use of the expression כל־שְׁאֵרִית יְהוּדה in vs. 5 of our passage must not allow us to forget that there were population groups who, with the coming of the Babylonians, certainly got a new government but not a new dwelling or a new style of living. Moreover, a not unimportant number of the population of the destroyed city of Jerusalem will have sought and found their refuge in areas nearby.

The verb גור, "stay as a stranger who is domiciled somewhere," generally with the idea of being admitted or received as a refugee, is used in vs. 2 for the proposed stay in Egypt, whither people sought to escape and where they hoped to get permission to stay. It is noticeable that the same verb (גור) is also used for the sojourn, in the Judean region, of those who returned from foreign parts and are mentioned as "the whole remnant of Judah" in vs. 5. The Greek, Syriac, and Aramaic translations of this fifth verse have clearly expressed this meaning. They use, respectively, the following verbs to render גור: κατοικεῖν, "to establish oneself, to settle down," also: "to found a colony"; 'mr, "to stay with as a stranger"; the Ittaf. of יתב, "to settle as a foreigner, to get permission to reside." We ought to discriminate between the region of Judah and its more or less permanent population, and what the author of this passage calls "the people" or "the remnant of Judah." The term "the region of Judah" is used in the foregoing translation in order to differentiate between Judah as the name of an area and as the name for those to whom the author confined himself. Not only in our passage but also elsewhere in the Old Testament these definitions for people and country ought to be more closely specified.[1]

Several sentences of the passage with which we are concerned leave the impression, after reading them, that they are a patchwork. In vs. 1, את כל־הדברים האלה is clearly an addition. It is also striking that a liberal use has been made of the word כל; in the seven verses of this passage it occurs eight times.

In the second verse, there are also additions. In this essay it is not my intention to go into supposed changes in the text. In the translation an attempt has been made to render all the words in the text into English. However, this does not mean that I presuppose that the original reading of the verse has been preserved. At any rate, a more or less possible sentence is achieved if the adjective with "men," הזדים, is recognized as having an adverbial meaning: the men talk in an excited way. This translation of זד, "excited," certainly expresses the fact that the normal limits of conversation are being exceeded— thus acknowledging the meaning of the root זוד/זיד, "to cook, cook over"—but not that this is condemned on religious or moral grounds. The usual translation "recklessly, audaciously, impudently," does just this. Even though זד did contain an element of blame (which cannot with certainty be deduced from the few places where it occurs), it

---

[1] L. Rost, "Die Bezeichnungen für Land und Volk im Alten Testament," in *Festschrift Procksch* (Leipzig, 1934), pp. 125-48, is instructive in this regard.

fits less well in the context of the passage in question. Johanan and his men may doubt Jeremiah's authority, but neither here nor in previous passages are they pictured as reckless fellows who audaciously rebel against YHWH. They seem more panic-stricken than presumptuous.

שׁקר, "lie," vs. 2b, has been rendered by "deceit," and I have tried to express the directness of the reaction to Jeremiah's words by letting the words and the speaker be expressed together: "Thou art an impostor." I refer to an obesrvation made by Klopfenstein who calls (sheker) "zwar eine Wortlüge . . . , aber nicht nur im negativen Sinn 'Unwahrheit,' sondern im positiv-aktiven Sinn 'Betrug.' " [2]

The verb בוא, "come, enter, reach," is used once in vs. 2 and twice in vs. 7. The old translations have rendered the Hebrew verb's meaning exactly. The Septuagint uses in all three places εἰσιέναι. The Peshiṭta uses ʿal; "to enter," in vs. 2 and ʾatʾa, "to come, to get to," in vs. 7. So also the Targum. The Vulgate uses ingredere in vs. 2 and vs. 7a, and venire in vs. 7b. In some recent translations the meaning "go to, to proceed to," at least in the vss. 2 and 7a, is attached to the verb בוא. This is done, among others, by A. Gélin in Bible de Jérusalem, in the RSV, in the version of the Dutch Bible Society, by J. A. Grispino in the Confraternity Version. In Brown-Driver-Briggs' Lexicon, the meaning "go, go to" is given. The evidence for this meaning of the verb is not convincing, however. Ps. 26:4, where the verb occurs with the preposition עם, and Prov. 22:24, where it appears with את, give the meaning "to come together with" a good sense, which moreover is in agreement with the parallel expressions ישׁב עם and התרעה את. The verb occurs several times after the imperative of the verb הלך, "to go." Thus it does in Isa. 22:15 where the RSV translates: "Come, go." But even in these cases, בוא keeps its own meaning. The translation of Isa. 22:15 should be vade ingredere (Vulgate). There exists one expression, preserved in Jon. 1:3, which seems to support the meaning "to go" for the verb בוא. It concerns the shipping term אניה באה תרשׁישׁ. In early translations the term was rendered by verbs meaning "to go": βαδίζον εἰς in the Greek of the Septuagint, דאזלא בימא in the Targum, euntem in Tharsis in the Vulgate. But it seems to me that in this expression also בוא does not mean "to go" but "come," "arrive." Jonah found a ship in the harbor of Joppa "bound for Tarshish." "Destined for," "bound for" are still the normal shipping terms. The expression does not refer to the journey, "the going," but

---

[2] M. A. Klopfenstein, Die Lüge nach dem Alten Testament, ihr Begriff, ihre Bedeutung, und ihre Beurteilung. Thesis Bern (Zürich, 1964), p. 102.

to the arrival, the goal of the voyage. In II Chron. 9:21 two verbs in connection with ships occur, הלך and בוא, distinguishing the journey of the ship (הלך) and its arrival (בוא). The parallel text in I Kings 10:22 only uses the verb בוא. In Jer. 43 the author is not interested in the journey to, but the stay in Egypt.

The literal translation of vs. 3 (end) is: "to kill us and to carry us into exile to Babel." The old translations all have the same sequence and join the two expressions by "and," *et*. We can find this literal rendering in several recent translations: the version of the Dutch Bible Society; E. Dhorme (Pléiade); B. N. Wambacq, Commentary (1957). However, there are also others who take the two phrases, about an expected death and about exile, as alternatives, changing the copulative *et* to *aut*. This is done, among others, by the Leiden Translation (1901); Volz, Commentary; Rudolph, Commentary; Gélin; RSV; Grispino. There is no language problem here, as *waw* can be rendered by *aut* in many places. One can also ascertain that when it is taken as an alternative the sense becomes more vivid. Yet the anticlimax remains.

The two infinitives with *lamed,* להמית and להגלות, are dependent on the previous phrase, i.e. the delivery into the power of the Babylonians. The opinion of these Judean men is that the consequence of this delivering into Babel's power will mean their death, their exile. In my translation, "exile which ends in death," I treat the two infinitives as belonging closely together, expressing one thought. That two verbal forms, whether or not joined by *waw,* can render one thought, and that in this way the first possesses an adverbial meaning, is a well-known feature of Hebrew style. In the detailed work on syntax by Eduard König and in Paul Joüon's useful *Grammaire,* to mention but a couple of studies, one can find examples of the adverbial meaning of verbs used in connection with other verbs.[3] This aspect is not limited to the *hiphil* forms of the verb, though these are the most clearly distinguishable, which also found their way into translations. T. J. Meek, dealing with the coordinate adverbial clause in Hebrew, refers to the common construction in Arabic, the so-called *hāl*-clause, expressing the state, condition, and also the manner in which the action of the main clause takes place.[4] In a study of II Sam. 12:25 I have summed up a fairly large number of cases of וישלח followed by

---

[3] Eduard König, *Historisch-Comparative Syntax der hebräischen Sprache* (Leipzig, 1897), pars. 332x, 361, 369. Paul Joüon, *Grammaire de l'hébreu biblique,* 2nd ed. (Rome, 1947), pars. 102g, 54d, "hifil adverbial."

[4] In *JAOS* XLIX (1929), 156-59.

a verbal form which carries the main thought of the sentence, like the Greek ἀποστέλλειν.[5] To mention yet a few more examples of this figure of speech, besides those mentioned in the literature referred to, I would point to the combination frequently in use: ויען ויאמר, usually rendered literally: "and he answered and said." Sometimes one finds: "and he answered," a single translation of the double expression. So one reads "and he answered" in RSV, Gen. 18:27; and the same, rendering the term ויען לאמור in Gen. 42:22. But in both cases the translators have wrongly chosen to translate the first verb of the combination. From the context, too, it seems to be clear that in Gen. 18 Abraham does not answer but "addresses the word to." And in Gen. 42:22 Reuben does not answer his brothers but addresses the word to them. Recognition of the adverbial meaning of one of the verbs, in this case of the verbal form ויען, would improve the translation of many sentences in both Old and New Testament. In Ps. 27:7b the psalmist begs: וחנני ועני. The translations render this literally: *miserere mei et exaudi me.* Here also an adverbial meaning for the first of the two verbs would express the unity of thought better. One could translate: "answer me mercifully."

Where in Jer. 43:3 we note the unity of thought expressed in two verbal forms, the two infinitives המית and הגלות, the first infinitive has an adverbial value connected to the carrying off into exile. Exile is feared as a fatal business, leading to ruin. "Exile which ends in death" is an attempt to do this figure of speech justice.

In the Syriac version of vs. 5, "all commanders of the forces" are counted in with those whom Johanan took. Probably the singular form of the verb has caused this rendering. Although "and all commanders of the forces" may be an addition, it more likely should be considered as belonging to the subject of the sentence. I have translated the verb as a plural, just as in vs. 4: "they did not obey." Those who are taken by Johanan are those who are led by him and his colleague commanders. In vs. 6 they are listed. The verb לקח indicates that those who are taken with them are carried away; not, however, that the carrying away takes place against their will. The picture of Jeremiah and Baruch being dragged away against their will cannot be derived from the wording of vss. 5 ff. It does not recognize the additional character of the last line of vs. 7 and tries to clear Jeremiah and Baruch of all blame.

Instead of "the daughters of the king," the princesses, which is the translation of the Hebrew text and also that of the Greek, Aramaic,

---

[5] In *Festschrift Vriezen* (Wageningen, 1966), pp. 27-28.

and Latin, I have translated: "the court," a rendering of בית המלך.
This is the reading of the Peshiṭta. Although I cannot give an absolutely convincing argument for choosing the Syriac reading, there
are some indications that we should bear in mind the possibility that
the handing down of the Hebrew text and the translations which depend on it do not preserve the original reading.

The phrase בנות המלך appears, apart from Jer. 43:6, also Jer. 41:10
and II Sam. 13:18; בנות מלכים occurs in Ps. 45:10. The two last-men-
tioned references deal with the splendor of the robes and the beauty
of the princesses. Jer. 41:10 uses the expression similarly in a summary. The Syriac translation of Jer. 41:10 does not have this phrase.

The context of Jer. 43 preserves another summary which has even
more similarity with our vs. 6, Jer. 41:16. The second part of this verse
runs: "soldiers, women, children, and eunuchs" (סרסים). The Syriac
translation renders this word with *mhymn'*, "the trusted ones." The
eunuchs belonged to the court as servants and guarded the house of
the king. Instead of the princesses in the lists of Jer. 41:10 and 43:6,
the text in Jer. 41:16 mentions the eunuchs. And this does make the
list more understandable: the men, the women, the children, and
the emasculated, the servants of the court. It is in no way strange
that they are mentioned in such a summary. But the mentioning of
the princesses does raise questions: Why are they mentioned and not
the king's wives, not the princes? If the intention was to report that
also among those who remained behind in the land there were members of the royal house, then it is possible that originally in place of
בית המלך: בנת המלך was written. The change of one letter could be the
reason for the form being preserved in the Hebrew tradition. In the
old writings a *nun* is not very different from a *yodh*. The *plene* writing בנות is a later appearance. I offer my choice of the Syriac tradition,
which finds some indirect support in the list in Jer. 41:16, for discussion.

III

REMARKS CONCERNING THE REDACTION

Paul Volz treated Jer. 42:1–43:7 as a unit, to which he gave the title:
"Die Juden wandern trotz Jeremias Rat nach Ägypten." [6] He changes
the sequence of the text by placing 43:1-3 before 42:19. Jeremiah's
threat, that Egypt will not be a place of refuge but a place of death
for "the remnant of Judah" (42:19-22), he considers a reaction of the

---

[6] *Der Prophet Jeremia*, Commentary, 2nd ed. (Leipzig, 1928), pp. 356-62.

prophet to the accusation: "Thou art an impostor." Many people have followed Volz's suggestion in their studies concerning Jeremiah. W. Rudolph has indicated this sequence of the reading in his treatment of the Hebrew text in the third edition of Kittel's *Biblia Hebraica* (1937), and in his well-known commentary the suggestion is accepted.[7]

This reorganization of the text seems attractive but at the same time raises new questions. Apart from the fact that the earliest history of the text preserves no witness that can be used to justify the change, it does seem strange that vs. 1 of chap. 43 so emphatically stresses that the oracle has come to an end and that Jeremiah has transmitted it in its entirety. In the passage 42:19-22, moreover, there is absolutely no reaction to the accusation of Jeremiah's falseness, nor to the accusation of Baruch's wicked intentions. Finally, changing the order makes an additional introductory sentence, such as "but Jeremiah said," or, "answered," necessary.

However, this attempt to strengthen the unity of a large passage makes it clear that Jer. 43:1-7 consists of two fragments. The lively, indeed, stirring style of the part which describes Jeremiah's share in what happened after the arrival of the Babylonians ceases after 43:3. Direct speech dominates this description. In 42:1-6 an oracle is asked for, promised, and accepted in advance; in 42:7-22 the oracle is given: If they stay in Judah, well-being is promised; should they settle in Egypt, they are doomed to total destruction. In 43:1-3, in just as emotional a manner, the veracity of the oracle is denied and Baruch accused.

The second part of Jer. 43:1-7, vss. 5-7, continues the report of the occurrences described in Jer. 40:7-16; 41:1-18. The information about Gedaliah's provincial governorship, his murder by Ishmael, Johanan's intervention and proposal to escape into Egypt, are continued in the same style in 43:5-7. Johanan and the other commanders carry away the group of Judeans who, because of the murder of Gedaliah, see no future for themselves in the land of Judah. Vs. 4 of chap. 43 attempts to connect up with the story that centers on the oracle. This verse omits Azariah, who does not appear in the report about what happened, but does come into the Jeremian passages, 42:1, and in 43:1-3 is the actual accuser of the prophet and Baruch. For Kareah's son Johanan is the leader after Gedaliah's death.

In vs. 6 the last line follows lamely. The words "and the prophet Jeremiah and Neriah's son Baruch" are obviously a redactional addi-

---

[7] *Jeremia,* Commentary, 2nd ed. (Tübingen, 1958) pp. 236-37.

tion. Just as in the report in II Kings 25 about the same events, Jeremiah does not appear in the fairly detailed report preserved in the book which bears his name. The subsidiary sentence in vs. 7, "for they obeyed not YHWH's command," comes from the same redactional hand. The last line, "and came to, *or* in Tahpanhes," may have served as connecting point for the prophetic story beginning in vs. 8.

Judging from style and content, the prophetic passages are independent units. Their connection with the description of events is secondary and stylistically weak. The intriguing question of whether the prophetic passages ought to be considered as a religious explanation of the events, or whether the events are to be taken as the fulfillment of prophecy—Zimmerli says, "das Geschehen ist verwirklichtes Wort, eingelöste Verkündigung"—is not solved by the exegesis of Jer. 43:1-7. The weak redactional links between the report of events and the oracles concerning these events indicate fairly independent circles, in which these two kinds of literature were handed down before they were joined together in the texts preserved for us.

13
JEREMIAH 45, VERSE 5

The number of problems in Jeremiah 45 is inversely proportional to the brevity of the chapter. The handing down of the test, the date in the introductory formula, the place of this chapter in the book of Jeremiah, the meaning of expressions used and, last but not least, Baruch's behaviour and Yhwh's reaction to it through the prophet Jeremiah have led to extremely various translations and explanations.

As far as the handing down of the Hebrew text is concerned, verse 5 shows no difficulties. But from early times its translation has occasioned problems. The Septuagint translates the first לך by a reflexive pronoun, σεαυτῷ "for yourself". The term לשלל is rendered by εἰς εὕρεμα, possibly with the intension of expressing Baruch's good fortune. Baruch may consider himself very fortunate that he is to stay alive. The Peshiṭṭa version adds "what is better (*or* more) than you (are)" to the prohibition "do not seek". The term לשלל in this version leads to the translation "that can save (thy life)". This notion of being saved (escape, safety, refuge) is also to be found in the Targum, שיזבא, and in the Vulgate which reads "(et dabo tibi animam tuam) in salutem".

CALVIN explains in the same spirit: Jubet eum hoc beneficio contentum esse. Satis sit tibi tali tempore vitam habere salvam. And GROTIUS joins him in his *Anno-tationes*. Yhwh's judgement of Baruch's attitude is imaginatively described by CALVIN in his comment *ad loc.*: Hic quasi in trutina deus constituit Baruch et totum popu-lum cum templo; An, inquit, tu praeponderabis? an vita tua illis pretiosior erit? tu ne solus immunis eris molestia? This accusation of selfishness is to be found in many descriptions of Baruch's personality. In this, says CALVIN, Baruch is not alone: sed solent homines sibi indulgere in amore sui.

In the previous verse Yhwh says that he will break down that which he has built, will pull out that which he has planted. This announcement is taken to be associated with verse 5 when dealing with it. DUHM [1] remarks that in verse 4 Yhwh's sadness is expressed as he has to destroy all his people. The last words of verse 4 as handed

---

[1] B. DUHM, *Das Buch Jeremia*, Tübingen, Leipzig 1901, p. 336.

down to us in the Hebrew text do not make clear sense. In the Septuagint and in some new translations including that of the Dutch Bible Society, they have been omitted. If they mean that Yhwh's destruction will affect the whole earth, they stress the accepted meaning of the beginning of the fifth verse. For it is not fitting that an individual should be out for his own safety or prosperity, to make a splendid career for himself in a time of destruction, in which God himself, with pain in his heart, is going to carry out punishment on his chosen people.

HEINZ KREMERS, after explaining in his thesis *Der leidende Prophet* [2] various parts of the book of Jeremia as being a history of his suffering written by Baruch, has published a full study about "Leidensgemeinschaft mit Gott im Alten Testament".[3] In Jer. 45 he sees the explanation of this history of suffering: after Baruch's complaint about his own misery Yhwh indicates to him his own, divine suffering. Through Jeremiah Baruch is admonished not to desire anything else but this suffering. "Nur sein Leben soll Baruch als Beute behalten dürfen. So stellt Jahwe in seinem Wort an Baruch diesen hinein in seine Gemeinschaft des Leidens mit ihm selbst." KREMERS sees in Philippians 3, verse 10 — κοινωνίαν παθημάτων αὐτοῦ — the fulfilling of what is mentioned in the Old Testament as only "Sonderfall". He ends his article with a quotation from BONHOEFFER's letters [4] in which is referred to Jer. 45 in this sense.

This explanation of the chapter therefore not only accepts Yhwh's rejection of Baruch's desire for "great things" by pointing out to him that he suffers far worse than the complaining Baruch, but that this reproof also is a consolation. Yhwh includes Baruch as well as Jeremiah in the company of those who have to bear the same suffering as he. WEISER, who has written similarly about this chapter,[5] also takes verse 5 as a reproach. Baruch must give up his egocentricity by turning his attention to God, who is forced to destroy his own work. Fate and mission go together. Baruch can draw strength from the thought that he too, like his master, suffers because of divine command.[6] BLANK also wrote several striking passages

---

[2] Göttingen 1952.

[3] Subtitle: „Eine Untersuchung der ‚biographischen' Berichte im Jeremiabuch", in *Evangelische Theologie* 13, München 1953, pp. 122-140.

[4] D. BONHOEFFER, *Widerstand und Ergebung*, herausgegeben durch E. BETHGE, München 1952, p. 248f.

[5] A. WEISER, „Das Gotteswort für Baruch, Jer. 45, und die sogenannte Baruch-biographie", in *Festschrift für K. Heim*, Hamburg 1954, pp. 35-46.

[6] G. VON RAD, *Theologie des Alten Testaments* II, München 1960, p. 220, concurs in Kremers' and Weiser's interpretation. A certain reservation appears from his words: „(diese Gottesrede) deutet fast ein Leiden an, das Gott über diesem Werk des Niederreissens des von ihm Gebauten empfindet". Further on in the same paragraph this reservation is no longer observed: „. . . . weil hier ein Mensch auf eine einzigartige Weise an dem göttlichen Leiden mitgetragen hat".

on this chapter under the heading "self-pity".[7] God expresses regret that he must do what he is to do. It is illuminating to quote Blank's 'paraphrasing in part' here. "You, Baruch, are saying: 'Alas! and Woe! God has added misery to my pain; I am worn out with my sighing and find no respite.' Well, now, consider! What I, myself, built I am about to demolish. What I planted I am about to uproot ... and would you seek personal advancement? Desist." At the end, with a promise, God softens the rebuke: "I will bring disaster down upon all flesh, God says, but I will give you your life as reward wherever you go." But it is the rebuke which carries the theme of self-pity. Pared of unessentials, God's ironic question to the complaining disciple is merely this: "What is your hurt, O man, compared to mine?".

Modern translations of Jeremiah 45, verse 5 certainly show some differences but are in the main in agreement. The beginning of the verse is taken either as a question without the questioning particle or as an exclamation. In both cases it serves as being in opposition to what Yhwh has said of himself in verse 4. The 'great things' which Baruch seeks for himself are taken as 'personal advancement' in which reward for faithful service to Jeremiah is thought of. The כִּי sentence is taken as being causal and therefore כִּי is translated by 'for', 'car', 'denn', 'want' in agreement with ancient versions, ὅτι, ܘ ܡܛܠ, *quia*. And the *waw* before the perfect form נתתי is rendered by 'but', 'mais', 'aber', 'maar', with a few exceptions as the New English Bible, 'and' GELIN, Bible de Jérusalem, 'et'. The expression את־נפשך לשלל (ונתתי לך) is rendered in the same way, albeit with some nuances: "... your life as a prize of war", Revised Standard Version; "... ton âme comme part de butin", DHORME, ed. Pléiade; "(accorder) pour butin ta propre vie", GELIN; "... dein Leben zur Beute", Zürcher Bibel, DUHM, RUDOLPH; "... lijfsbehoud ten buit", Leiden Translation, JANSEN, Canisius Translation; "your life ... as booty", GRISPINO, The New American Bible, Confraternity Version. The NEB proposes a different division of the whole of the sentence. The expression under discussion is rendered by: "and I will let you live wherever you go, but you shall save your life and nothing more", evidently a paraphrastic translation.

A fresh examination of the syntax and of the meaning of the expressions used leads one, I believe, to doubt whether the translations and explanations usually given are right. And herewith the sketch of Baruch's personality and the theological train of thought mentioned above become open to discussion.

1. גדלות. This term occurs once more in the book of Jeremiah, in chapter 33, verse 3. There Yhwh says to the prophet: "If you call me I will answer you and tell you great

---

[7] S. H. BLANK, *Jeremiah, Man and Prophet*, Cincinnati 1961, p. 32 and pp. 143ff., „The Theme of Self-Pity".

and hidden (*or*, mysterious) things which you have not known (*or*, do not understand)." גדלות here is synonymous to בצרות, "inaccessible, impenetrable facts". They belong to the realm of the deity. The same is true for the naming of God as "He who is doing great things", עשה גדלות, a rather frequently used epithet of the deity, Ps. 71, verse 19; Ps. 106, verse 21; Job 5, verse 9; 9, verse 10; 37, verse 5; and Deuteron. 10, verse 21. In Job נפלאות, 'wondrous works, marvels', is used as synonym of גדלות. In Ps. 106, verse 22 נוראות, 'terrible things', is found beside the synonymous term 'marvels'. This 'terrible things' also serves as a synonym of גדלות in Deuteron. 10, verse 21, the great and terrible things done in favour of God's people. Furthermore in II Kings 8, verse 4 where the king asks Elishah's servant to tell him the marvels that Elishah, the man of God, has done, Gehazi uses the same expression, 'the great things'. Elishah had restored the dead to life, a clearly supernatural act. The prophet, as a man of God, was enabled by the deity to do miracles, 'great things'.

When it is said of ordinary people that they speak untruths, flattering and with a double heart, Ps. 12, verse 4, then Yhwh is asked to cut off all flattering lips, the tongue that makes great boasts; literally: the tongue speaking great things. 'Great things' in the mouth of man are *hybris*, cf. Ezek. 8, verse 6: 'great abominations'. A pious man says: "I do not occupy myself with things that are beyond me, that are too marvellous for me", Ps. 131, verse 1.[8] In this Psalm verse נפלאות, 'supernatural acts' are again synonymous with גדלות.

We may conclude that in the Hebrew handed down to us the term גדלות means divine, superhuman acts. Man who is thinking of having such great things at his disposal falls into sin, hybris. It is God alone, and man only as a servant of God, איש האלהים, who controls 'great things'. God is doing the 'great things, terrible things, marvels' in favour of his people. They may ask him to act in their favour but they never have 'great things' at their disposal. גדלות is not used in the Old Testament to indicate high social positions or great rewards. When one reads in Jer. 45, verse 5 that Yhwh rejects Baruch's personal ambitions, this reading can not be derived from the meaning of גדלות. If the coherence of chapter 45 is original—a question we need not go into—, one could transform Baruch's complaint, verse 3, into desires which we can suppose Baruch had—for a life without worries and sorrow, without weariness and restlessness. If we justify this interpretation, we are still nowhere near high ambitions or desire for great rewards. Yhwh's words given as an answer to Baruch's complaint have rightly been compared with the answers which the prophet Jeremiah got to his complaints, viz. rejection of the pleas.[9] Moreover, I believe that we

---

[8] See the present writer on Psalm CXXXI 2 in *V.T.* XVI, 1966, p. 288.

[9] See W. BAUMGARTNER, *Die Klagegedichten des Jeremia*, Giessen 1917, p. 75 and the present writer's *Jeremia's twijfel*, Leiden 1957, pp. 22ff., (24ff.).

should not loose sight of the fact that these very personal complaints are closely connected to the sorrow felt towards the people whose fate is to be proclaimed.

2. תבקש־לך. The meaning of גדלות makes it very unlikely that תבקש־לך is meant to reflect Baruch's selfishness. It is also just as unlikely that Jeremiah's 'spiritual care' of Baruch by using a divine oracle to reject the 'overtones' of his complaints—a qualification of BLANK's [10]—can be derived from Yhwh's words. Yhwh's answer to Baruch interprets his complaint as an indirect prayer to alter fate, his own destiny and that of his people. The answer can also be a reaction to a prayer of Baruch which has not been preserved. In any case, it is only Yhwh who can do 'great things' or who can put his servant in a position to carry out wonders. Consequently I take the meaning of the verb בקש to be asking of God, prayer for God's intervention. In this disastrous situation with the threat of extermination, the prayer for 'great things' can mean nothing else but for an alteration of destiny by a superhuman, divine act. The meaning of גדלות makes it impossible to attach a selfish meaning to לך in the question. ־לך can also be an ethical dative, which is probably used too in I Sam. 28, verse 7: "Find me—בקשו־לי—a woman who is a medium, and I will go and inquire through her." That such a change to the good by Yhwh can be expressed by 'great and mysterious things' is shown in Jer. 33, verse 3: "If you call to me I will answer you, and tell you great and mysterious things . . .". In this verse a change in sentence by Yhwh himself is promised as an answer to a plea to him. In the verse under consideration here, the request is turned down by the deity. The fact that further on in the verse it is said that Baruch will remain alive anyway stands independent from his complaint and from his plea.

3. ונתתי לך את־נפשך לשלל This expression in this form occurs only in Jer. 45 verse 5, but some other similar expressions have been preserved. They can be found in texts which as far as character and date are concerned differ little from Jer. 45. היה לשלל occurs in Jer. 49, verse 32 together with היה לבז, and in Jer. 50, verse 10, with the sense of 'be abandoned, given up'. Yet closer to Jer. 45, verse 5 are Jer. 21, verse 9 and Jer. 38, verse 2 והיתה־לו נפשו לשלל and Jer. 39, verse 18 והיתה לך נפשך לשלל. 'Having life as a prize of war' means that only life shall be spared, cf. the paraphrastic rendering of the NEB, "he shall take home his life and nothing more". The expression clearly means: to have a narrow escape from a dangerous situation, to be saved from a dangerous situation by the skin of one's teeth.

4. כי הנני plus participle, continued with ונתתי In most translations and commentaries כי is taken causally, 'for', 'car', 'denn', 'want'. But the sentence "Behold, I am

---

[10] BLANK, o.c., p. 146.

bringing disaster upon all flesh" does not give the reasons why Yhwh has commanded Baruch "do not ask". The first part of the כי sentence gives in other words what has been said in verse 4: He who builds and plants, but also breaks down and uproots, the Almighty, will now show his destructive side to the people, bringing disaster upon everybody. The continuation, beginning with ותתי, is taken in the translations and commentaries as an independent sentence. The conjunction is rendered by some as 'and' (NEB), 'et toi' (GELIN) but by most as 'but', 'mais', 'aber', 'maar'.

In my opinion neither the meaning of כי nor the connection of the two parts of the sentence are done justice to in this way. I take it that כי possesses a concessive meaning here.[11] The construction of the sentence can be compared to that of Ezek. 11, verses 16, 19: "... though I removed them far off among the nations, and though I scattered them among the countries and I have been a sanctuary for a while to them in the countries where they have gone, ... (19) I will give them a unified (or, new) heart" etc. Verses 17 and 18 are secondary in this context.[12] In the construction of verse 17 account has been taken of the concessive character of כי in verse 16. The כי-phrase is continued in this later added verse with וקבצתי, 'I will gather', ואספתי, 'I will assemble', and ונתתי, 'I will give'.

The subject of the first part of the sentence, Jer. 45, verse 5b, as well as that of the second is Yhwh. He rejects Baruch's request to remit the condemnation he had pronounced. Then he continues: "Though, behold, I am bringing disaster upon everybody—says Yhwh—I will let you capture your life as a prize." If, in this way, the composition and unity of the sentence are correctly described, then there is less need to read between the lines than has been necessary in the usual translations.

— . — . —

After this attempt to explain words and expressions used, I would like to suggest the following translation for the verse:

"And you ask for mighty acts?—do not. Though, behold, I am bringing disaster upon everybody— says Yhwh—I will let you capture your life as a prize wherever you go".

Based on this translation, Baruch must be acquitted from selfishness. He is not out for personal advancement. Neither the scanty evidence elsewhere in the book of Jeremiah, nor that which is related about him in chapter 45 give reason to regard him as an egocentric personality. In the oracle the immutability of God's decision to destroy the country is expressed. Baruch's complaint is interpreted by God, or by

---

[11] See P. JOÜON, *Grammaire de l'hébreu biblique*, 2e éd., Rome 1947, Par. 171b.
[12] See W. ZIMMERLI, *Ezechiel* I Neukirchen 1969, p. 251. I cannot agree with his change of place and translation of כי, "Gewiss —", *o.c.* pp. 190 and 249.

Jeremiah as Yhwh's prophet, as a penetrating plea for a favourable change. It is clear that the oracle presupposes that Baruch has called upon God, who can do 'great and unsearchable, mysterious things', marvels in favour of his people. But his God keeps this side of his being hidden. He rejects the plea. Baruch's attempt to intercede with God who had pronounced his sentence is in vain. Yhwh will reveal himself as devastator.

Baruch's complaints are similar to the complaints of Jeremiah and the result is on a par with his master's idle intercession too. His master dies during the period in which Yhwh's sentence is carried out, but Baruch's difficult life is not ended.

The translation and explanation offered here undermine the right to speak of Jeremiah's personal spiritual care of his selfish scribe. The supposed idea of God's suffering too, and that of community with God's suffering, cannot be derived from Jer. 45. But in their place comes the sketch of a man who remains faithful to his master, following his steps. It seems likely that we owe many prophecies of Jeremiah to him who escaped with his life from the destruction.

14
QUELQUES REMARQUES SUR L'ARC DANS LA NUÉE

(GENÈSE 9,8-17)

Le déluge dont seul Noé fut sauvé avec les êtres vivants qui l'accompagnaient dans l'arche est, suivant le rédacteur du récit, un châtiment dû à la corruption des hommes. « La terre se corrompit à la face d'Elohim et la terre fut remplie de violence ».

Elohim décide donc la fin de toute chair. L'introduction à ce qui est nommé en 6,9 « l'histoire de Noé », *tôledôt nōaḥ*, énonce cette explication théologique avec encore plus de netteté : « Yahvé vit que la malice de l'homme sur la terre était grande et que tout l'objet des pensées de son cœur n'était toujours que le mal. Yahvé se repentit d'avoir fait l'homme sur la terre et il s'irrita en son cœur.... Mais Noé trouva grâce aux yeux de Yahvé ». (*Genèse* 6,5-6.8) [1].

Dans le passage intitulé «histoire de Noé», 6,9ss., Elohim révèle à Noé sa résolution de détruire toute chair, verset 13. Il est cependant manifeste dès le début qu'elle ne le concerne pas, car Noé est une exception parmi les hommes, un homme juste, parfait parmi ses contemporains, qui marchait en compagnie d'Elohim, comme il dit au verset 9. L'expression *hithallēk 'et* se trouve dans *Genèse* 5,22, « Hénoch marcha en compagnie de l'Elohim », et dans l'histoire de David où elle s'applique aux relations intimes que David et ses gens entretiennent avec les bergers de Nabal, *1 Samuel* 25,15.

Elohim donna donc des instructions à son familier Noé pour qu'il construisit l'arche, grâce à laquelle il se sauverait et assurerait aussi l'avenir de sa famille et des autres vivants sur la terre, car « toute ce qui est sur la terre expirera », (v. 17).

Cette prédiction et ces instructions ne sont pas une « grâce » car elle est en harmonie avec les relations intimes avec Elohim. En ces jours Elohim ne fait pas sa *bĕrît* avec Noé, mais il maintient son pacte avec son

---

1. Traduction de DHORME dans *La Bible*. Pléiade, Paris, 1956.

intime ami. En effet, on lit dans *Genèse* 6,18 non pas *kārat běrît*, mais la forme hiphil de *qûm*, *hēqîm běrît*, à comparer avec l'emploi qui est fait de ce verbe entre autres en *1 Samuel* 13,14, dans ces mots que Samuel dit à Saül : « et maintenant, ta royauté ne tiendra pas ». En divers endroits, on lit la forme *hēqîm* avec le sens de tenir : tenir sa promesse, rester fidèle à son serment, *Gen.* 26,3, *Jér.* 11,5 etc. Ainsi donc, Elohim maintient sa relation avec Noé et, en conséquence, lui donne des instructions pour la construction de l'arche.

Cette « histoire de Noé » ne fournit qu'une seule indication sur la nature de la *běrit*, les mots du verset 9 qui déclarent que Noé marchait en compagnie d'Elohim. C'est du fait que Noé était un homme juste, parfait, *ṣaddîq tāmîm*, que découlaient ces relations intimes. En conséquence, la *běrit* entre Elohim et Noé n'est nullement, à mon avis, quelque chose de nouveau, mais le maintien d'une relation existante. La traduction de *Genèse* 6,18 par 'établir' ou 'conclure une alliance' me paraît fautive.

L'histoire de Noé et de l'arche s'achève en *Genèse* 8,18 et 19. Noé exécute alors l'ordre intimé par Elohim de quitter l'arche. Dans la présentation qui nous est faite du récit, vient ensuite la scène du sacrifice de Noé sur l'autel bâti à Yahvé. Il est notable qu'en ce passage qui, à plus d'un égard, rappelle l'introduction yahviste à l'histoire de Noé, à savoir *Genèse* 6,5-8, l'explication théologique du déluge, châtiment de la corruption humaine, a disparu. Yahvé se fait cette réflexion, constate — littéralement ' dit en son cœur ', comme le texte le porte — que le mal est demeuré. Le déluge n'a donc pas répondu au but de dieu. Les causes pour lesquelles Yahvé « se repentit d'avoir fait l'homme » (6,6) n'ont pas été supprimées. Yahvé accepte l'échec et se résigne au fait que *jēṣer lēb hā'ādām ra'*, que l'objet du cœur de l'homme soit le mal (8,21). Il déclare : « Je ne recommencerai plus à frapper tout vivant comme je l'ai fait » (8,21). Au lieu d'une proposition théologique suit maintenant une conclusion philosophique, comme Dhorme l'a bien montré en sa note sur le verset 22 : ' La nature a ses lois qui sont définies par la succession régulière des saisons, des travaux et des jours, comme dans le poème d'Hésiode ' [2].

> « Tous les jours que la terre durera
>   Semailles et moissons, froid et chaud,
>   Été et hiver, jour et nuit,
>   Point ne cesseront. » (*Gen.* 8,22)

Je n'éprouve aucune difficulté à parler, en ce cas, de philosophie, à condition toutefois de ne pas oublier que cette philosophie de la nature

2. *La Bible*, t. I, p. 27.

ou des lois de la nature, est fondée sur un sentiment religieux de la nature, pour parler comme Kristensen — 'een godsdienstig natuurgevoel' [3].

Nous ne rendons pas justice à la foi, et certainement pas à celle des époques primitives de la Bible, lorsque nous la rattachons seulement à des intuitions morales, même si nous déclarons que ces intuitions sont ressenties par le croyant comme venant de son dieu. Nous nous fermons même l'accès à la foi de l'ancien Israël, si nous prenons pour règle de sa croyance les conceptions morales sur le dieu et sur ' le peuple élu ' des siècles plus récents et d'un temps où un groupe de Juifs menacés de disparition interpréta les mythes en fonction de son existence et de son avenir national.

Le début du chapitre suivant, *Gen.* 9, caractérise en quelques lignes la vie sur la terre. Les hommes, c'est-à-dire les descendants de Noé, dominent les animaux et se nourrissent de plantes et d'animaux. Ils ne peuvent manger de la chair avec son âme, c'est-à-dire avec son sang. S'ils versent le sang d'un homme, ce meurtre sera sanctionné par la mort du meurtrier.

Cette sorte de description cadre avec ce qui a été dit à la fin de l'histoire de Noé et de l'arche, 8,15-17 : « Elohim parla à Noé en disant : Sors de l'arche, toi et ta femme, tes fils, etc. avec toi, tous les animaux... Qu'ils foisonnent sur la terre, qu'ils fructifient et se multiplient sur la terre », 9,1 ; et 9,7 : « Quant à vous, fructifiez et multipliez-vous, foisonnez sur la terre, et soyez nombreux en elle ». (La Septante lit : ayez autorité sur elle ; suivie par Dhorme). Mais ultérieurement, il n'est plus fait mention de l'histoire de Noé, sauf lorsque le texte parle des hommes comme de « Noé et ses fils ».

Par contre, les versets 8 à 17 du même chapitre sont nettement rattachés au récit du déluge. Les êtres vivants sur la terre, désignés au verset 12 par l'expression : « Les générations à jamais », reprennent les mots « Noé et ses fils avec lui » du verset 8 et les mots « avec tout animal qui est avec vous » du verset 10.

Toutefois, l'idée dominante du passage, sur laquelle je désire faire quelques observations, est la promesse qu'Elohim fera en sorte que sa *běrît* soit effective: il tiendra sa *běrît*. Il semble que le rédacteur fasse ici allusion à la promesse faite par Elohim à Noé au début du récit sur le déluge, en 6,18 : « Je tiendrai ma *berît* etc. ». On retrouve un emploi des mêmes termes : *hěqîm 'et-běrîtî'et.* Comparer 6,18 et 9,9.11 et aussi 17.

Il n'est pas parlé ici d'un fait nouveau. Soit dit en passant, il en va de même, me semble-t-il, pour la circoncision, au chapitre 17, et le sabbat, en *Exode* 26,13-17 ; ce ne sont pas des institutions nouvelles.

---

3. W. B. KRISTENSEN, e.a. dans *The meaning of religion*, The Hague 1960. Voir General index s.v. '' religious sense of nature ''.

Nouvelle est l'interprétation des faits ; ils comportent maintenant une signification et une obligation imposées par Elohim. Dans les prescriptions sur le sabbat, il pourrait cependant y avoir une systématisation en ce que le repos est prescrit tous les sept jours, systématisation qui est probablement d'origine sacerdotale.

Par contre, en *Osée* 2,20, il s'agit bien d'une réalité nouvelle : « Je conclurai — littéralement couperai — pour eux une *bĕrît* en ce jour-là avec la bête sauvage, l'oiseau des cieux, le reptile du sol ; l'arc, l'épée, la guerre, je les briserai loin du pays et je les ferai dormir en sécurité » (je permettrai aux gens de dormir en sécurité, Dhorme).

Comme il fallait s'y attendre, Osée emploie en ce cas les mots *kārat bĕrît* puisqu'il annonce un nouveau type de relation, un comportement nouveau de la part de Yahvé. Semblablement — entre autres — Yahvé et Abram, *bajjôm hahu'*, *Gen.* 15,18 ; Laban et Jacob, *Gen.* 31,44 ; et en Jérémie, lorsqu'il est parlé expressis verbis d'une *bĕrît ḥadāšā*, on trouve les mots *kārat bĕrît*.

En notre péricope (*Genèse* 9,8-17) nous devrions donc renoncer à traduire , établir ' ou , conclure mon pacte ' et opter pour la traduction : , tenir, ou maintenir ma *bĕrît* [4]. Le pronom possessif, *bĕrîti*, ma *bĕrît*, confirme la thèse du maintien d'une relation existante. La conséquence de ce maintien est exprimée clairement au verset 11 : « qu'il n'y ait plus de déluge pour détruire la terre », mots à comparer avec ce qui est dit au verset 15, un des doublets de notre péricope, « qu'il n'y ait plus d'eaux pour un déluge pour détruire toute chair ». Mais la question se pose aussi de savoir si ce passage comporte des éléments qui permettent d'en déduire la signification précise de l'expression *bĕrîti*.

Dans ce qui est nommé ' l'histoire de Noé ', la *bĕrît* indique une relation intime entre Elohim et Noé, *'îš ṣaddîq tāmîm*. Cependant, bien que les hommes soient regardés dans notre péricope comme la descendance de Noé, ils n'en sont point pour autant déclarés « justes et parfaits » ! Si Elohim maintient sa *bĕrît*, la raison doit donc, dans notre péricope, être ailleurs. Si je vois bien, la *bĕrît* d'Elohim avec les hommes et les animaux est ici une *bĕrît* d'Elohim avec la terre, en parallélisme avec le thème de *Genèse* 8,22 : la nature a ses lois.

On sait que divers interprètes du passage s'efforcent d'en tirer une conception morale de la divinité, à partir de la restriction alimentaire : « Vous ne mangerez point la chair avec son sang » et de la déclaration : « qui répand le sang de l'homme, son sang sera répandu ». Ainsi seraient indiquées les conditions auxquelles l'homme devrait satisfaire pour appartenir à la *bĕrît* d'Elohim. Mais il n'existe, en fait, dans notre passage, aucun mot ou allusion qui renferme une telle idée. Le signe de la *bĕrît*,

---

4. Voir E. KÖNIG, *Die Genesis eingeleitet, übersetzt und erklärt*, Gütersloh [2,3]1925, p. 386 : " einen Bund aufrecht erhalten ".

l'arc-en-ciel, n'est nullement lié à une obligation imposée à l'homme et a fortiori aux animaux. C'est, à mon avis, un non-sens que d'établir un rapport entre l'interdiction de manger de la chair avec son sang, plus celle de tuer l'homme, et la *bĕrît* de cette péricope.

La *bĕrît* de notre péricope indique, en réalité, une relation entre Elohim et la terre, ou plus précisément, la vie sur la terre. L'effet de cette relation est une protection de la vie sur la terre : aucun cataclysme — *mabbûl* — n'anéantira plus jamais la vie sur la terre, savoir la vie animale et humaine. Mais nous ne sommes pas informés clairement sur le caractère propre de cette relation. Est mentionné seulement un phénomène naturel qui est le signe, *'ôt*, de la *bĕrît* d'Elohim avec la terre, savoir « mon arc dans la nuée ». Si nous pourrions nettement déterminer la signification de l'arc dans la nuée, nous y gagnerions une idée plus précise de ce que signifie *bĕrît* dans notre péricope.

Avant de faire quelques remarques sur l'arc-en-ciel, portons notre attention un moment sur le verbe *zākar*. Le verbe s'y trouve deux fois avec le mot *bĕrît* comme complément, à savoir aux versets 15 et 16. ' Rappeler ' me paraît fournir un sens plus juste que , se souvenir ' employé par Dhorme et de Vaux [5]. *Zākar* signifie : faire présent, effectif ; je me permets de renvoyer à mon étude *Gedenken und Gedächtnis in der Welt des Alten Testaments* [6]. L'emploi de *zākar* est une indication supplémentaire qu'il ne s'agit nullement là d'une nouvelle *bĕrît*, mais du maintien d'un rapport déjà existant [7].

Le signe de la *bĕrît* est l'arc-en-ciel. Puisque le maintien de la *bĕrît* signifie l'exclusion de tout nouveau déluge, ce à quoi il est fait nettement allusion, il s'ensuit normalement que le signe de cette *bĕrît* soit regardé comme un message de salut. Le commentaire habituel sur ce texte fait l'observation suivante que je cite d'après de Vaux, dans *La Bible de Jérusalem* : « L'alliance noachique, dont le signe est l'arc-en-ciel, s'étend à toute la création ; l'alliance avec Abraham, dont le signe sera la circoncision, n'intéresse que les descendants du patriarche, *Genèse* 17 ; sous Moïse, elle se limitera au seul Israël avec, en contre-partie, l'obéissance à la loi (*Exode* 19,5; 24,7-8) et notamment l'observation du sabbat (*Exode* 31,16-17) ».

Si nous considérons les autres signes, *'ôtôt*, ce qui en différentie « mon arc » apparaît aussitôt. L'humanité et les animaux forment, dans notre péricope, un ensemble aussi vaste que le monde ; quant au signe de cette *bĕrît*, il est complètement hors de la portée des hommes.

5. *La Sainte Bible* (« la Bible de Jérusalem »), Paris 1956.
6. Stuttgart, 1962.
7. Voir encore le texte illustratif de *Deutéronome* 8,18 : « Rappelles-toi de Yahvé ton dieu, car c'est lui qui t'a donné cette force — afin de maintenir sa *bĕrît*, jurée à tes pères, comme aujourd'hui ». Cf. *Gedenken und Gedächtnis*, p. 37.

L'Ancien Testament n'a pas de mot propre pour désigner l'arc-en-ciel. Il emploie le mot *qešet* pour désigner une arme, celle du tireur à l'arc, du chasseur. On m'a appris que l'accadien n'a pas non plus de terme propre pour désigner l'arc-en-ciel. La langue arabe possède un terme qui désigne l'arc-en-ciel, présage du temps [8]. On y connaît les proverbes suivants : ' arc-en-ciel au matin : voyage sans inquiétude ; arc-en-ciel au soir : recherche un creux bien chaud '. ' Arc-en-ciel d'Orient en Occident : sommeille en chemin ; arc-en-ciel du Midi au Nord : détache le bœuf de la charrue (il va pleuvoir) '.

En dehors de notre péricope, l'arc, *qešet*, désignant l'arc-en-ciel, se trouve au premier chapitre d'Ezechiel. La gloire de dieu se manifeste dans une apparition éblouissante : « comme la vision de l'arc qui se forme dans la nuée un jour de pluie, telle était la vision de la clarté environnante : c'était la vision de l'image de la gloire — *kābôd* — de Yahvé » (*Ez.* 1,28.) Le Siracide emploie le mot *qešet* d'une manière semblable : en 43,12 et 13, il est regardé comme une des merveilles de la création ; en 50,8 il est une image de la gloire multicolore du grand prêtre Simon.

Les mots d'Ezechiel *bějôm haggešem*, rendus par le Père Auvray « les jours de pluie » [9], par le professeur Zimmerli « am Regentage » [10] ne se rencontrent pas ailleurs dans l'ancien Testament. Il est évident que l'arc-en-ciel suppose un temps pluvieux. Et ceci nous fournit la raison pour laquelle il est si peu parlé de l'arc-en-ciel dans la littérature du Proche-Orient. L'arc-en-ciel est effectivement assez rare en Palestine [11]. La Palestine possède moins que nos régions les conditions nécessaires à la formation de l'arc-en-ciel. Elle se trouve, en effet, à 20 degrés de latitude plus au sud. Il y a donc une vingtaine de degrés de différence dans la hauteur du soleil par rapport à nos régions. Ainsi, les circonstances atmosphériques comme la situation géographique expliquent que l'arc-en-ciel soit relativement rare dans le Proche-Orient.

L'arc, les flèches et l'épée sont les marques distinctives de la guerre. Je cite à nouveau *Osée* 2,20 : « Et je conclurai pour eux un pacte, en ce jour-là, avec la bête sauvage, l'oiseau des cieux, le reptile au sol ; l'arc, l'épée, la guerre, je les briserai loin du pays et je les ferai dormir en sécurité ». Ce texte est à rapprocher de la prophétie de Gog en *Ezechiel* 39,3ss.: « Je briserai ton arc dans ta main gauche et je ferai tomber les

---

8. *qos quzaḥ*, voir G. DALMAN, *Arbeit und Sitte* I, 2, Gütersloh, 1928, p. 647, et la littérature citée à cet endroit.

9. *La Sainte Bible*, 1957.

10. W. ZIMMERLI, *Ezechiel* I, 1969, p. 30.

11. Les pluies sont relativement rares ; elles n'ont lieu qu'en début ou en fin d'année, *hā'ēt gešāmîm* (*Esr.* 10,13). Il pleut dans cette période souvent un jour entier, mais il y a aussi de fortes ondées tandis que le soleil n'apparaît qu'avant où après ces pluies.

flèches de ta main droite. Tu tomberas sur les montagnes d'Israël... ». Et au verset 9 : « Alors les habitants des villes d'Israël sortiront : ils feront un feu, ils l'alimenteront avec les armes, le petit et le grand bouclier, l'arc et les flèches, le javelot et la lance... ». Comparer le bouclier de Saül dans l'élégie de *2 Sam.* 1 ; l'épée de Goliath avec quoi le Philistin était décapité, dans le temple de Nob, *1 Sam.* 21. Les armes du vaincu sont brisées et brûlées : celles des vainqueurs honorées.

Lorsqu'Elohim met son arc dans le ciel, c'est d'un arc bandé qu'il s'agit, non de l'arc détendu et mis de côté, signe de la fin du combat. Ceux qui voient un signe de paix dans l'arc apparaissant dans la nuée, à savoir la fin du châtiment d'Elohim par le déluge, sont amenés à cette conclusion par l'interprétation théologique du déluge qui se lit dans l'introduction yahviste du récit (Genèse, 6,5-8) et leur manière de voir semble être corrobée par les mots qui, dans notre péricope, suivent le maintien par Elohim de sa *běrît* « pour qu'il n'y ait plus d'eaux pour un nouveau déluge pour détruire toute chair», 9,15.

Cette interprétation est fréquente depuis Wellhausen. Mais elle semble, à mon avis, perdre de vue le fait que l'arc n'est pas remisé, détendu, mais est montré au contraire comme un arc bandé. Elohim montre son arc bandé, assurément comme un signe de combat, non contre les hommes et la vie sur la terre, mais contre une puissance menaçante pour cette vie, celle des hommes et des animaux. Le combat d'Elohim signifie qu'il maintient sa *běrît* avec la terre, plus précisément avec la vie existant sur la terre.

Il se pourrait bien qu'il y ait un sens à une différentiation que nous pouvons constater dans le texte, tel qu'il nous est transmis. Nous lisons, en effet, au verset 8 : *wajjōmer 'ᵉlōhîm 'el-nōăḥ wᵉ'el-bānāw 'ittô* et au verset 17 : *wajjōmer 'ᵉlōhîm 'el-nōăḥ* mais au verset 12 nous ne lisons plus que les mots : *wajjōmer 'ᵉlōhîm* sans que Noé soit mentionné. Il n'y a là qu'une hypothèse, je le reconnais, mais qui a l'avantage de mieux rendre compte de l'image de l'arc, si l'on admet, comme il est vraisemblable, que le passage central de cette péricope se trouve aux versets 12, 13 et 16.

Il aura existé un ancien mythe décrivant un combat entre Elohim et une puissance adverse, un combat analogue à celui de Baʿal et Môt mais non identique, qui, à l'époque des pluies, a été décidé en faveur d'Elohim. Elohim est le dieu de la vie sur la terre, celles des humains et des animaux. Lorsqu'il montre son arc, c'est le signe qu'il maintient sa *běrît*. Il se porte garant de la vie des hommes et des animaux qui s'est trouvée en péril. Du contexte, on peut conclure que l'ennemi d'Elohim n'est pas une puissance comme Môt, le dieu de la sécheresse, mais une puissance comme Yâm, l'inondation, le déluge, *mabbûl*. La victoire doit être remportée à nouveau chaque année.

Au temps des pluies, le croyant fait l'expérience d'une puissance qui détrempe la terre, remplit les citernes, alimente les sources : c'est le dieu qui apporte la vie. Mais il fait aussi l'expérience d'un autre aspect, une puissance qui inonde et ravage. C'est le dieu qui anéantit. Le croyant se confie dans le dieu qui maintient sa *bĕrît* avec la terre et il nourrit sa foi par le récit, le mythe, qui fait voir dans l'arc-en-ciel un signe de ce dieu. « Et Elohim dit : Je mets mon arc dans la nuée et il sera le signe de pacte entre moi et la terre. » *(Gen.*, 9,12.13).

Il me paraît en outre possible que le verset 16 ait gardé quelques mots de l'ancien mythe. Le texte lit : *wĕhajtā haqqešet be'ānān urĕ'îtîhā lizkōr bĕrît 'ôlām bēn 'elōhîm ubēn ⟨kol bāśār 'ašer 'al⟩ hā'āreṣ*. En effet, si l'on prend Elohim, l'Elohim qui a mis son arc dans la nuée, comme sujet de la forme verbale *urĕ'îtîhā*, ainsi que le suggère le texte actuel, la phrase devient étrange : « l'arc sera dans la nuée et je (Elohim) le verrai pour me rappeler la *bĕrît* entre Elohim et tout animal vivant en toute chair, qui est sur la terre ». La Septante traduit au lieu de « entre Elohim »: *entre moi* et est suivie par plusieurs interprètes, entre autres par SPEISER, sans qu'il avertisse qu'il s'écarte ici du texte hébreu [12].

Eerdmans voyait dans ce verset une trace de polythéisme, puisque le sujet du verbe est autre que Elohim [13]. En fait, si une partie du verset 16 provient de l'ancien mythe où Elohim maintient sa *bĕrît*, mais où d'autres puissances entrent aussi en jeu, le sujet de la forme « je le verrai » pourrait être la puissance qui, à la vue de l'arc-en-ciel, reconnaît — *zākar* — le pacte entre Elohim et la terre.

De plus, l'absence de pronom possessif au terme *berît*, alors qu'Elohim parle au verset 13 de « mon arc », s'expliquerait mieux ainsi ; c'est l'autre puissance qui parle de l'arc-en-ciel. Quant aux versets 14 et 15, ils paraissent dépendre de l'ancien mythe. La difficulté du sujet pour le verbe *rā'ā* y est éliminée. On lit le passif : *wĕnir'ătā*.

J'ai conscience de corroborer l'hypothèse d'un ancien mythe israélite, si je pouvais rapporter un tel mythe accadien, ou plutôt ugaritien. Dans ce cas il faudrait remarquer que « Israël » a usé le mythe sans croire à sa réalité, comme une expression poétique. De cette manière on affaiblit les textes mythologiques de la Bible, n'est-ce pas ? Il n'est pas nécessaire de dire que je n'ai pas de confiance en cette pratique car le mythe supposé dans notre péricope n'a pas de pareil dans la littérature de l'ancien Proche-Orient, à ma connaissance. Plus important, je crois, seraient des traces d'un mythe semblable à celui que je suppose, dans les textes de la Bible même.

Possiblement l'Ancien Textament nous a gardé la mémoire du mythe ou d'une idée semblable dans quelques lignes du livre de Job et dans les Psaumes. Yahvé donne l'ordre à la mer

---

12. E. A. SPEISER, *Genesis*, Anchor Bible, 1964.
13. B. D. EERDMANS, *Alttestamentliche Studien* I, Giessen, 1908, p. 29.

« jusqu'ici tu viendras et ne continueras point
ici se brisera l'orgueil de tes flots » (*Job.*, 38,11) [14].

L'expression *gĕ'ut hayyām* se trouve aussi dans *Deutéronome* 33,26 ;
Ps. 46,4 et Ps. 89,10 [15]. Ps. 89,10 lit :

« c'est toi — Yahvé, 'elohe Seba'ot — qui domines l'orgueil
de la mer ».

Si l'hypothèse qu'il reste des traces d'un ancien mythe dans la péricope
Genèse 9,8 à 17 se situe dans une bonne voie d'interprétation, il devient
alors évident que l'amalgame de cet ancien mythe avec le récit de Noé
est secondaire. La question se pose alors de savoir pourquoi le rédacteur
n'a-t-il pas complètement éliminé ce vieux mythe. Je n'y vois qu'une
seule réponse. Manifestement, la foi suscitée par l'étrange phénomène
de l'arc-en-ciel était si fortement ancrée jusque dans les milieux pour
lesquels écrivait le rédacteur, qu'il n'a pas pu le passer sous silence.

Par l'introduction de ce mythe dans la présentation des récits sur Noé
le pacte d'Elohim avec la terre s'identifie avec le pacte entre Elohim
et Noé. Deux significations dissemblables du terme *bĕrît* sont égalisées.
Ainsi s'établit un lien entre l'ancienne et la nouvelle foi, et le vieux dieu
israélite est assimilé au dieu d'un cercle juif, toujours plus restreint,
qui aboutit à ce qui est, suivant l'écrivain sacerdotal, le véritable
« Israël », le « peuple élu du dieu unique ».

Le terme *bĕrît* n'a certainement pas eu la même signification tout au
long des siècles. Dans l'ancien mythe, que je suppose intégré dans notre
péricope, la notion de *bĕrît* peut être définie comme une relation entre
Elohim et la terre, relation maintenue par dieu, grâce à laquelle la vie
continue d'exister sur la terre et dont le croyant voit le signe dans
l'arc-en-ciel [16]. L'arc-en-ciel est la manifestation multicolore du dieu

---

14. Traduction de DHORME, *o.c.*

15. M. DAHOOD, Anchor Bible, *Psalms*, 1966, rend avec « le dos de la mer ».

16. Quoiqu'il n'ait pas été le but de cette étude à discuter les sens du terme *bĕrît*,
une description puisse expliquer ici l'expression « relation entre Elohim et la terre »
et l'expression usée plus haut, « relation intime entre Elohim et l'homme ». *bĕrît*
signifie, je crois, la relation entre deux parties de quoi l'une est plus forte que
l'autre. On peut observer que cette relation est unilatérale, un décret, une ordonnance. Le décret règle les obligations du vassal. Le décret divin établit et garantit
les lois de la nature. L'ordonnance de dieu avec son peuple ou avec son serviteur
signifie aussi toujours des obligations imposées par le dieu. Mais la relation peut
être aussi bilatérale, avec des obligations pour les deux parties. On peut traduire
cette relation avec pacte. Les pactes sont régulièrement assurés avec des actes
religieux, comme des sacrifices et des serments. Les obligations et les conditions
pour le pacte sont en premier lieu à remplir par la partie faible. Mais la partie plus

vainqueur qui arrête net les forces de destruction. Au contraire, dans la présentation du rédacteur sacerdotal, la *bĕrît* n'est plus qu'une garantie de la persistance de la vie humaine sur la terre, parce qu'il faut qu'existe « le peuple élu ».

Supplementary Notes by Marc VERVENNE

The thesis defended in de Boer's contribution on Gn 9,8-17 is taken up and rectified by C.J.L. KLOOS, *The Flood on Speaking Terms with God*, in *ZAW* 94 (1982) 639-642. It is Kloos's opinion that the Priestly writer accorded the concept of the 'flood' (*mabbûl*) as an instrument of God with the concept of the 'sea' (*yam*) as the defeated arch-enemy of God, by conceiving of the flood as an independent power, which was temporarily released to punish mankind and to force them to renewed obedience. Compare also L. DEQUEKER, *L'alliance avec Noé (Gen 9,1-17)*, in J. CHOPINEAU (ed.), *Noé, l'homme universel* (Publications de l'Institutum Iudaicum Bruxelles, 3), Brussels, 1978, pp. 1-19.

A study of the structure and theme of the pericope is done by A. BONORA, *La promessa-impegno di dio con il mondo (Gen. 9,8-17); Proposta di struttura letteraria*, in *TItSett* 7 (1982) 37-45.
See moreover:
G.J. WENHAM, *The Coherence of the Flood Narrative*, in *VT* 28 (1978) 336-348, and comp. the critical examination of this and other attempts to defend the unity of Gn 6-9 by J.A. EMERTON in *VT* 37 (1987) 401-420 and 38 (1988) 1-21.
L. NEVEU, *Entrelacs bibliques sur le déluge. Recherches sur la structure littéraire de Gn 6,5-9,17*, Angers, 1981.
For a 'new approach': see R. COUFFIGNAL, *La geste de Noé. Approches nouvelles de Genèse, vi-ix*, in *Revue Thomiste* 85 (1985) 607-619.

In regard to the *bᵉrît* terminology, reference should be made to the bibliographical supplements to the contributions of E. Kutsch (p. 213), D.J. McCarthy (p. 214) and L. Dequeker (p. 217). For the *bᵉrît ḥādāšāh* in Jeremiah, see the supplementary note by R. Martin-Achard (p. 218).

The *tôledôt* formulae (*supra*, p. 105) are discussed by S. TENGSTRÖM, *Die Toledotformel und die literarische Struktur der priesterlichen Erweiterungsschicht im Pentateuch* (Coniectanea Biblica; Old Testament Series, 17), Gleerup, 1982, as well as P. WEIMAR, *Struktur und Komposition der priesterschriftlichen Geschichtsdarstellung*, in *Biblische Notizen* 23 (1984) 81-134, pp. 88-98.

---

forte s'oblige aussi aux certaines obligations. Dans la relation intime avec dieu le croyant a aussi le courage de compter sur des obligations à remplir par son dieu. On trouve des exemples de cette croyance audacieuse dans l'intercession, voir mon étude *De voorbede in het Oude Testament*, Leiden, 1943.

15

I SAMUEL 8, VERSE 16B

ועשה למלאכתו belongs to the catalogue of the customs of a king, I Samuel 8,11-16 (17). The sentence is a continuation of the statement that a king takes slaves, male and female, and the elite of the young men together with asses. Its construction is imperfect forms continued with perfect with *waw*, verses 11, 14, 15 and in verse 16, and can be compared with imperfect forms continued with *lamed* plus infinitive, verses 12 and 13.

The ancient versions render verse 16b in various ways. The Septuagint reads καὶ ἀποδεκατώσει εἰς τὰ ἔργα αὐτοῦ, ועשר instead of ועשה, a rendering which rightly did not find followers.[1] The usual translation of the sentence, 'doing his work', is given in the Peshiṭta, *wnᶜbd ᶜbdh*, and in the explanatory reading of the Targum למהוי עבדין עבידתא. The Vulgate renders *et ponet in opere suo*, which recalls (*tollet*) *et ponet* of verse 11.

Budde thinks ועשו במ' an easier reading[2] and similarly Segal suggests correcting the masoretic text into ועשה (ועשו) במ'.[3] Smith speaks of an unusual construction. He says: We should expect לעשות במ'.[4] The reading of 4QSamᵃ approaches Budde's wish and others suggestion, ועשו למלאכתו.[5] The Qumranreading takes מלאכה as work, labour, similar to the

---

[1] J. WELLHAUSEN, *Der Text der Bücher Samuelis*, Göttingen 1871, 70 observes that the expression 'the best, elite, of the young men' already marks the Septuagint reading as incorrect. The Septuagint reading 'your herds' instead of 'your young men' does not lessen the power of Wellhausen's remark.

[2] K. BUDDE, commentary, Tübingen/Leipzig 1902, 56, 'leichter wäre ועשו במ''.

[3] M. S. SEGAL, commentary, Jerusalem 1956, סג, 'perhaps to correct ...'.

[4] H. P. SMITH, commentary, Edinburgh 1899, 3rd ed. 1912, 58.

[5] Reproductions of the photographs of these fragments are kindly made available to me by Professor F. M. CROSS Jr in view of Biblia Hebraica Stuttgartensia, Samuel, which is expected to appear in 1974.

ancient versions. The reading 'and they will do his work' is possible. In later style *lamed* is used in the sense of את, indicating the direct object.

It is improbable that the Qumran fragment has preserved the original reading, however. The late style forms a reason to mistrust its originality. Moreover the construction of the masoretic text is similar to that used in verses 11, 14 and 15. All these statements have the same subject, the king. It would be very improbable to assume a deviation in verse 16. The object of the verb יקח would become the subject of the verb following.

Is 'doing his work' a correct rendering of our sentence? A review of a series of translations from the last century[6] shows an almost common opinion in rendering עשה ל with 'to use for'. Klostermann's 'einstellen für' (put into use); Buber-Rosenzweig's 'übermachen' (transfer to); and Stoebe's 'einspannen für' (assign to) differ from the usual rendering. This usual rendering 'to use for' (to put to, employer à, verwenden) might be influenced by מלאכתו. עשה ל means 'to make, *or* appoint, to'. If we try to fix the meaning of מלאכתו we see in the translations the idea, the works of the king, or the royal housekeeping, household, As far as is known to me only Stoebe translates differently, 'seine Vorhaben', his intentions, plans, projects. In his original and elaborate study of the first book of Samuel Stoebe distinguishes the statements of verses 11-15 from the directive in verse 16. In his opinion vv.11-15 contain the permanent obligations imposed by the king and verse 16 speaks of incidental

---

[6] Revised Version, 1884, 'and put them to his work'; *idem* Revised Standard Version, 1952; The Confraternity Version, 1965:
A. KLOSTERMANN, 1887, 26 'und für seine Wirtschaft einstellen';
S. R. DRIVER, 1889, 2nd ed. 1913, 68, 'and use them for his business';
Leiden Translation, 1899 'en ze bij zijn werk gebruiken';
W. NOWACK, 1902, 37, 'und für seine Wirtschaft verwenden'; *idem* A. SCHULZ, 1919, 122; R. KITTEL, 1922;
P. DHORME, 1910, 72, 'pour les employer à ses travaux';
W. CASPARI, 1926, 93, 'um arbeiten zu lassen';
Zürcher Bibel, 1931, 'und für seine Hofhaltung verwenden';
JOH. DE GROOT, 1934, 47 'om ze voor zich te laten werken';
M. BUBER-F. ROSENZWEIG, (no date), 'und seiner Wirtschaft übermachen';
Canisius Translation, A. VAN DEN BORN, 1939, 'om die voor zijn eigen werk te gebruiken';
Dutch Bible Society, 1951, 'en gebruiken voor zijn werk';
Bible de Jérusalem, R. DE VAUX, 1956, 'et les fera travailler pour lui';
Pléiade, DHORME, 1956, 'et les affectera à ses travaux';
A. VAN DEN BORN, 1956, 48, 'en ze voor hem laten werken';
H. W. HERTZBERG, 1965, 54, 'und (sie) für seine Arbeit verwenden';
New American Bible, 1969, 'and use them to do his work';
New English Bible, 1970, 'and put to his own use';
H. J. STOEBE, 1973, 185, 'und sie für seine Vorhaben einspannen'.

projects, probably building plans of the king.[7] I do not think that Stoebe
gives sufficient evidence for a new meaning of מלאכה, a meaning which
cannot be derived from the basic sense of the word, nor is found elsewhere in Hebrew or in a cognate language. מלאכה is a derivation of the
root l'k, known in Ugaritic, Arabic and Ethiopic, to send, to charge with a
mission. מלאך is a messenger, and מלאכה an instruction, agency, charge.
From the basic sense the various meanings of the term are comprehensible:
The execution of orders, assigned duties, work, employment, in some cases
including the results of work, property or stock (Ex.22,7.10; Gen.33,14;
I Sam.15,9). In Ezech.15,3 Zimmerli suggests 'to make to a product
of work',[8] עשה לעשות למלאכה. nif. with למלאכה occurs in Ezech.15,5
and Lev.7,24.

I think that in I Sam.8,16b מלאכה means the royal property, including
his servants, acres, cattle, court. The royal property is required, recruited
from families. Thenius was in my opinion not far from the correct sense:
'nach der gew. Bedeutung von עשה ל er wird sie zu seiner Habe (I Sam.
15,9) machen, d.i. sich aneignen; [möglicher Weise auch: er wird sie zu
seiner Botschaft machen, d.i. zu seinen Beschickungen und Geschäften
überhaupt verwenden.][9]

The rendering '(Your slaves, male and female, the elite of your young
men and your asses he will take) and make his property' suits to the
basic sense of the terms used and is in agreement with the context.
The rendering seems to be supported by the description of the contrast,
the ruin of royal power. Ruin of royal power is expressed by the return
of the king's soldiers and servants to their ancestral families. 'And all
Israel fled every one to his tent', after Absalom's death, II Sam.18,17b,
cf. II Sam.19,8. Rejecting their king is expressed with: 'We have no
portion in David – every man to his tent, O Israel', II Sam.20,1.

---

[7] STOEBE, Das erste Buch Samuelis, Gütersloh 1973, 184-189.
[8] W. ZIMMERLI, commentary 1969, 325f. 'Wörtl. zum Werk (stück?) zu machen'.
[9] O. THENIUS, commentary 1842, 29.

16

THE PERFECT WITH *WAW* IN 2 SAMUEL 6:16

The usual translation of 2 Sam. 6:16 reads:

As the ark of the Lord was entering the city of David, Saul's daughter Michal looked down through the window and saw king David leaping and dancing before the Lord, and she despised him in her heart.

There are some differences in the modern translations, but these involve the division of the sentence. Dhorme (1910: 323ff.) distinguishes three clauses,

Comme l'arche de Iahvé entrait dans la cité de David, la fille de Saül, Mical, regardait par la fenêtre. Elle vit le roi David dansant et gambadant devant Iahvé. Alors elle le méprisa en son cœur.

Kittel (1922) connects the last two clauses and translates,

Während nun die Lade Jahwes in die Stadt Davids einzog, hatte Sauls Tochter Michal durchs Fenster geblickt. Und als sie den König David sah, wie er vor Jahwe hüpfte und tanzte, empfand sie Verachtung für ihn.

It appears that differences in translation exist, too; the rendering of *meP̄azzēz ūmekarkēr* may or may not be in connection with the reading of the parallel text in 1 Chron. 15:29. Those differences will not be considered here.

The following verses (2 Sam. 6:17-19) continue and complete the story of the bringing up of the ark. Verse 19 ends with the common final line of narratives, "all the people departed every one to his house". In the recension to be found in the Chronicles version, verse 20a, "And David returned to bless his house" is taken into the final sentence of the story. Then follows (2 Sam. 6:20-23) the scene in David's palace. The Chronicler, dropping this scene, adds, after the blessing of the people by David, a long passage of liturgical character, in which large parts of some Psalms – 105, 96, and others – are incorporated. Evidently he could not use David's punishment of Michal in his picture of the chosen king.

Michal's observation of David and her resultant feelings (2 Sam. 6:16b) anticipate the story of her reprobation because of her criticism of David's behaviour. Smith (1912:295) observes,

The verse [16] is designed to prepare for the scene at home. As it breaks the thread of the narrative, and is introduced awkwardly [16a], it is perhaps a redactional insertion.

Budde (1902:231) and Dhorme (1910:323) do not accept Smith's opinion but fail to argue why they take verse 16 as belonging to the original narrative.

Almost every translator and commentator changes the first word of verse 16. Instead of *wᵉhāyāh*, perfect with *waw*, one reads *wayhî*, imperfect with *waw*.[1] The Revised Version (1884) is an exception in trying to maintain the Masoretic text, rendering, "And it was so, as the ark of the Lord came into the city of David, that...."

The emendation, reading *wayhî* instead of *wᵉhāyāh*, is supported by the recension in 1 Chron. 15:29 and by the rendering in the Septuagint, while the rendering of the Vulgate, "cumque intrasset arca domini civitatem David" might also reflect the reading *wayhî*. Peshiṭta and Targum, using perfect forms, do not support the Masoretic reading being *whw'* and *whwh* the rendering both of *wᵉhāyāh* and *wayhî*. Recently a fragment from Qumrân, 4QSamᵃ, has been found to strengthen the emendation.[2] It seems certain that in the future few people will continue to prefer the Masoretic reading of 2 Sam. 6:16a.

A difficult question remains unanswered, however. Why is an understandable reading changed into a form which at first sight does not make sense? This question is rarely taken into consideration. Klostermann

---

[1]   Without striving for completeness I mention a number of commentaries and translations from the latest time: Klostermann (1887:153); S. R. Driver (1913:270); Het Oude Testament (Leiden Translation) (1899); Smith (1912:295); Budde (1902:231); Dhorme (1910:323); Schulz (1920:72); Kittel (1922); Caspari (1926:473); Das Buch Schmuel (n.d.); Die Heilige Schrift (1931); de Groot (1935:21); Revised Standard Version (1952); de Vaux (1956); Dhorme (1956); Goslinga (1956:78,86f); van den Born (1956:153); Grispino (1965); Hertzberg (1965:226); The New American Bible (1969); The New English Bible (1970).

[2]   See the Notes to the New American Bible. I could check the reading on a xerox of the photograph, kindly made available to me by Professor F. M. Cross, Jr., in view of the Biblia Hebraica Stuttgartensia, Samuel, which is expected to appear in 1974 (de Boer i.p.).

(1887:153) supposes, "*wᵉhāyāh* ist vermutlich aus *wᵉhinnēh* entstellt", but he did not have confidence in his guess; *wᵉhinnēh* is wrongly spelled *wᵉhāyāh*, as appears from his translation "Es geschah aber", as in the reading in 1 Chron. 15:29. Budde (1902:231) suggests as original reading *wᵉhā'ārôn* instead of *wᵉhāyāh* *'ᵃrôn yhwh*. Cod. Vaticanus of the Septuagint, leaving Yahweh unrendered, is no real support for this suggestion because of its καὶ ἐγένετο. Joüon (1947: paragraph 119z, 336) thinks that graphic resemblance between *wᵉhāyāh* and *wayhî* "peut expliquer en partie certains *wᵉhāyāh* anormaux" (1 Sam. 1:12; 10:9; 13:22; 17:48; 25:20; 2 Sam. 6:16; 2 Kings 3:15; Jer. 37:11; Amos 7:2). He adds to 2 Sam. 6:16, "mais parall. 1 Chron. 15:29 correctement *wayhî*". Joüon's reservation "en partie" discourages real discussion. The supposition of a possible orthographic variant seems to me arbitrary. If *wayhî* is taken as a variant of *wᵉhāyāh* in 2 Sam. 6:16 we ought to speak of a real variant reading and not of an orthographic one. The same applies, in my opinion, to the other quoted texts, where the Septuagint renders καὶ ἐγένετο or καὶ ἐγενήθη. Such variants, in most cases emendations, are of the category: *wᵉḳatalti* instead of *wayyiḳtōl*. The difficult question, why a perfect with *waw* has been chosen instead of the usual imperfect with *waw*, which is according to the later witnesses a smoother reading, remains unanswered.

Those who maintain the Masoretic reading seem to be compelled to credit *wᵉhāyāh* here with the meaning of *wayhî*. Gesenius-Kautzsch (1885) concludes the "Gebrauch des Perfect" in the Grammatik with

Dass jedoch *wᵉhayah* auch zur Fortführung der Erzählung verwendet werden kann, lehrt Gen. 30:41; 38:9; 1 Sam. 13:22 (überall in Bezug auf eine in der Vergangenheit wiederholte Handlung); 1 Sam. 1:12; 13:22; 25:20; Jer. 3:9; 37:11; 38:28; Hiob 1:1.

An explanation is not given. Davidson (1902:81, paragraph 54, Rem. 1 (2)) distinguishes perfect with strong *waw*, and mentions herewith, "Details are often introduced or a new start made in the narrative by *wᵉhāyāh*." And further on (1902:85, paragraph 58), "The use of *waw* perf. as freq. is exceedingly free; it may occur in any connexion, introducing an additional trait or an entirely new fact"; and perfect with simple *waw*. In the latter he states that there are many cases where *waw* with perfect appears in simple narrative, and is merely copulative. The usage becomes more common as the language declines and comes under the influence of Aramaic. But Davidson does not dismiss lightly the difficulty by everywhere supposing Aramaic influence.

Even in early style, the form *wehāyah and it was* is not quite rare. Amos 7: 2; 1 Sam. 1: 12; 10: 9; 17: 48; 25: 20; 2 Sam. 6: 16. In Gen. 38: 5[3] read *wehî'* with Septuagint (1902: 85).

Davidson's remark in the same paragraph of his important *Syntax* seems to me elucidating," The perfect with *waw* seems occasionally to resume and restate briefly an event previously described in detail; Judg. 7: 13 *wᵉnāp̄al*; 1 Kings 20: 21; Gen. 15: 6.(?)" He finds Judg. 3: 25 and 2 Sam. 13: 18 to be curious. I shall return to Davidson's remark below.

Joüon (1947: 335) observes,

Même en tenant largement compte des altérations possibles du texte conso-nantique, il reste un assez grand nombre de *wᵉḳataltî et j'ai tué* anormaux, c'est-à-dire contraires à l'usage.

Next to the supposition of errors through graphic resemblance concerning *wayhî* and *wᵉhāyāh*, in my opinion an impossible idea (see above), he takes into account the influence of Aramaic and post-Biblical Hebrew. But he reckons also with other factors. Paragraph 119z of his useful *Grammaire*, however, does not explain those cases where no influence of Aramaic or post-Biblical Hebrew is supposed.

It is incorrect, in my opinion, to detach the cases of *wᵉhāyāh* in question from the rather many cases of perfect with *waw* in simple narrative. Let us first look at some of those cases. In 2 Kings 23: 4, 5, 10, 12, and 15, five cases occur. They are considered to be incorrect forms and translated as imperfects with *waw*, see Klostermann (1887: 479ff); Benzinger (1899: 192ff), and others. Klostermann supposes in some cases – also in 2 Kings 14: 7 – an original reading *(wᵉ) hû'* plus verb, to get rid of the "impossible perf. cons.". Davidson (1902: 85) considers *waw* here and in similar cases as merely copulative (see also Montgomery-Gehman 1951: 529ff; Gray 1970: 730ff). It is possible that perfect with *waw* in the quoted texts indicates late additions or a late redactional influence. Such seems more likely than to suppose similarity in meaning between the perfect with *waw* forms and the imperfect with *waw* forms. I prefer, however, following Davidson's remark about some other texts quoted above, reckoning with a special meaning of perfect with *waw*: an attempt to express a brief resumption of an event described in detail previously, or to express a kind of conclusion or making a record, a statement, or to indicate the conditions for a following narrative.

[3] The Septuagint reading is αὐτη δὲ ἦν. καὶ ἦν is usually the rendering of *wayhî* but occurs sometimes as rendering of *wᵉhāyāh*, indicating a durative, see Gen. 38:5; Num. 11:8; Judg. 2:18, and 2 Kings 18:7.

In several studies the additional character of the perfect with *waw* cases in 2 Kings 23 has been proven. But, even as additions to an earlier story, the forms may preserve a special meaning. It seems possible, I think, to paraphrase the verses in question as follows: verse 4, "Well, thus he has carried their ashes to Bethel" – a scoffing allusion to Bethel's cult, anticipating Bethel's destruction mentioned in verses 15ff. Verse 5, "Well, thus he has stopped the heathen priests" (of Jerusalem's surroundings). Verse 10, "Well, thus he has desecrated Tefet." Verse 12, "Well, thus he has thrown their ashes into the wadi Kedron", indicating the definitive end of the cult. Verse 15, "Well, thus he has burnt Ashera", here using intentionally the name of the goddess to state the total destruction of Bethel's cult.

wᵉnāp̄al hā'ōhel, at the end of verse 13 in Judges 7, whether or not it is an addition, is in my opinion another example of a conclusive statement expressed by perfect with *waw*, "Well, thus the tent has collapsed." Similarly preserved is a final statement in 1 Kings 20: 21, "Well, thus he has smitten the Aramaeans with great slaughter" – a resumption of the preceding story. Gen. 15: 6, in Davidson's work mentioned with a question mark, might mean as a record, "Well, he was a believer in Yahweh, therefore he – Yahweh – planned righteousness – blessing – for him."[4]

In Judg. 3: 23 *wᵉnā'al* may have the meaning, "Well, thus it – the door – was tied up", a repetition of the idea expressed with the verb *šāgar*, indicating the durative. But in 2 Sam. 13: 18 the use of *wᵉnā'āl* is curious. Davidson (1902: 85) rightly observes that verse 18 states how the *two* injunctions of verse 17 were literally carried out. It would seem we are forced to suppose here a record of Amnon's definite decision. In Ezek. 37: 2, 7, 10 one may assume a condition, expressed by the construction with perfect with *waw*. I think that Zimmerli (1969: 886) is right in his comments,

eine die Vorbedingung beschreibende Aussage im perf. mit *waw* führt vorbereitend hin zu der eigentlich akzentuierten Hauptaussage.
Man wird also keineswegs schon mit einer völligen Einebnung des perf. mit *waw* in der allgemeinen Gebrauch des perf., wie sie dann etwa in der späten Sprache Kohelets zu finden ist, zu rechnen haben.

---

[4] The pointing of the Masoretic text, *wᵉhe̊'ᵉmīn* read a hiph. perf. with *waw*. This meaning is found in the Septuagint, moreover adding the name Abraham. See, too, the quotation in Rom. 4:3; Gal. 3:6, and James 2:23. The spelling of the Hebrew text handed down to us suggests a reading *wᵉhā'ᵃmēn*, imperative hiph. Such would give a totally different idea.

Such a condition, expressed in an introductory clause, is usually followed by a nominal sentence, introduced with w^{e}hinnēh or by sentences using imperfect with *waw*. 1 Sam. 5: 7, "Well, thus they have said", and 2 Sam. 16: 5, ūbā' picturing a situation which is the condition for the following story, seem to me to be in the same category.

w^{e}hāyāh occurs several times to express frequency, repetition, or iteration: Gen. 38: 9; Exod. 17: 11; 33: 7, 8, 9; Num. 21: 9; Judg. 6: 3; 1 Sam. 16: 23; 17: 48; 2 Sam. 14: 26; 15: 5; 2 Kings 3: 15. In cases as Exod. 17: 11; 33: 7; and 1 Sam. 16: 23, the similarity of the construction with other perfect with *waw* forms is underlined.

w^{e}hāyāh occurs, too, as the indication of a brief resumption. Hannah's prayer, previously mentioned at length, is in 1 Sam. 1: 12 briefly repeated in order to introduce Eli's intervention. Jer. 40: 3, "Therefore this thing is come upon you" is a conclusive sentence, resuming the preceding record. In Jer. 3: 9, "It has been the staff[5] of her infidelity – adultery, metaphorically used – by which she..." is a resumption as well as a condition for what follows (cf. further Jer. 37: 11; Amos 2: 7 (?); 1 Sam. 10: 9; 13: 22). 1 Sam. 25: 20a seems to me also to be a conditional clause, a clear picture of the situation, introducing the unexpected meeting, "then she met him" (verse 20 end). w^{e}hāyāh in verse 20a is followed by further nominal sentences, constructed with participles: she, Abigail, riding and coming down, and David and his men coming down, kept hidden from each other by a hill in between.

It is time to return to our starting point, 2 Sam. 6: 16. If I am right that several perfect with *waw* clauses possess an intentional meaning and are erroneously understood as mistakes or as additions from a period that did not distinguish between perfect and imperfect with *waw*, 2 Sam. 6: 16a also might indicate a brief statement of the situation, resuming the event of the bringing up of the ark previously described in detail. This should be expected after verse 19, the end of the story.

The reading of the Peshitta suggests verse 16a to be a final statement. In cod. Ambrosianus, sixth or seventh century, we find two marks,

---

5   I read makkēl (z^{e}nūtāh), cf. Hos. 4:12. The staff will be used by sorcery . (see AJirku 1914). C. H. Cornill (1905:37ff.) shows that the pointing makkēl, instead of the difficult mikkōl of the Masoretic text, has been suggested already by J. D. Michaelis (1793), who was followed by Hitzig (1841:26). Michaelis (1793): "Quod, si legatur makkēl baculus est scortatio eius: i. e. cum baculo divinatorio (sacris sortibus) scortatur. Confer Hos. IV, 12 'ammî b^e^{c}ēṣô yis'al ūmakk^{e}lô yaggîd lô. Nec vero baculus h. l. idolum est, sed ut apud Hoseam instrumentum divinatorium, sagitta ex qua vaticinabantur. Egregie confirmant hanc meam interpretationem, verba quae statim sequuntur." The editor, Schleusner, adds a note wherein he declines, Michaelis' reading.

$-\overset{|}{|}- \ -\overset{|}{|}-$, to indicate the end of the story. Other ancient manuscripts do not have these marks. But three of the lectionaries available to me, all of the Nestorian rite, support the final character of verse 16a in Syrian use of the Bible.[6] These liturgical books do not contain the Michal episode. One of the lectionaries mentioned[7] continues the reading after 2 Sam. 6: 16a with 2 Sam. 7: 1 - 5 and 8 - 11. "Thus was the ark of the Lord in David's house" is considered to be the end of the story of the bringing up of the ark.

The Peshiṭta version gives us a slightly deviating text. The Hebrew *bā'* is not rendered and instead of "town of David" Peshiṭta reads "house of David". The dropping of *bā'* can be caused by taking verse 16a as a final statement. The variant "house (palace) of David" might be a correction of the Hebrew tradition, or a reminiscent of a lost tradition. A survey of the term *'îr dāwid* suggests that the term is not original in the Books of Samuel. In the story of David's capture of the strong-hold Ṣiyyôn, 2 Sam. 5: 7, "this is David's town" is evidently a gloss. In 2 Sam. 5: 9 the clause, David giving the stronghold Ṣiyyôn the name "David's town", is secondary. The stronghold is named *after* David, not *by* David, as appears from the many occurrences of the term in the stories about the time following, preserved in the Books of Kings. Finally, in 2 Sam. 6: 10 and 12, the term is not at all required, but is mere adornment.

2 Sam. 6: 16 is unnecessary for the scene at David's house in verses 20 to 23. This, together with a consideration of the place at which it interrupts the story of the bringing up of the ark, indicates its secondary character. The placement might have been influenced by the description of David's and the people's exuberant behaviour (verses 13-15). We should not forget that the author is writing in glorification of king David. The composer, who might have added verse 16 to connect the story of the bringing up of the ark with the scene at David's house, shows his religious zeal in giving David's cultic behaviour as the reason for Michal's contempt. The story of Michal's criticism of the chosen king and David's humiliation of Saul's daughter aims at dishonour for the house of Saul, diminishing, almost dissolving, David's connection with the clan of the rejected king. The context exhibits the glorification of David as founder of the cult in Jerusalem.

---

[6] These lectionaria have the sigla 13/1, 15/1 and 16/2 in the Leiden edition of the Peshiṭta (de Boer i.p.).
[7] 13/1.

Saul's daughter Michal saw king David leaping and dancing before the Lord, and she despised him. 2 Sam. 6: 16a seems to preserve an intentional construction, a perfect with *waw* followed by two participles, expressing the condition by picturing the situation and introducing the verbal clause – she despised him. "Well, thus it was, the ark of the Lord coming into David's city, and Michal, Saul's daughter, looking down through the window...."

REFERENCES

Translations

The Revised Version (Oxford: The University Press, 1884).
Het Oude Testament (Leiden Translation) (Leiden: Brill, 1899).
Die Heilige Schrift des Alten Testaments, E. Kautzsch and A. Bertholet (eds.), 4th ed. (Tübingen: Mohr, 1922).
Das Buch Schmuel, by M. Buber and F. Rosenzweig (Berlin: Schneider, n.d.).
Die Heilige Schrift (Zürich: Zwingli Verlag, 1931).
Revised Standard Version (New York: Oxford Press, 1952).
La Sainte Bible (Bible de Jérusalem) (Paris: du Cerf, 1956).
La Bible, Ed. Pléiade (Paris: Gallimard, 1956).
Confraternity Version (New York: Guild Press, 1965).
The New American Bible (Paterson: St. Anthony Guild Press, 1969).
The New English Bible (Oxford and Cambridge: University Press, 1970).

Other Literature

Benzinger, I.
1899 "Die Bücher der Könige", in K. Marti (ed.), *Kurzer Hand-Commentar* (Freiburg i. B.: Mohr).
Boer, P. A. H. de (ed.)
i.p. The Old Testament in Syriac. Peshiṭta Version, publication on behalf of the International Organization for the Study of the Old Testament by Peshiṭta Institute, Leiden University (Leiden: Brill).
Boer, P. A. H. de
i.p. Samuel. Biblia Hebraica Stuttgartensia (Stuttgart: Württembergische Bibelanstalt).
Born van den
1956 "Samuël" in van den Born, Grossouw, and van der Ploeg (eds.), *De Boeken van het Oude Testament* (Roermond: Romen).
Budde, K.
1902 "Die Bücher Samuel", in K. Marti (ed.), *Kurzer Hand-Commentar* (Freiburg i. B.: Mohr).
Caspari, W.
1926 "Die Samuelbücher", in E. Sellin (ed.), *Kommentar zum Alten Testament* (Leipzig: Deichert).
Cornill, C. H.
1905 *Das Buch Jeremia* (Leipzig: Tauchnitz).
Cross, F. M.
1969 "Textual Notes to the Books of Samuel", (*The New American Bible*) (Paterson: St. Anthony Guild Press).

Davidson, A. B.
  1902 *Hebrew Syntax*, 3rd ed. (Edinburgh: Clark).
Dhorme, P. (E.)
  1910 *Les Livres de Samuel* (Paris: Gabalda).
  1956 Translator of La Bible, Ed. Pléiade (see Translations above).
Driver, S. R.
  1913 *Notes on the Hebrew Text and the Topography of the Books of Samuel*, 2nd ed. (Oxford: Clarendon).
Gesenius, W., — Kautzsch E.
  1885 *Hebräische Grammatik*, 24th ed. (Leipzig: Vogel).
Goslinga, C. J.
  1956 "De Boeken Samuël", *Korte Verklaring der Heilige Schrift* (Kampen: Kok).
Gray, J.
  1970 *I and II Kings* (London: SCM Press).
Grispino, J. A.
  1965 Translator of the Books of Samuel in the Confraternity Version (see Translations above).
Groot, de
  1935 "II Samuël", *Tekst en Uitleg* (Groningen: Wolters).
Hertzberg, H. W.
  1965 "Die Samuelbücher", *Das Alte Testament Deutsch* 10 (Göttingen: Vandenhoeck and Ruprecht).
Hitzig, F.
  1841 "Der Prophet Jeremia", *Kurzgefasstes exegetisches Handbuch* (Leipzig: Weidmann).
Jirku, A.
  1914 *Materialien zur Volksreligion Israels* (Leipzig: Diechert). Reprinted in *Von Jerusalem nach Ugarit, Gesammelte Schriften* (Graz: Akademische Druck- und Verlagsanstalt, 1966).
Joüon, P.
  1947 *Grammaire de l'hébreu biblique*, 2nd ed. (Rome: Institut Biblique Pontifical).
Kittel, R.
  1922 Translator of the Books of Samuel in Die Heilige Schrift des Alten Testaments (see Translations above).
Klostermann, A.
  1887 "Die Bücher Samuelis", in H. Strack and O. Zöckler (eds.), *Kurzgefasster Kommentar* (Nordlingen: Beck).
Michaelis, J. D.
  1793 "Observationes philologicae et criticae in Jeremiae Vaticinia et Threnos" J. F. Schleusner (ed.), (Göttingen: Vandenhoeck and Ruprecht).
Montgomery, J., — H. S. Gehman
  1951 "The Books of Kings", *The International Critical Commentary* (Edinburgh: Clark).
Schleusner, J. F. (ed.)
  1793 see Michaelis.
Schulz, A.
  1920 "Die Bücher Samuel", in J. Nikel (ed.), *Exegetisches Handbuch* (Münster in Westf.: Aschendorff).
Skehan, P. W.
  1969 "Textual Notes to the Books of Samuel", (*The New American Bible*) (Paterson: St. Anthony Guild Press).

Smith, H. P.
    1912   "The Books of Samuel", *The International Critical Commentary*, 3rd ed.
           (Edinburgh: Clark).
Vaux, R. de
    1956   Translator of the Books of Samuel in La Sainte Bible (See Translations
           above).
Wellhausen, J.
    1871   *Der Text der Bücher Samuelis* (Göttingen: Vandenhoeck and Ruprecht).
Zimmerli, W.
    1969   "Ezechiel", *Biblischer Kommentar* (Neukirchen-Vluyn: Neukirchener Verlag).

17

EGYPT IN THE OLD TESTAMENT
SOME ASPECTS OF AN AMBIVALENT ASSESSMENT

In addition to his earlier publications,[1] R.J. WILLIAMS gave a clear survey of the relations between Egypt and Palestine in a paper presented to the Congress of the IOSOT at Edinburgh in August 1974[2]. Once again, it strikes one how much in her relations with Palestine, Egypt was the giving party and Palestine the receiving one. Although Egypt may have had political and economic interests in Syria and Palestine and may have profited from foreigners, groups, and individuals forcibly or voluntarily "sojourning" in Egypt, an Egyptologist looking at the Old Testament will note Israel's receptivity to influences from Egypt, especially in the tenth and seventh centuries B.C., which were important periods in the relatively short span of Israel's history[3]. WILLIAMS realizes full well that these Egyptian influences were not always direct. In this connection, he mentions the transmitting role of the Phoenicians.[4] He could also have drawn attention to the Philistines and to Canaanite culture in general. I am referring here to the city-states, to the social and economic situation in Palestine before the establishment of a state under the control of Hebrew tribes and of a government concentrated in one or two capitals. Owing to the lack of archaeological evidence, a clear break in the historical development and socio-economic situation of Palestine in the centuries under discussion cannot be demonstrated and seems indeed unlikely. In the Book of Zephaniah we still read, "O Canaan, land of the Philistines" (ii 5b), and the El Amarna letters inform us about both Egyptian influence and native culture and policy in early times. There are also arguments for the hypothesis that Egypt served as an example for the administration of the Hebrew state in the tenth century B.C., a subject

---

[1] E.g. "Egypt and Israel", in: *The Legacy of Egypt*, ed. J.P. HARRIS, Oxford ²1971, pp. 257–290.

[2] R.J. WILLIAMS, " 'A people come out of Egypt', An Egyptologist Looks at the Old Testament", *SVT* 28 (1975), pp. 231–252.

[3] Cf. S. MORENZ, "Ägypten und die Bibel", *RGG*³I, col. 117–121.

[4] WILLIAMS refers to A. BARUCQ, *L'expression de la louange divine et de la prière dans la bible et en Égypte*, Cairo, 1962, and to W.F. ALBRIGHT, *Yahweh and the Gods of Canaan*, London, 1968.

which cannot be discussed in this paper. WILLIAMS's well documented paper rightly concludes that "... the evidence is overwhelming that Israel drank deeply at the wells of Egypt. In a very real sense the Hebrews were 'a people come out of Egypt' (Num. xxii 5, 11)".[5]

Surveying the Old Testament texts that deal with the land of Egypt and the Egyptians, one can make the following classification:[6]

Firstly mention should be made of Egypt's wealth: $g^\jmath wn \; m\c{s}rym$, the pride of Egypt (Ez. xxxii 12). Egypt is a rich country. The result of her labour, her acquired wealth, the fruit of toil (ygy^c Isa. xlv 14), is mentioned in parallel with the merchandise of Kush, etc. The enumeration of Egypt, Kush, and Saba is not an accidental one. The mere mention of these countries calls to mind a picture of power and wealth.[7] Unlike many parts of the surrounding regions, Egypt's well watered country is a source of life and prosperity. The Jordan Valley, shown to Abram's nephew Lot (Gen. xiii 10), "well watered everywhere", is compared to a $gn \; yhwh$, a mighty garden,[8] and to the land of Egypt. The abundant inundation of Egypt was proverbial: "to rise like the Nile and be tossed about and sink again, like the Nile of Egypt" (Am. viii 8; ix 4; cf. Exod. xvii 1 – 7). Egypt had water to drink, unlike Rephidim and unlike the wilderness of Zin in Kadesh (Num. xx 5). Water means food, bread, vegetables, and fruit (see also Num. xxi 5). Canaan is not like Egypt, from which the people came who are addressed in Deuteronomy: "Where you sowed your seed and watered it with your feet, like a garden of vegetables" (xi 10)[9]. The image of Egypt as a land of grain, figs,

---

[5] WILLIAMS, *art. cit.*, p. 252. Cf. also John MacDONALD, "Egyptian Interests in Western Asia to the End of the Middle Kingdom: An Evaluation", *AJBA* (Sydney) 5 (1972), pp. 72–98; and H. ENGEL, "Die Vorfahren Israels in Ägypten. Forschungsgeschichtlicher Überblick über die Darstellungen seit Richard Lepsius 1849", *FThSt* 27 (1979).

[6] Geographical occurrences such as "... as far as Shur, to the land of Egypt" (1 Sam. xxvii 8) and "... along the Brook of Egypt to the Great Sea" (Ezek. xlvii 29) may be left out on the grounds that they are irrelevant to the subject under discussion, the assessment of Egypt.

[7] I may refer to my *Second Isaiah's Message*, Leiden, 1956, pp. 49f.

[8] On the tetragrammaton used as an epithet expressing the superlative, see my article in *VT* 24 (1974), pp. 233–235.

[9] Let me observe, incidentally, that the usual explanation of "watering with the feet" in the sense of carrying water could be replaced by a comparison with the watering of fields on different levels by opening low earthen walls between the fields with the feet, a system of watering in use for rice fields, e.g. in Indonesia.

vines, pomegranates, and drinking water can be deduced from the Hebrews' dispute with Moses in Num. xx 5; compare also Lam. v 6, "We have given the hand to (we came to terms with, NEB) Egypt and to Assyria, to get bread enough ...". Moreover Egypt provided them with fish (Num. xi 5) and meat (xi 18). "Would that we had died by the hand of Yhwh in the land of Egypt, when we sat by the fleshpots and ate bread to the full ..." (Ex. xvi 3). "Why did we come forth out of Egypt?" (Num. xi 20). And in Num. xiv 2ff. the Israelites, after hearing the negative report about the land of Canaan which has been spied out, cry out in dismay, "Would that we had died in the land of Egypt! ... would it not be better for us to go back to Egypt? ... Let us choose a captain, and go back to Egypt." Many more fine and valuable products of Egypt are mentioned in the Old Testament, such as linen (Ez. xxvii 7; Prov. vii 16), bronze (Ps. lxviii 32), and vines (Ps. lxxx 9 (8)). The fact that Egypt remained a relatively rich country is confirmed in the Mishna.[10]

Secondly, some old Testament passages refer to intermarriage between Hebrews and Egyptians. The narrative of Joseph in Egypt, culminating in his attaining a high position (though only after a series of adventures), must have been intended to inspire desperate people who lived in foreign countries or were dominated by foreigners with new hope for the future. Joseph married the daughter of an Egyptian priest, and his father Jacob, who had been rescued by his naturalized son together with his family, gave his blessing to the sons out of this mixed marriage (Gen. xlviii). Abram took Sarai's Egyptian maid Hagar (Gen. xvi) as a concubine. Sheshan had daughters but no sons, as we read in the genealogies from Adam to David opening the book of Chronicles (1 Chron. ii 34), and gave his daughter in marriage to his Egyptian slave Jarha. The most striking example of intermarriage is to be found in 1 Kings iii 1, where we read that Solomon allies himself with Pharaoh, king of Egypt, by marrying the latter's daughter. "There can be no doubt", as Williams rightly observes, "that the marriage alliance itself is evidence of a close association between Egypt and the Hebrew kingdom."[11]

---

[10] A number of tractates mention Egyptian products and specialities, e.g. *Kil.* 1,2; *Maas.* 5,8; *Shab.* 9,7; *Pes.* 3,1; *Ned.* 17,8; *Maksh.* 6,3.

[11] WILLIAMS, *art. cit.*, p. 232. Cf. Gezer as dowry (*šlḥym*) in 1 Kings ix 16. See also D.B. Redford, "Studies in Relations between Palestine and Egypt during the

Thirdly attention must be drawn to people's sojourns in Egypt in times of threat and disaster. Egypt was not the only country where people in difficulties sought refuge. The prophet Elisha advised the Shunnamite woman to go to the country of the Philistines (2 Kings viii), and "she went with her household and sojourned in the land of the Philistines seven years" (*wtgr b'rṣ plštym*). And Elimelech, his wife, and his two sons went and stayed in the country of Moab (Ruth i 1). Here again the verb *gwr* is used to denote a temporary stay in a foreign country where one receives hospitality. A *gr* is a temporary resident with certain privileges, but without the right of inheritance. Abram went down to Egypt to live there for a while because of the severe famine in Canaan (Gen. xii 10). Jacob and his sons went to Egypt for the same reason. After being presented to Pharaoh by Joseph, Jacob's five sons said to the Egyptian king, "We have come to sojourn in the land (*lgwr b'rṣ b'nw*), ... let your servants dwell in the land of Goshen" (Gen. xlvii 4).

According to David DAUBE, who in his monograph *The Exodus Pattern in the Bible* offers a highly instructive treatment of the terminology used in the exodus narrative (ch. 3, pp. 22–38), the verb *yšb*, "to dwell", also has a legal meaning. The derivative noun *tšwb* is of particular interest in so far that it denotes a "resident alien" or "sojourner", and "in not a few passages throughout the Old Testament the verb definitely has the connotation 'to live as a subject'".[12] In the announcement to Abram (Gen. xv 13), DAUBE interprets the noun *gr* in a technical sense, as a "temporary, tolerated alien"[13], but he explains the permission to dwell in Goshen in Egypt (Gen. xlv 10; xlvi 34; xlvii 4, 6, 27; 1 22) as dwelling "surely as a kind of guesttribe"[14]. The favourable position of the Jacobites in Egypt is expressed in the verse "Thus Israel dwelt in the land of Egypt, in the land of Goshen; and they gained possessions in it (*wy'hzw bh*), and were fruitful and multiplied exceedingly" (Gen. xlvii 27). In Deuteronomistic style we read of their wandering Aramaean forefather who went down to Egypt and lived there until they became a great, powerful, and numerous nation (Deut. xxvi 5).

First Millennium B.C. II. The Twenty-Second Dynasty", *JAOS* 93 (1973), pp. 3–17.
[12] David DAUBE, *The Exodus Pattern in the Bible*, London, 1963, p. 24. See also his *Studies in Biblical Law*, Cambridge, 1947.
[13] *Exodus Pattern*, p. 26.
[14] *Op. cit.*, p. 24.

This is followed by the remark on their humiliation and slavery (v. 6; cf. Ps. cv 23): "Then Israel came to Egypt; Jacob sojourned in the land of Ham (*gr bʾrṣ ḥm*), and Yhwh made his people very fruitful, and made them stronger than their foes." The sequel describes the Egyptians' cruelty and is similar to Deut. xxvi 5f. This negative assessment of Egypt does not refer to the Hebrews' sojourn as refugees, but only to their growing power and their position of authority in the country where they had sought shelter.

I am inclined to explain the argument "for you were strangers (*grym*) in the land of Egypt" of the social instructions of Exod. xxii 20, xxiii 9, Lev. xix 33f., and Deut. x 19 as a positive appreciation of the hospitality met in Egypt. This hospitality is to be reciprocated: "You shall not regard an Edomite as an abomination, for he is your brother [your own kin, NEB]; nor an Egyptian, for you were a sojourner in his land; the third generation of children born to them may enter the assembly of Yhwh [may become members of the assembly of the Lord, NEB]" (Deut. xxiii 8f.). CARMICHAEL states, "Deuteronomy's willingness to have relations with the Egyptians rests on the time of sojourn, initially one of expansion and well-being. The slavery to which Israel was subjected in Egypt appears in D's unenthusiastic statement that the Egyptians are not to be abhorred, and in the admission into the assembly only after three generations."[15] VON RAD says, "It is difficult to discover the reason for the preferential treatment of the Edomites and the Egyptians. It is unlikely to be found in certain positive political connections of these nations with Israel. Here the determining factor was probably really of cultic origin which was comparatively independent of the fluctuating goodwill or ill-will in political relations."[16] One rubs on'e eyes in astonishment at hearing these words from the lips of someone who in other books, and especially in his *Theology of the Old Testament*, explains the liberation from Egypt as Israel's creed, its ancient confession of faith. Is the saying of this confession—which according to VON RAD is the very beginning of Israel's faith—supposed to have a setting in life outside the cult, or does VON RAD suggest that what he calls a creed can be combined with a favourable statement like that of Deut. xxiii 8f.? Both explanations seem rather awkward.

---

[15] Calum H. CARMICHAEL, *The Laws of Deuteronomy*, Ithaca-London, 1974, p. 176f.

[16] G. VON RAD, *Deuteronomy. A Commentary*, London, 1966, p. 146.

In *Midrash Rabbah*, the problem of the favourable attitude taken to both Edomites and Egyptians, as opposed to Moabites and Ammonites, is smoothed over by the observation that the Moabites and Ammonites advanced against the Israelites with transgressions, inviting them to idolatry, and that the Edomites and Egyptians advanced against them with the sword (Num. xxi 4). RASHI's explanation is in the same line: idolatry applies to life in this world as well as to life in the world to come, but murder only to life in this world.

The favourable attitude shown to the Egyptians is quoted in yet another midrash, on Deut. xx 10 (m. Deuteronomy v 15), the famous passage on the power of peace: "If a man injures his neighbour he never forgets it; but not so God. Israel were in Egypt and the Egyptians enslaved them with lime and bricks. After all the evil they had done unto Israel, God had pity upon them and decreed, 'Thou shalt not abhor and Egyptian, because thou wast a stranger in his land' (Deut. xxiii 8) but pursue after peace, as it is said: 'Seek peace and pursue it' (Ps. xxxiv 15)."[17] Especially an attempt like this to reconcile the differences of opinion points to the authenticity of a positive judgement on Egypt, which had provided refuge in times of despair.

As a refuge, Egypt further appears in the stories about Solomon's adversaries in 1 Kings xi. In agreement with his religious views, the pious author presents these stories under the heading "Yhwh's anger at Solomon's sins", in order to explain the disasters which befell the Israelites after Solomon's reign. One of Solomon's adversaries, Hadad, fled to Egypt, where Pharaoh gave him a house and land, and his own wife's sister in marriage. Hadad took flight after David's massacre in the country of Edom (1 Kings xi 14–22). According to 1 Kings xi 26–29, Jeroboam son of Nebat, an Ephraimite, was encouraged by the prophet Ahijah to rebel against Solomon, again with the argument that the king had forsaken the true worship of Yhwh. This is probably also an attempt to explain the miserable state of the kingdom. Jeroboam received the following divine promise: "I will take you ($w^{\supset}tk$ $^{\supset}qqh$) and I will make you king over all that your soul desires; you shall be king over Israel" (1 Kings xi 37). "Solomon sought therefore to kill Jeroboam; but Jeroboam arose, and fled to Egypt, to Shishak king of Egypt, and

---

[17] *Midrash rabbah.* Vol. 7: Deuteronomy. Translated by J. Rabinowitz, London, 1939.

was in Egypt until the death of Solomon'' (v. 40). It is not unreasonable to suppose that Jeroboam was made welcome in Egypt. It seems probable that he was treated like Hadad of Edom. After Solomon's death, the assembly of Israel sent for him (*wyšlḥw wyqrʾw lw*, 1 Kings xii 3), to negotiate with Solomon's successor Rehoboam. But the latter refused to listen to Israel, and Israel rebelled against the house of David. Once again Jeroboam's return from Egypt is recorded (1 Kings xii 20): "And when all Israel heard that Jeroboam had returned, they sent and called him (*wyšlḥw wyqrʾw ʾtw*) to the assembly and made him king over all Israel." In Jer. xxvi 20ff., we read that the prophet Uriah son of Shemaiah, from Kiriath-jearim, prophesied against the city of Jerusalem. When king Jehoiakim tried to put him to death, he fled to Egypt. He was less safe there from the agents of the king of Jerusalem than Hadad and Jeroboam had been, possibly because he was a prophet and not a prince or one of the king's rivals. In this connection, it may be advisable to pay attention to the military support Israel expected and received from Egypt. In the OT, 2 Kings xvii 4 and 2 Chron. ix 28 deal with this subject. Ezek. xvii 5 refers to Zedekiah's rebellion against Nebuchadrezzar "by sending ambassadors to Egypt, that they might give him horses and a large army ...''. Ahab of Israel received military support, which was sent by Osorkon II in 853 B.C. against the Assyrians at Qarqar. The Assyrian threat made many Israelites seek refuge in Egypt (Hos. vii 11; ix 6). Attempts to obtain military help from Egypt were also made during Hoshea's reign in Samaria, at the time of Shalmaneser's threat.[18] Indirect evidence of Egyptian support for the policy of Jerusalem's kings can be found in the harsh and critical words spoken by Isaiah and Jeremiah. In Isa. xxx 2f., we read that taking refuge in Pharaoh's protection and seeking shelter in the shadow of Egypt will result in disaster, shame, and humiliation: "For Egypt's help is worthless and empty" (v. 7a). The same negative judgement is found in the narratives about Hezekiah's attempt to escape Assyrian domination (2 Kings xviii; par. Isa. xxxvi). I quote Rabshakeh's words: "Behold, you are relying now on Egypt, that broken reed of a staff [a splintered cane, NEB], which will pierce the hand of any man who leans on it. Such is Pharaoh king of Egypt to all who rely on him" (2 Kings xviii 21; par. Isa. xxxvi 6).

---

[18] WILLIAMS, *art. cit.*, p. 233. Cf. 2 Kings xvii 4.

The events during the last years of the Judaean kingdom offer the same picture. According to Jeremiah, Pharaoh's army, coming to its aid against Nebuchadrezzar's threat, is of no value, for the Egyptians are about to return to their country (Jer. xxxvii 7). Nevertheless after Judah's downfall, a number of people afraid of the Chaldaeans went to Egypt (2 Kings xxv 26). According to the records of the Book of Jeremiah, they did so against the prophet's advice to stay in the country. Jer. xlii 13ff. offer a very vivid picture of his warnings, a picture which is reflected at the same time in the expectations of those who wished to seek refuge in Egypt: "No, we will go to Egypt, where we shall see no sign of war, never hear the sound of the trumphet, and not starve for want of bread; and there we will live" (Jer. xlii 14, NEB).[19]

I shall conclude this section about Egypt offering refuge and help with two lines taken from the Book of Ezekiel. The first is from a lament about Egypt: "You consider yourself a lion among the nations" (Ezek. xxxii 2). This illustrates the expectations of both the kings and their subjects during the period of the Hebrew kingdoms. The second is from ch. xxix, a prophecy against Pharaoh and against all Egypt—in Ezekiel's view, Egypt's future will be disastrous—: "It shall never again be the reliance (*mbṭḥ*) of the house of Israel" (v. 16). The wording of this text reflects the appreciation of Egypt felt until the very end of Judah's existence.[20]

Summing up, it can be said that:

a) Egypt is mentioned in several Old Testament texts as a rich country, of whose wealth many foreigners and foreign countries, including the Israelites, profited;

b) The Egyptians are described as servants and concubines in a number of biblibal narratives and genealogies, and one of Pharaoh's daughters even married the king of Jerusalem;

c) Egypt was a place of refuge for families and groups in times of famine and war, and for groups as well as for individuals in times of threat and disaster;

---

[19] On the lively, stirring style of the passage describing Jeremiah's share in what happened after the arrival of the Babylonians and on the rather extensive prosaic report of the occurrences in Jer. xl 7–16; xli; and xliii 5–7, see my remarks on Jer. xliii 1–7 in *Translating and Understanding the Old Testament*, Essays in Honor of H.G. May, Nashville and New York 1970, pp. 71–79.

[20] Cf. S. Morenz, "Ägypten und die Bibel", *RGG*³I, col. 117–121.

d) Egypt was trusted by both Israelite and Judaean kings, because of the military support it gave them.[21]

It is a remarkable fact that the prophecies against Egypt which reject and condemn the desire and practice of many Israelites to seek refuge in Egypt and also the requests for Egyptian support do *not* bring in the argument that Egypt is the land where the Israelites were humiliated, the land of cruelty and slavery, the house of bondage. They only warn for Egypt's inability to save: "For Egypt's help is worthless and empty" (Isa. xxx 7a).[22] The absence of a condemnation of Egypt as Israel's oppressor and exploiter in prophecies clearly directed against Egypt and against the pro-Egyptian policy of Israel's leaders is even more conspicuous when one realizes that the majority of Old Testament texts mentioning Egypt are intended to glorify Israel's god, who delivered his people from the house of bondage, from Egypt. Their main tenor is that the Egyptians dealt harshly with the Israelites, but were forced to acknowledge Yhwh's miraculous power and to let his people go. The Book of Deuteronomy is our primary source for the thought that the liberation and the exodus from Egypt lie at the root of Israel's origins and existence. "The Egyptians treated us harshly," we read in Deut. xxvi 6ff. (to quote one obvious example), "and afflicted us, and imposed upon us cruel slavery, but (. . .) Yhwh heard our voice, and saw our affliction, our toil, and our oppression, and Yhwh brought us out of Egypt, with a strong hand and an outstretched arm, with great terror, and with signs and wonders." The same argument is advanced in support of the concept of obedience to the "statutes and ordinances": " . . . then take heed lest you forget Yhwh, who brought you out of the land of Egypt (*ʾšr hwṣyʾ k mʾrṣ mṣrym*), out of the house of bondage (*mbbyt ʿbdym*) (Deut. vi 12; cf. also v 15; vi 21; xiii 6; xxix 24).

Parallel to the verb *yṣʾ*, "to go out", the verb *ʿlh* is used to denote the exodus from Egypt.[23] Sometimes the two verbs occur in the same sentence or context (e.g. Jer. xi 4; Ps. lxxxi 6, 11), but usually

---

[21] For some aspects of the influence of Egypt on Israel and Canaan (!) which are not discussed here, now see R. GIVEON, *The Impact of Egypt on Canaan: Iconographical and Related Studies*, OBO 20, Göttingen, 1978.

[22] Cf. Jer. ii 18, 36; iii 1; Ezek. xvi; xxiii.

[23] *yṣʾ* qual is used 23 times in this category of texts; in hiphʾil the verb occurs even more frequently. *ʿlh*, sometimes used in qal (Judg. xix 30; Num. xxxii 11; Hos. ii 7), is mostly used in hiphʿil.

there is reason to distinguish, with J. WIJNGAARDS, "a twofold approach to the Exodus"[24]. H. LUBSCZYK sees the $h^c lh$ texts as belonging to the prophetic tradition, and the $hwsy^{\flat}$ texts as part of the priestly tradition.[25] The terminology of the exodus narratives has been studied by several scholars. DAUBE's important contribution has already been referred to.[26] It is tempting to discuss these terminological studies at length, and to one of them, DAUBE's *Exodus Pattern*, I shall come back later. Here, however, it is sufficient to note that in spite of the large number of texts alluding to the deliverance from Egypt and despite the gradations in the expressions used, the assessment of Egypt (which is the subject of this paper) is always the same: the land of Egypt and its king are charged with cruelty, and it is Yhwh, Israel's god, who brings his people out of the "iron furnace"[27], the place of humiliation, the house of bondage. This wholly negative judgement of Egypt and the glorification of Yhwh as Israel's saviour together make up the kernel of what has been called "the fundamental creed", "das Urbekenntnis Israels"[28], according to formula of Martin NOTH, repeated in many variations by a number of scholars.

Opinion differs with regard to the origin of this exodus *credo*. Some scholars actually credit the people who escaped with its formulation,

---

[24] J. WIJNGAARDS, "$hwsy^{\flat}$ and $h^c lh$, A Twofold Approach to Exodus", *VT* 15 (1965), pp. 91–102.

[25] H. LUBSCZYK, *Der Auszug aus Ägypten. Seine theologische Bedeutung in prophetischer und priestlicher Überlieferung*, Erfurter Theologische Studien 11, Leipzig, 1963. LUBSCZYK continued his treatment of the subject in "Die Einheit der Schrift. Zur hermeneutischen Relevanz des Urbekenntnisses im Alten und Neuen Testament", in: *Sapienter Ordinare*, Festgabe E. Kleineidam, Leipzig, 1969, pp. 73–104.

[26] It did not escape DAUBE's notice that both ysb and gwr/gr occur very rarely in the narratives about the deliverance from the land of slavery. "The preponderance of $^c ebedh$ and $^c abadh$, 'slave' and 'to serve', over $yashabh$, 'to dwell', is striking," he declares on p. 25 of his *Exodus Pattern*, and with reference to gwr and gr (p. 26) he observes, "The verb is not met once in the actual epic of the exodus, nor is the noun ger, 'sojourner'." Cf. also his *Studies in Biblical Law*. Mention should be made here of P. HUMBERT, "Dieu fait sortir. Hiphil de $yaṣa$", *ThZ* 18 (1962), pp. 357–361 and of the "Note complémentaire" on pp. 433–436; of W. Richter, "Beobachtungen zur theologischen Systembildung in der alttestamentlichen Literatur an Hand des kleinen geschichtlichen Credo", in: *Wahrheit und Verkündigung, Festschrift M. Schmaus* I, München-Paderbron-Wien, 1967, pp. 175–212; and of Heribert RÜCKER, *Die Begründungen der Weisungen Jahwes im Pentateuch*, Erfurter Theologische Studien 30, Leipzig, 1973, esp. pp. 39–44.

[27] Deut. iv 20; Jer. ix 4; 1 Kings viii 51; cf. Isa. xlviii 10 "the furnace of affliction" (= the exile).

[28] M. NOTH, *Überlieferungsgeschichte des Pentateuch*, Stuttgart, 1948, pp. 50–54.

referring to Miriam's song after the narrative of the Egyptians' drowning in the Red Sea (Ex. xv 21); others believe that it stems from the so-called Yahwist, who is supposed to have composed a "history of salvation" in the tenth or ninth century B.C. Let me quote E.W. NICHOLSON's instructive monograph, which excels in careful phrasing: "So central and so ancient is the confession that Yahweh delivered Israel from Egypt, and so very much is it the *sine qua non* of Israel's faith as presented in the Old Testament, that few commentators have doubted that Yahweh belonged to the exodus tradition from the outset or that he was in fact attributed with the deliverance from bondage from the beginning."[29] Historians have not failed to draw attention to the difficult question of the identity of the Hebrews who escaped from Egypt. The total lack of sources contemporary with the period suggested by tradition explains why only assumptions can be put forward. One of these is that the ancestors of the Rahel tribe participated in the escape, and according to Rainer SCHMITT they were the first adherents of this creed.[30] After their arrival in Palestine, it was handed down to the other Israelites, and very soon the exodus tradition must have been "nationalized". The exodus creed became the *credo* of the whole of Israel. "In der Herausführung aus Ägypten hat ... Israel für alle Zukunft die Gewähr, die unverbrüchliche Bürgschaft von Jahwes Heilswillen gesehen ..."[31]

A long period of time elapsed between the supposed (but fictitious) date of the deliverance from Egypt and the Deuteronomistic paraenetic use of the exodus motif, and not everybody will agree with the assumption of the immutable character of Israel's faith. But it is a fact that in Jewish piety, in conformity with the paraenetic use of the exodus motif in the Book of Deuteronomy, the deliverance from Egypt is the nucleus of religious practice. In the *geullah* prayer of the morning and evening services, in the *qiddush* of the evening

---

[29] E.W. NICHOLSON, *Exodus and Sinai in History and Tradition*, Oxford, 1973, p. 57.

[30] Rainer SCHMITT, *Exodus and Passah*, Göttingen, 1975, p. 14.

[31] G. VON RAD, *Theologie des Alten Testaments* I, München, 1957, p. 178. It is refreshing to read Mario LIVERANI's realistic statement "Non sappiamo e non sapremo mai in qual percentuale gli abitanti della Palestina nel XIII sec. a. C. (e poi nel XII, nell' XI, e così via) ritenessero che esistesse un' etnía 'Israele', ritenessero di farne parte, ritenessero che fosse caratterizzata de certi elementi, e quali" (M. LIVERANI, "Le 'origini' d'Israele: Progetto irrealizzabile di ricerca etnogenetica", *Rivista Biblica* 28 (1980), p. 15).

of Sabbath, and in the Passover *haggadah*, the exodus from Egypt is an essential element.[32] The combination of the old religious ceremony of Passover with the exodus motif, which probably originated just before or after the fall of the kingdom of Judah, underlines the importance of the exodus motif; and the experiences of the Babylonian exile and the preaching of the so-called Second Isaiah can be seen as its main causes. It is through this religious practice that the early Christians could regard the exodus motif as a biblical promise fulfilled in Christ's act of salvation. It became the heart of their liturgy, and has always remained central in the faith of the leading denominations of the Christian Church.[33]

One is forced to doubt whether pre-exilic Israel saw the Exodus as the fundamental tenet of its faith, and it seems necessary to put a question mark at the almost generally accepted negative assessment of Egypt as central to Israel's faith from the outset. The social setting ("Sitz im Leben") of the appreciation of Egypt from David till Zedekiah as the refuge and reliance of both individual people and groups and the policy adopted by Israel's leaders are incompatible with an assumed religious practice that remembered Egypt as an enemy, viz. the people's pre-eminent enemy, to whose cruelty and power Yhwh's miraculous acts put an end. Even the prophet's warnings against Egypt do not allude to the exodus creed, but only argue that Egypt's help is worthless and empty. The words spoken by Rabshakeh have the same prophetic colour: "You are relying on a broken reed of a staff, which will pierce the hand of any man who leans on it."

DAUBE's treatment of the terminology of the exodus narratives seems to me a very valuable contribution to a new understanding of the subject under discussion. In the third chapter of his *Exodus Pattern*, he lays out the legal and social backgrounds of the terms used by the narrators of the exodus. He demonstrates that the sources represented in the Pentateuch offer illustrations "of that construction of the exodus, as the freeing of a slave in accordance with social legislation or practice"[34]. The legal pericopes which are the terminological source of the exodus narratives have been preserved in

---

[32] DAUBE, *Exodus Pattern*, p. 34, mentions "the post-Biblical technical expression *yeṣiʾath miṣrayim*, 'the exodus from Egypt'".

[33] See e.g. H. HAAG, *Vom alten zum neuen Pascha*, SBS 49, Stuttgart, 1971.

[34] *Op. cit.*, p. 14.

the so-called Book of the Covenant and in passages with a historical nucleus, notably Jer. xxxiv 8–20, about the release of slaves during the siege of Jerusalem in 588 B.C. The prophetic utterance that follows when the slave holders change their minds refers to the law about the release of slaves (Exod. xxi and Deut. xv): "a decree (*bryt*) ... when I brought your fathers out of the land of Egypt, out of the house of bondage" (Jer. xxxiv 13). It remains uncertain whether we should speak of Deuteronomistic influence or of a late enlargement of the text. The argumentation of the prophet's words is certainly not borrowed from the exodus narratives, but from the legal institutions. The exodus narratives describe Yhwh as acting in conformity with the practice of freeing slaves. In my opinion, this sheds new light on the "Werdegang" or genesis of the biblical narratives. Has there ever been an exodus narrative that did not yet presuppose the social practice or legislation known from the Palestinian period? DAUBE thinks this is a legitimate question, but states, "This is not improbable, though it would have to antedate any of the sources represented in the Pentateuch ...'' He suspects that the approach he chose to determine the background of the terminology will necessitate a radical revision of the current theories as to the setting of the exodus and the narratives referring to it.[35] "The principal reason for the fascination exercised by the exodus is that here was depicted ... the first ... deliverance, indeed the birth of the nation."[36] We should indeed not forget that stories about the birth of a nation belong to the fascinating field of mythological literature or to ideological schemata, and that they are not historical sources.[37]

In wisdom literature, the theological motif of the exodus is lacking. If we should be willing at all to reopen the discussion about the dating of the Pentateuch and prepared to recognize considerable Deuteronomistic influence in the so-called historical books (and, as it happens, the recent study by the young Finnish scholar Timo VEIJOLA entitled *Die ewige Dynastie*[38] encourages us to do both), we are left with the poetic text of Exod. xv and a few prophetic utterances in the Books of Amos, Hosea, and Micah which apparently

---

[35] *Op. cit.*, p. 15.

[36] *Op. cit.*, pp. 12f.

[37] Cf. D.W. THOMAS, "The Sixth Century B.C.: A Creative Epoch in the History of Israel", *JSS* 6 (1961), pp. 33–46.

[38] Timo VEIJOLA, *Die ewige Dynastie: David und die Entstehung seiner Dynastie nach der deuteronomistischen Darstellung*, Helsinki, 1975.

allude to Israel's slavery in Egypt and its deliverance by Yhwh. I shall conclude my paper with some remarks on these texts, which are usually thought to be as old as the eighth century B.C.

The main body of the song, said to be sung by Moses (one line is sung by Miriam), does not seem to have anything to do with Egypt. It is apparently Palestinian and possibly Phoenician, reflecting a divine battle against Yam, the Sea. The horse and its rider thrown into the sea do not correspond with the narrative of Exod. xiv, which uses different terms. "The enemy said, 'I will pursue, I will overtake; I will divide the spoil, I will glut my appetite upon them; I will draw my sword, I will rid myself of them'" (Exod. xv 9, NEB). Evidently these lines are not spoken by Pharaoh pursuing slaves in flight in order to subdue them; they are the words of a boasting king-warrior in pursuit of his enemy. The song may have been related to the narrative by the addition of the lines about Pharaoh and the flower of his officers (vv. 4f.). In this context, I shall confine myself to these remarks.

I shall pass over the texts of Amos (ii 10; iii 1; ix 7), of Micah (vi 4), and of Hosea (xii 14): all of them may well be of Deuteronomistic origin. I have not as yet gained a clear insight into the difficult text of Hos. ii 16f. (14f.). But I think I have some arguments for a new understanding of Hosea xi 1, which in the current translations runs as follows:

> When Israel was a child, I loved him,
> and out of Egypt I called my son. (RSV)

This is the beginning of a poem on Ephraim, the beloved people now fallen prey to sin. The king of Israel will be swept away. The people will return to Egypt, and Assyria will be their king (v. 5). I assume that the return to Egypt is really a flight, an escape to the traditional place of refuge, at the time when Ephraim's king is swept away and Assyria dominates the country, "is its king" (ʾ*ššwr hw*ʾ *mlkw*). The frequently quoted first line of the poem describes Ephraim's (Israel's) birth as a kingdom in loving terms. It was Yhwh himself who called his son out of Egypt. The term used here is *qr*ʾ *l*, which means "to summon", "to call". It does not have a legal meaning, or at any rate does not belong to the terms used for the release of slaves.

It is usual to explain "my son" as referring to the people as the "son of god", Cf. the Targum reading *qr*ʾ*ty lhwn bnyn*: "I called them sons''. Support for this explanation can be found in later texts, such as Exod. iv 22f., ''. . . Israel is my firstborn son, and I say to you [Pharaoh], 'Let my son go that he may serve me' '', where the legal terms for the release of slaves are used. In Jer. xxxi 9 and 20, Ephraim is Yhwh's beloved child, for whom he feels compassion. In my paper "The Son of God in the Old Testament"[39], I counted Hos. xi 1 as one of the texts in which Egypt is associated with slavery, but fresh consideration of the passage in the context of this paper has led me to suggest that this text should be moved from the large category of texts in which Egypt is the house of bondage to that in which Egypt is a more or less sympathetic country, prepared to receive refugees. My arguments are:

a) qr° l, "to summon" or "to call", is never used to denote a deliverance from slavery (cf. Gen. xii 18; xxxi 4; and many other texts);

b) In the Book of Hosea, Egypt is never the country where the Israelites were kept in bondage, but several times it occurs parallel to Assyria to express Israel's dependence: Egypt seems to be one of the foreign countries in which one is forced to stay because of the deplorable situation in one's own country;

c) The first king, the Ephraimite Jeroboam, who is called by a prophet to rebel against Solomon and is given the promise that he will be king over Israel (1 Kings xi 36 – 39), fled to Egypt and was called back from it by the assembly of Israel ($wyqr^{\circ}w$ lw) to be made king over Ephraim (1 Kings xii 3 and 20). Hosea xi 1, the beginning of the poem, describes the fulfilment of Ahijah's prophecy. In Hosea's time the destruction of the kingdom is a real threat: Assur will be its king. The messianic interpretation of Hos. xi 1 which led to the miraculous story of Joseph and Mary's flight to Egypt with their child as recorded in the Gospel of St. Matthew (ii 13 – 15) is presumably right in explaining "my son" as referring to a king, even if the actual application cannot be accepted as a valid exegesis.

From the foregoing it seems evident that there is a twofold and ambivalent assessment of Egypt in the Old Testament, which reflects some obvious aspects of the genesis of the biblical records. The positive assessment of Egypt should be dated before the stereo-

---

[39] P.A.H. DE BOER, "The Son of God in the Old Testament", in: *OTS* 18 (1973), p. 198.

typed, negative view which was to dominate both Judaism and Christianity. I should like to conclude this paper by quoting Isa. xix 24, in which the contradiction between the two opposing views is solved by Yhwh, who blesses three nations without any form of discrimination:

Blessed be Egypt my people,
and Assyria the work of my hands,
and Israel my heritage.

18

A NOTE ON ECCLESIASTES 12:12a

Jerome's translation of the Hebrew text הַזָּהֵר עֲשׂוֹת סְפָרִים הַרְבֵּה אֵין קֵץ
... *ne requiras faciendi plures libros nullus est finis* made Hugo Grotius
observe: Si hoc eâ aetate dixit, quid nunc diceret, si nostras biblio-
thecas inspiceret[1]? Now that in our age libraries have resorted to
microfilms and microcards as substitutions for books, the truth of
Eccles. 12:12a seems unshakable. But is it indeed true that the text
refers to the writing of many books? I think there is reason to doubt
this.

Jerome's rendering of the Hebrew text is substantially the same as
that of the Septuagint: ... φυλάξαι τοῦ ποιῆσαι βιβλία πολλά· οὐκ
ἔστιν περασμός, the only difference being that the Latin version has
the pausa at the same spot as the Masoretic text. Both versions render
הרבה, an adverb frequently used in Ecclesiastes, by an adjective, *many*
(books); both also understand the phrase עֲשׂוֹת סְפָרִים as *to make
books*. Now ποιεῖν is the verb used for the writing of poetry while
that for the writing of prose is generally (συγ)γράφειν. So there is
reason to wonder what was the intention of the literal translation of
עשׂה by ποιεῖν. The pupil—called the son in the terminology of the
teaching of worldly wisdom—is warned, *clare et distincte,* הזהר ,
against 'the making of many books because such is without end',
runs the usual paraphrase of the text. The Syriac version had already understood עֲשׂוֹת סְפָרִים as the writing of books : ܠܡܥܒܕ ܣܦܪ̈ܐ
ܣܓܝ̈ܐܐ

The Western translations show hardly any variation: 'faire beaucoup
de livres', or, 'faire des livres en grand nombre'; 'making of many
books'; 'das viele Büchermachen'. Some German and Dutch translators prefer 'schreiben', 'schrijven' (to write), to 'machen', 'maken'[2].

---

[1] *Annotata ad Vetus Testamentum* (Paris 1644), I, p. 540.
[2] K. BUDDE in *Die Heilige Schrift des Alten Testaments* II, ed. E. KAUTZSCH und
A. BERTHOLET (Tübingen 1923); K. GALLING in *Handbuch zum Alten Testament* XVIII
(Tübingen 1940); H. W. HERTZBERG in *Kommentar zum Alten Testament* XVII, 4

Gordis explains his translation with 'the composing of many books'[3] but this does not differ from the usual rendering.

In Midrash Rabba, Eccles. 12, 12, 1 the question which books could have been meant in the phrase עשׂות ספרים is answered as follows: they are the books excluded from the rabbinic canon, such as the Book of Ben Sira and the Book of Ben Tagla. If one sticks to the meaning 'to write', influenced by the term 'books' and the Greek 'poetry writing', the phrase עשׂות ספרים does not mean according to the midrash 'to write, compose books' but to copy or transcribe books. A similar remark can be made on Barton's suggestion that 'heathen libraries' should be considered[4]. If this is what the 'writings' refer to, then the text does not deal with the writing, composing of these books. Drusius must have felt the same hesitation, explaining *faciendi libros* with *comparandi, emendi*[5].

In his well-known book, *The Legacy of Canaan*[6], John Gray has produced arguments for an entirely new translation. His translation is inspired by an article by M.J. Dahood, who presumes Canaanite-Phoenician influence also in Ecclesiastes[7]. Dahood refers to a Ugaritic text wherein the terms *spr* and *hg* occur both with the meaning 'number, reckoning'. Gray thinks that in Eccles. 12:12 there is no reference to 'the making of books ... and much study' and suggests the translation,

> In much casting of accounts there is no end,
> And much reckoning is a weariness of the flesh.

Although the Ugaritic text with *spr* and *hg*, qua time and place, is very far away from Ecclesiastes, this translation has a clear meaning and maintains the connection between verse 12a and 12b. The warning against too much attention to financial activities, however, does not fit into the passage. The saying would be an independent maxim in this context, and moreover, I do not know a suitable place for it in Ecclesiastes' book.

(Gütersloh 1963); B. ALFRINK (Nijmegen 1939); J. VAN DER PLOEG, *Der Prediger* (Roermond 1953); New translation, Kath. Bijbel Stichting (Boxtel 1975).

[3] R. GORDIS, *Koheleth—the Man and His World* (New York 1950), p. 344.

[4] G.A. BARTON, *A Critical and Exegetical Commentary on ... Ecclesiastes, International Critical Commentary* 18 (New York 1908).

[5] J. DRUSIUS, *Annotationes in Coheleth. Opus Posthumum* (Amstelrodami 1635). He continues, however, *aut componendi, conscribendi*.

[6] *Vetus Testamentum* [Supplements v. 5] (Leiden 1957), p. 201 (2nd ed. 1965, p. 275).

[7] *Biblica* 33 (1952), pp. 30-52 and 191-221.

The Aramaic version offers some interesting traits. The rendering is paraphrastic and serves a didactic purpose. The text is as follows

איזדהר למעבד ספרי חוכמתא סגי עד לית סוף ולמעסק בפתגמי אוריתא

The term ספרים is explained as 'books of wisdom'. The phrase עשׂות ספרים is repeated in different words to exclude any misunderstanding, 'namely being industriously engaged in lessons'. The verb עשׂה is literally rendered by עבד , to do, make. There are not sufficient grounds, in my opinion, to suppose that the Aramaic עבד also possesses the meaning 'to write' as suggested by Ginsberg[8]. He refers to line 22 of Papyrus 9 of the Brooklyn Museum Aramaic Papyri, edited by Kraeling[9]. In Hoftijzer's *Dictionnaire*[10] the same suggestion has been made, translating the line : 'ce document, que j'ai fait (i.e. écrit) pour toi'. Kraeling himself is more reluctant. He translates the line of the document in which the owner of a house is disposing of a part of it by will to his daughter by '... this document which I made out to thee'. In a note he suggests a Paᶜel meaning, 'prepared?'[11]

The writing of documents, however, is always expressed by the verb כתב , also in this papyrus. As far as I know עבד never possesses the meaning 'to write'. In the passage quoted, the owner of the house is not, I think, attending to the writing of the document, but to the legality, the validity of the disposition written down in it. In my opinion the correct paraphrasing of the text is that no other document than the one with which he is engaged in pinning down his daughter's rights can be brought out against her[12].

The Hebrew verb עשׂה with ספרים as the object does not have the meaning 'to write, make, compose books'. Phrases like עשׂה שפטים 'to do acts of judgment, act judicially' (Exod. 12:12, Num. 33:4, Ezek. 5:10, 15, 11:9, 16:41, etc.); עשׂה חיל , 'to act mightily' (I Sam. 14:48, etc.), 'to do efficiently' (Prov. 31:29); עשׂה אבל 'to mourn' (Ezek. 24:17) point to the possibility of rendering עשׂה ספרים with 'to read' or, 'to study books', 'be at work on books', 'work at books'. The midrash and the Aramaic paraphrase indicate the right meaning of the phrase, I think. It seems to me possible that the Septuagint

---

[8] H.L. GINSBERG, *Koheleth* (in Hebrew) (Tel Aviv-Jerusalem 1961), p. 135.

[9] E.G. KRAELING, *The Brooklyn Museum Aramaic Papyri* (New Haven 1953), p. 238.

[10] C.F. JEAN et J. HOFTIJZER, *Dictionnaire des inscriptions sémitiques de l'ouest* (Leiden 1965), p. 200.

[11] Op. cit., p. 243.

[12] On עבד see also R.A. BOWMAN, *Aramaic Ritual Texts from Persepolis* (Chicago 1970), p. 65 : 'bdw... 'he worked' or 'he used' the object. See also ibid., pp. 39f.

version shows a Hebraism. Or did the translator have a different Hebrew text, compare the Peshiṭta version? The plain reading of the Syrian version, however, more probably is an elucidation of the obscure Greek.

If one rejects John Gray's ingenious rendering and chooses the meaning 'writings', 'books' for ספרים in this text—books of wisdom according to the Targumic explanation—then the following translation may be worth consideration :

(Furthermore, my son,) be warned : much working at books is without end,
(and much reading aloud is weariness of the flesh).

This rendering is very close to R.B.Y. Scott's translation in his commentary : 'Beyond this, my son, be warned; book learning is an endless occupation (and much study is exhausting)'[13]. It is regrettable that the Notes added to the translation of the Anchor Bible Series are very short. They often do not contain the arguments for the proposed translation. In our case we read only : 'Literally "much use of books is endless"'. The New English Bible considers the first adverbial הרבה to be superfluous but except for this omission explains the verse similarly. Its rendering is : 'One further warning, my son; the use of books is endless (and much study is wearisome)[14].

Professor Vööbus has flung Ecclesiastes' warning to the winds. His work on documents, manuscripts often discovered by himself in far away regions, is indefatigable and we, his fellow students, are grateful for his contributions.

---

[13] R.B.Y. SCOTT, Proverbs and Ecclesiastes, Anchor Bible 18 (New York 1965), p. 256.

[14] The late Professor THEOPHILE J. MEEK observed in an article, 'Translating the Hebrew Bible', Journal of Biblical Literature 79 (1960), p. 335, that the correct translation of עשׂה ספרים is 'to make use of books'. His translation of the whole sentence, however, is different : 'Be well instructed from them, my son, to make much use of books without end and to study diligently until the body is weary'. O. LORETZ follows MEEK's rendering of verse 12a in Gotteswort und menschliche Erfahrung, eine Auslegung der Bücher Jona, Rut, Hoheslied und Qohelet (Freiburg im Breisgau 1963), p. 185.

19

Einige Bemerkungen und Gedanken zum Lied in 1. Samuel 2, 1-10

Wie jede Übersetzung zugleich auch Auslegung ist, so will auch die folgende Wiedergabe vom Liede der Hanna ein Versuch sein, das Gedicht zu verstehen. Der eigentlichen Wiedergabe füge ich ein paar Bemerkungen zu, die meine Übersetzung erläutern. Für einen ausführlichen Kommentar, in dem die Auslegungsgeschichte und die eigene Auffassung des Kommentators sorgfältig erörtert werden, verweise ich auf das neue Buch von Hans Joachim Stoebe, Das erste Buch Samuelis (Gütersloh 1973) 100—107.

I.

(1) Ich empfinde Triumph durch Jhwh, fühle mich riesenstark durch Jhwh.
Ich verhöhne meine Feinde
— denn ich bin durch deine Rettung voll Lebensfreude —.
(2) So strahlend wie Jhwh tritt niemand auf
— denn es tritt kein Gott auf außer dir —
und solch einen Schutz, wie unseren Gott, gibt es nicht.
(3) Sie sollen nicht immer wieder hochmütig reden und dünkelhaft prahlen
— denn Jhwh nimmt es sich sehr zu Herzen,
und die bösen Taten haben keinen Bestand —.

(4) Der Bogen der Krieger ist zerbrochen,
aber Strauchelnde laufen voll Kraft.
(5) Die satt waren, gehen zur Arbeit um Nahrung,
aber die Hunger hatten, hören auf mit Sklavenfron.
Eine Unfruchtbare gebärt sieben Söhne,
aber die viel Söhne hatte, wird eine verwelkte Frau.

(6) Jhwh ist es, der tötet und lebendig macht,
der niederfahren läßt in das Totenreich und daraus emporsteigen läßt.
(7) Jhwh ist es, der arm macht, aber (auch) reich,
der erniedrigt, aber auch erhöht,

(8) der den Schwachen aus dem Staub erhebt,
    den Armen aus der Aschengrube emporholt,
    (ihnen) einen Platz gibt unter den Honoratioren,
    ja ihnen einen erblichen Ehrenplatz gibt.
    — Denn die Fundamente (?) der Erde gehören Jhwh,
    er hat die Welt auf ihnen errichtet —.

(9) Den Lebenslauf dessen, der ihm ergeben ist, macht er sicher,
    aber Übeltäter erstarren in der Finsternis
    — denn nicht durch Kraft ist ein Mensch mächtig . . . —.

(10) Was Jhwh betrifft:
    sie erlahmen vor Schreck, (jeder) der mit ihm rechtet,
    über solchen läßt er seinen Donner in der Luft widerhallen.
    Was Jhwh betrifft:
    er richtet weit und breit, und er gibt Kraft seinem König,
    ja er macht seinen Gesalbten riesenstark.

II.

ad Vers 1. *lēb* bezeichnet nicht das im Innern Verborgene, sondern den Stolz, der sich nach außen kundtut. ‚Das Horn erhöhen‘ bedeutet stark machen. Das Gegenteil heißt ‚das Horn abhauen‘, vgl. Jer 48,25: ‚das abgehauene Horn‘ und ‚der gebrochene Arm‘ sind Bilder für die gebrochene Kraft. Die Wiedergabe von *'lṣ* mit ‚stark sein‘ in den alten Übersetzungen kann man als zutreffende Erklärung ansehen. ‚Den Mund öffnen gegen‘ kann mit ‚schelten‘ übersetzt werden, aber der Zusatz über die erneute Lebenskraft läßt mich ‚verhöhnen‘ vorziehen.

ad Vers 2. Jhwh hat sich als mächtig zugunsten des Dichters erwiesen: *qādōš*, glanzvoll, strahlend und unantastbar. Dieser Qualifikation der Gottheit entspricht die Parallele *ṣūr*. Der Fels ist der Ort, an dem man sicher ist. Als Epitheton oder Metapher für Gott meint *ṣūr* Sicherung, Schutz, vgl. Jes 44,8.

ad Vers 3. ‚Immer wieder‘ versucht die Wiederholung von *gᵉbō-hā* wiederzugeben. Als Grundbedeutung von *jādaʿ* nehme ich an ‚sich kümmern um‘, ‚eingehen auf‘, ‚sich zu Herzen nehmen‘. Die Mehrzahl *dēʿōt* wird durch ‚sehr‘ wiedergegeben, Intensität ausdrückend. Der Ersatz von *wᵉlō'* durch *wᵉlō* scheint mir keineswegs „eine einleuchtende Verbesserung". Wenn man mit den alten Übersetzungen *ʿᵃlīlōt* zu Jhwhs Taten macht, kann man die Lesart *wᵉᵉl* annehmen und übersetzen: ‚ein Gott, dessen Taten überlegt sind‘.

ad Vers 4. Wenn seine Waffe zerbrochen ist, ist der Krieger besiegt. Im Gegensatz dazu werden strauchelnde Männer zum Laufen befähigt, mit Kraft umgürtet.

ad Vers 5. ‚Sklavenfron'. Diese Übersetzung beruht auf der Konjektur *ᶜᵃbōd* von Reifmann.

ad Vers 8. Für die Zufügung ‚ihnen' (seinen Platz geben) vgl. Targum und das Suffix des Verbs *nḥl*. ‚Einen erblichen Ehrenplatz' bedeutet eine bleibende Befähigung zur Machtausübung.

ad Vers 9. ‚Lebenslauf' als Übersetzung von *raglájim* versteht das Wort als Metapher der dadurch bezeichneten Aktionsart ‚Schreiten', ‚Gangart'.

ad Vers 10. Was die weitläufige Erörterung der griechischen und altlateinischen Versionen betrifft, darf ich auf meine Artikel verweisen: *Confirmatum est cor meum*, Oudtestamentische Studiën 13 (1963) 178, 182 f., und 14 (1965) 207 f. und: Een verdwenen bijbeltekst, Theologie en Praktijk 23, 2 (1963) 45—57. Der Exkurs hat den Text aus Jer 9,22 f. nicht unverändert gelassen.

‚Weit und breit', wörtlich: ‚die Enden der Erde', bis dahin, wo das Land endet und das Meer beginnt, ebenso wie *qᵉṣōt hā'āræṣ* und *'ijjīm*, ‚Küstenländer', Jes 40,28; 41,1 Bezeichnung der ganzen bewohnten Welt.

III.

Das Lied setzt wie ein Gelegenheitsgedicht ein, das die Erfahrungen eines Individuums zum Gegenstand hat. Es beschäftigt sich von Anfang bis Ende mit Jhwh und seinen mächtigen Taten. Jedoch ist das Lied keine Einheit, sondern aus verschiedenen Teilen zusammengesetzt. Die Unterschiede treten sowohl in der Form als im Inhalt zutage.

Die Verse 1—3 haben sichtlich persönlichen Charakter. Der Dichter, obwohl von Feinden umringt, fühlt sich stark, weil er Jhwhs Stärke empfangen hat. Deshalb wagt er es, seinen Feinden höhnisch zu raten, den Mund nicht so weit aufzureißen. Man erhält nicht den Eindruck, daß es sich um ausländische Feinde handelt.

Dieser Teil wird dreimal durch Sätze erweitert, die durch die Konjunktion *kī* eingeleitet sind. Die beiden ersten Kausalsätze weichen von dem Gedicht, das über Jhwh in der dritten Person spricht, dadurch ab, daß sie ihn in der zweiten Person anreden, der dritte fügt der persönlichen Erfahrung des Dichters eine allgemeiner gehaltene Äußerung über das Tun Jhwhs hinzu.

Die Verse 4—8 enthalten eine Reihe von Aussagen, die in Form

und Inhalt einheitlich sind. Jede besteht in einer Antithese. Innerhalb der Reihe ist außerdem ein Unterschied festzustellen: im Gegensatz zu den ersten Antithesen, v. 4—5, wird in v. 6—8 die Par-
tizipialkonstruktion benutzt und Jhwh als Verursacher der durch
die Antithesen ausgedrückten Zustände ausdrücklich genannt.
Trotzdem tragen alle Antithesen denselben Charakter und drük-
ken eine allgemeine Feststellung aus. Alle sind von der Stellung
des Schwachen, Benachteiligten aus formuliert, der mit einer radi-
kalen Wendung seines Schicksals rechnet, und bilden für den, dem
es gut geht, eine Warnung. In Vers 8, wo ausführlicher über die
erwartete günstige Wendung gesprochen wird und die damit ver-
bundene Erhöhung als ‚Platz unter den Honoratioren‘ und weiter
als ‚erblicher Ehrenplatz‘ beschrieben wird, fällt auf, daß auf jene
nicht eingegangen wird, die von der Ungunst der Wendung betrof-
fen werden. Offenbar sind sie innerhalb der Reihe nicht die Feinde aus dem ersten Teil.

Auch v. 4—8 sind in Vers 8 Ende durch einen mit *kī* beginnen-
den Satz erweitert: es handelt sich um eine Zeile aus einem
Schöpfungshymnus, die Jhwhs Macht hervorhebt, aber mit dem
Vorhergehenden nicht in innerem Zusammenhang steht. Solche
Sätze findet man öfter in den poetischen und prophetischen Teilen
des Alten Testaments. Sie können mit einem späteren Gebrauch der
Texte in der Liturgie zusammenhängen.

Die Gotteserfahrung des ersten Teiles ist stark persönlich ge-
färbt, während man in der Reihe von Antithesen eher an die Gottesvorstellung der Weisheitsbücher, vor allem an das Buch Qohelet, erinnert wird.

In Vers 9 wird die Lehre des Deuteronomisten ‚böser Tat folgt
böser Lohn‘ ausgesprochen. Wenn wir dem Konsonantentext von
Vers 3 folgen, dann haben wir sie auch schon dort in der kausalen
Zufügung angetroffen. Der Satz schließt sich an die ziemlich lan-
ge Reihe der Antithesen an. Dadurch erweckt er den Eindruck
eines Versuches, die unberechenbare Macht zu rechtfertigen, die in
den Schicksalswendungen zum Vorschein kommt; er sieht somit
nicht wie ein Ergebnis der im ersten Teil ausgedrückten Glaubens-
erfahrung aus, das dessen Fortsetzung bilden könnte.

Der Kausalsatz in diesem Vers stammt, wie die Erweiterung in
den griechischen und altlateinischen Versionen bestätigt, aus anderer Quelle. Auch dieser Satz weist eher auf einen weisheitlichen
Aspekt als auf die Gotteserfahrung der Anfangsverse.

Vers 10 besteht aus zwei Teilen. Der erste Teil schließt sich weder an v. 1—3 noch an v. 4—8 an, auch nicht an Vers 9. Viel-
leicht sind die benutzten Ausdrücke eine Erinnerung an das Buch

Hiob. Der zweite Teil erinnert jedoch an Vers 1 mit dem Gebrauch der Redewendung ‚das Horn erhöhen‘, die ich mit ‚sich riesenstark fühlen‘ wiedergegeben habe. Möglicherweise hat der Bearbeiter, der diese Zeile angefügt hat, das Gedicht bereits in seiner erweiterten Form mit den Antithesen vor sich gehabt, und wollte seiner Hoffnung auf das Wiedererstehen des Volkes zu einer selbständigen Existenz im eigenen Land nach dem Exil Ausdruck geben. Sollte diese Annahme richtig sein, dann haben wir hier ein Echo der Erwartung Deuterojesajas: Jhwh wird den Verachtetsten zum Allerhöchsten machen, Jes 52,13.

Wenn in v. 1—3 der älteste Teil des Textes erhalten ist — ein auf den Einzelnen bezogener Hymnus auf die von Jhwh empfangene Lebenssicherheit in einer dem Dichter feindlichen Umgebung —, dann bildet die Aussage über die nationale Selbständigkeit, die dadurch zustande kommt, daß Jhwh dem gesalbten König große Kraft gibt, nicht „den entscheidenden Abschluß des Gedichtes", wie Stoebe, aaO 102, will. Stoebe bestreitet, meiner Meinung nach mit starken Argumenten, die Erklärung des Versteiles als Bezugnahme auf den „messianischen König der Endzeit"; seine Annahme, daß mit dem gesalbten König ein Fürst gemeint ist, der als Nachkomme Davids angesehen wird, hat sicherlich ihr Recht. Daß jedoch David selbst gemeint sein könnte — aaO 105 —, ist ausgeschlossen, wenn man den kompilierten Charakter des Textes und die Verschiedenheit der Gottesvorstellung in den einzelnen Teilen wahrgenommen hat.

IV.

Auch der älteste Teil des Textes gibt uns keinen Hinweis auf die Entstehungszeit. Dies hat das Lied mit den meisten Psalmen gemein. Seine Einfügung in die Geburtsgeschichte Samuels ist ebensowenig eine Hilfe für die Datierung. Diese Geschichte selbst ist ja kein vertrauenswürdiger Maßstab für einen frühen Ansatz des Gedichts. Außerdem ist das Lied sichtlich sekundär gegenüber der Erzählung, wenn es auch an sich ganz oder teilweise älter als dieser Kontext sein kann. In Hinsicht auf die Zufügungen besteht Anlaß, an andere Bibelteile zu denken. Ausdrücke wie ‚denn es tritt kein Gott auf außer dir‘, Vers 2, ‚die Enden der Erde‘, Vers 10, und der Zusatz in Vers 10b weisen mit Wahrscheinlichkeit auf Einfluß von Text und Gedankenwelt von Deuterojesaja hin, Vers 9 auf die deuteronomistische Rezension großer Teile des erzählenden Stoffes des Alten Testamentes. Bei den Redewendungen mit weisheitlichem Charakter ist die nachexilische Datierung weniger sicher, wenn auch nicht unmöglich. Vgl. Ps 33,16 ff.; 147,10; und Lk 1,51—53. Ich bringe in diesem Zusammenhang Antoine Causses Arbeit: Les „pauvres" d'Israël (1922) in Erinnerung.

Die Nachwirkung des Liedes zeigt sich bis hin zum Lobgesang der Maria in Lk 1,46 ff. Hat das Lied oder Teile von ihm aber auch Bedeutung für die Ausdrucksformen unseres eigenen Glaubens? Für den Schreiber dieser Zeilen beruht diese Bedeutung allerdings nicht darauf, daß das Lied ein biblischer Text ist, wohl aber darauf, daß die Aussage, wie ich sie verstehen zu müssen glaube, in positivem und negativem Sinn weiter reicht als seine Entstehungszeit.

a) Im ältesten Teil des Liedes erkenne ich den Ausdruck eines Gefühls, das von Gottes Kraft erfüllt ist, einer Teilnahme an mehr als eigener Macht. Diese Verbindung mit Gott ist kein Hochmut, denn der Mensch bleibt darin von Gott abhängig. Ob das zur Verhöhnung meiner Feinde führen darf, ist mir zweifelhaft, aber es kann mir dadurch zur Pflicht werden, der Anmaßung anderer entgegenzutreten.

b) In den weisheitlichen Partien des Liedes erkenne ich die unberechenbare Launenhaftigkeit des Schicksals. Dies führt mich nicht zum deuteronomistischen Versuch, diese Seite der Gotteserfahrung sittlich zu rechtfertigen, wie das in Vers 9 geschieht, sondern zur Bejahung des Wortes von Allard Pierson „Gott ist groß und wir begreifen ihn nicht", Hiob 36, 2b.

c) Das antike Königtum ist in der Verbindung mit dem eigenen Gott, dem Volksgott oder dem Reichsgott, die Verkörperung nationaler Selbständigkeit. Auch nach den schrecklichen Erfahrungen mit Faschismus und Nationalsozialismus bleibt der Nationalismus eine der Geißeln unseres Jahrhunderts. Der Verbindung, erst recht der Identifizierung eines Volkes oder Staates, jedes Volkes oder Staates, auch jeder gesellschaftlichen Ordnung mit Gott, mit dem göttlichen Recht, muß man Widerstand leisten.

„Die wissenschaftliche Arbeit am Alten Testament und die Auslegung für die Gemeinde sind zuzeiten auf weit voneinander getrennten Wegen gegangen. Diese Trennung ist nicht vom Guten", hat Walther Zimmerli im Vorwort zur ersten Auflage seiner Auslegung von Genesis 1—11 geschrieben. Dieses Wort aus seinen Zürcher Jahren ist für sein Leben bezeichnend. Seine Annahme des Rufes nach Göttingen führte zu einem bedeutenden Beitrag zur Wiederherstellung der alttestamentlichen Forschung im Nachkriegsdeutschland, aber auch zu einer Herausstellung des ‚Alten

Testaments als Anrede'. Daß ich es gewagt habe, diesem kurzen exegetischen Beitrag zu seiner Festschrift einen Abschnitt über die Gegenwartsbedeutung der behandelten Perikope zuzufügen, möge ihm zeigen, daß sein Anliegen auch außerhalb der Grenzen seiner Kirche als berechtigt empfunden wird.

20

DOES JOB RETRACT?
(Job xlii 6)*

I

The story of Job is one of the most famous parts of the Bible. Our language has borrowed expressions from it (a Job's comforter, the patience of Job) and it has been used in novels, short stories, poems and plays. Hedwig, the main character of Frederik van EEDEN's novel *Van de koele meren des doods* (''The Cool Lakes of Death''), reprinted many times since its publication in 1900 and now put on as a play by the theatre group *Centrum*, is given ''counsel in her distress'' by a Job-like figure called Joob who is incurably ill. He rebukes Hedwig for not daring to be and not daring to say what she feels she is. Let me quote the passage in which he says to Hedwig: ''Job's pals had no guts—for sheer fear of being punished people dare not be what they really are—, and they did not want to offend Yaweh and said, 'You must have done something wrong, Job, you must. Did you mean to say that the Lord punishes innocent people?' But Job said, 'God damn it, no! I haven't done anything wrong, and the Lord just punishes anyone he pleases'. Mind you, Job had courage and was honest, he was not afraid to say what he thought. And in the end the Lord said, 'Well said, Job! You're nothing but a perfect ass, but at least you're sincere.' And his respectable, pious pals got a real rap on the knuckles and were sent home like naughty children.''[1] Some beautiful drama has been written by the American poet Archibald Macleish: *J.B.* (Boston, 1958). The Dutch poet

---

* This is the text of a lecture for Leiden University foundation day delivered to the alumni of this university on the 5th of February 1977. (Some remarks in the notes were added later (*editor's note*).)
[1] Dutch text of this fragment: ''Hiob's vrinde waren zulke lammelingen—uit lammenadige bangigheid voor straf durven de mensen niet te zijn zooals ze zijn— die wouën Jaweh niet beledigen en zeien: 'Je hebt stellig kwaad gedaan, Job, dat mot wel. Wou je zeggen, dat de Heer onschuldigen straft?' maar Job zei: 'Nee, godverdomme! Ik heb geen kwaad gedaan en de Heer straft net wie hij wil.' Zie je, Job durfde en was eerlijk, en vreesde niet te zeggen wat ie dacht. En toen 't uit was zei de Heer: 'Jij hebt goed gepraat, Job! Je bent een nieteling en een ezelsveulen, maar je bent oprecht.' En de brave, godvruchtige vrindjes werden als stoute kinderen met een uitbrander naar huis gestuurd.'' (*Translator's note.*)

H. de Bruin[2] concludes his epic about Job with a poem called *De Nakomeling*. Two stanzas of this poem are reproduced here:

Men roept mij op, men tempert het gefluister
dat overal nog rondwaart, men verwacht
van mij te horen, uit de beste bron,
hoe Job na al dat lijden werd getroost
met nieuw bezit en even talrijk kroost—
Is er een wisseling van leed en luister
gelijk van licht en donker, dag en nacht?;
doch keert wel iemand ooit waar hij begon?

Zie niet op mij, mijn hoorders: *onvermogen*,
dat werd een diep besef in mijn geslacht
zodra het om de vraag ging naar Gods raad,
met name om het antwoord van hun kant
omtrent de Macht, de Weldaad van Zijn hand.—
Jobs kinderen zijn beschroomde theologen
en weten niet zoveel als men verwacht,
ondanks de trek van Jobs beproefd gelaat.

(I am called for, they soften the whispers
which still are all around, they expect
to hear from me, the most reliable source,
how Job found comfort after all these sufferings
in new property and equally numerous offspring—
Do sorrow and splendour take turns,
just as do light and darkness, day and night?;
but does anyone ever return whence he came?

Do not look to me, O my hearers: *impotence*
is what struck my generation's mind
as soon as people raised the question of God's counsel,
and asked us to provide an answer
concerning the Power, the Blessing of His hand.—
Job's children are bashful theologians,
and do not know as much as one expects,
despite the lines in Job's afflicted face.)

And of course one thinks of Abel Herzberg's recent novel *Drie rode rozen*. Painting and sculpture have also been inspired by the story of

---

[2] H. DE BRUIN, *Job*, Baarn, 1943.

Job. Out of the wealth of examples only a few may be mentioned here: the 4th century murals in the catacomb of Domitilla in Rome; a sculpture by Donatello in Florence, 14th century; a carved chair by Jörg Syrlin the Elder, from Ulm on the Danube, 15th century; engravings by Fischer from the southern Netherlands, 16th century; a drawing by Rembrandt, etc., up to our own age.

II

At the meeting of God's court, Job is God's pride: no one is as sincere or as religious as he is. One of God's courtiers, who is called the Adversary, satan, dares to voice his doubts about this. It is true that Job is god-fearing, but this is not "for nothing": it serves his own interests. "Do you, God, not give him all sorts of things? Take away his riches and then see if he will still be religious!"

You are all familiar with the story and with the succession of disasters by which Job is struck. He passes the test. "Naked I came from my mother's womb, and naked shall I return [into the bowels of the earth]; the Lord gave, and the Lord has taken away; blessed be the name of the Lord."

Once again the Adversary succeeds in getting permission to test Job's loyalty, this time by ruining his health. Job is afflicted with sores. Probably because of the danger of infection, he stays out of doors, scratching himself with a shard and sitting among the ashes. Job's wife advises him to curse God this time and then die. Job, however, thinks her advice is foolish. "If we accept good from God, shall we not accept evil?" Job stands this test, too. His illness has affected him so badly that his three friends, coming to condole with him, but also to comfort him—that is, to help him see matters in perspective—, do not recognize him. They sprinkle dust on their heads and silently mourn with him for seven days and seven nights, having seen "that his suffering was very great".

The Adversary is not able to substantiate his doubts about the sincerity of Job's piety: he loses, God wins. Now one expects a passage confirming that God was right. It is not there. Leafing through the whole of the book, one will read on the last page that God shows favour to Job, and then Job appears to be home again and, although this is not explicitly told, cured as well. "All Job's brothers and sisters and his acquaintance of former days came and feasted with him in his home. They consoled and comforted him for all the misfortunes which the Lord had inflicted on him, and each of them gave him a pound of silver and a gold ring'' (xlii 11ff.). God, too, acquitted himself well: Job acquired even more cattle than he had formerly owned, had another seven sons and three daughters, who were the most beautiful women in the land, and lived very happily ever after. We hear no more about the Adversary. Part of the narrative must have been lost, perhaps at the time when a long series of poems was built into it.

As in many other Old Testament texts, the image of God in this narrative has been borrowed from the form of government: the powerful king, who can give and who can take away. In this King-God's court, however, there is someone who has the ability to raise doubts. And the human who is the king's most sincere subject is forced to prove that God has a right to call himself king. If Job, who is the only real character of the narrative—his wife, his children, his slaves, his friends, and his relatives are only extras—, had not stood the test, if, deprived of his possessions and his health, he had lost his sincere faith and cursed or renounced God, God would have been proved wrong before the Adversary. In other words, the rule of this King-God is made dependent on the human subject Job. By his attitude Job robs the Adversary of his autonomous role. The demonic does not have a personality apart from or in opposition to God. The sincere believer incorporates the disaster that deprives him of his property and health into his image of God, which includes both good and evil: prosperity and health as well as disaster and ruin.

III

When Job's friends have sat with him for seven days and seven nights without speaking a word, they change from extras to interlocutors. The change beginning at ch. iii becomes clear by the transition of narrative prose to poetry. In the long series of poems (taking up over 39 chapters of the total 42 chapters of the book) Job himself is a different person from the Job of the narrative. Job's reaction to this miserable fate is in complete contrast with that of the first chapters. In his *Tischreden* about Job in the poems Luther says, ''Es redet sich nicht also in der Anfechtung'', and he is right: these poems belong to literature, they are a poetical expression of a problem that worried the poet. Yet in many stanzas those who listened to his poetry and, later, the readers of the poems, recognized the pains that people suffer when they receive no answer to the question of the whys and wherefores of their lot in life. Like Jeremiah Job curses the day of his birth: let that day be darkness. "Why was I not stillborn, [. . .] or why was I not concealed like an untimely birth?" Let me quote Job iii 20 – 26 in A. de Wilde's recent and in many ways superb translation:[3]

> Warum gibt er dem Leidbeladenen das Licht,
> das Leben den Seelenbetrübten
> die auf den Tod harren, ohne dass er kommt,
> die nach ihm graben, mehr als nach Schätzen,
>
> die sich ihres Grabsteins freuen würden,
> frohlocken, fänden sie das Grab;
> dem Manne, dem sein Weg verborgen,
> den Gott ringsum eingehegt?
>
> Denn mein Seufzen ist mein Brot geworden,
> und für (mein) Wasser ergiesst sich mein Schreien;
> denn was mich beben macht, trifft mich,
> und wovor mir bangt, das fällt über mich her;
> ich habe keinen Frieden, keine Ruhe,
> kein Rast, immer kommt neue Erschütterung.

The existence of similar literature in Babylonia, Egypt, and Greece[4] has rightly been pointed out. This may be illustrated with a few lines by Sophocles (from *Oedipus at Colonos*, 1225f.):[5]

> Not to be born at all
> Is best, far best that can befall.
> Next best, when born, with least delay
> To trace the backward way.

This lament is of all ages, but there are some periods in history that provide support for the assumption that there must have been mutual influence between its poetical expressions. Job's three friends turn into opponents in the course of the series of poems. The oldest of them, Eliphaz, initially speaks in a sensible and dignified manner.

---

[3] A. DE WILDE, *Das Buch Hiob* (OTS 22), Leiden, 1981, p. 96 (translator's note: the original Dutch translation used by DE BOER has been replaced here by the later German one).

[4] See e.g. the valuable introduction to S. TERRIEN, *Job* (Commentaire de l'Ancien Testament), Neuchatel, 1963, pp. 5 – 27, from which I have borrowed the quotation from Sophocles.

[5] Quoted from the English translation by F. STORR, B.A., in *Oedipus the King, Oedipus at Colonus, Antigone*, Loeb Classical Library No. 20, London, 1981, p. 261.

Bildad is more combative, and the youngest one, Zophar, more fanatical, less civilized and accordingly poorer in thoughts and shorter of speech. In his replies—there is a sort of dialogue, even though it shows little or no development: all speakers repeat their own views using different words and images—, Job admits that no one is able to resist God. However, he persists in calling his fate unfair. His lament turns into a complaint and he asks for a judicial verdict, which, according to his firm conviction, would put God in the wrong. His accusers' tone begins to show irritation rather than love. In their opinion, no one suffers innocently. God does not pervert justice, he has a wise reason for everything. Those who resist him are wicked and will perish. The prosperity of the wicked never lasts. According to the teachings of Job's friends, one can only conclude from Job's fate that he is being punished for his sins.

Two things may be noted in the arrangement of the series of poems. Firstly the accusers, who seem to think that they can draw conclusions about man's moral value from his fate, fail to convince Job. Job's share in what can hardly be called conversations increases steadily. His lament turns into an complaint, sometimes bordering on derision. His friends' voices subside.

The second remarkable aspect of the arrangement of the property is that the common element in the words spoken by these four people, by Job and his three friends, is not their friendship but their shared respect for wisdom. One of the friends says (xi 5ff.),

> But if only God would speak
> and open his lips to reply,
> to expound to you the secrets of wisdom,
> for wonderful are its achievements!
> (...)
> Can you fathom the mystery of God,
> or attain to the limits of the Almighty?

Job has the same respect for divine wisdom. Wisdom—where does it come from? Where can it be found? No mortal being knows the way to it. Only God knew that way and used it when he ordered the world, says ch. xxviii, a poem which may have been inserted at a later stage but fits very well into the thoughts that the poet makes Job express. In a lecture he gave for the Amsterdam *V.C.S.B.* in 1928, KRISTENSEN said this about it: "The passage dwells on the exalted and infathomable nature of divine wisdom; no human being or creature knows its place, even destruction and death do not know where it resides. And then the poem ends abruptly and on an altogether new note with this one verse: "And he said to mankind, 'The fear of the Lord is wisdom, and to turn from evil, that is understanding!' That is all it says. Of course modern criticism (though not the *Leidse Vertaling*) has wanted to omit the verse because of its odd place in the text. It seems to me that it clarifies the purpose of the whole book in an excellent manner. Man has not been initiated into divine wisdom. But he knows all he needs to know, namely that true human wisdom consists of the fear of the Lord and justice. This is the law of *his* life. The question what law applies to God is an infathomable mystery for him; it is not his business."[6]

Job's friends repudiate his lament and consider his complaint improper. In their eyes there are no contradictions between divine wisdom and the law God has imposed on man. Therefore Job must have sinned, and only if he shows remorse may he hope for forgiveness and recovery. In his lament and complaint, Job himself also starts from the idea that what applies to men as the law and justice given by God must also apply to God. God must be bound by the same form of justice. The friends' accusing voices die down because Job takes their teachings seriously: sincere religion should guarantee one's happiness in life. He raises his voice in protest and accuses God of injustice, because their doctrine has not been violated by him but by God. New voices are heard when the friends have fallen silent. The first one belongs to a character who has not been mentioned before and is introduced as a young man called Elihu. The meaning of his poems is not always clear. Job does not reply to them. In many ways Elihu's words give the impression of being first of all a kind of continuation of what has been said by the three friends. Job's suffering might be a stage in his life teaching him something. His lament and complaint do not show wisdom or understanding; it might all be just a dark and narrow tunnel at the end of which there will be light again. "*Wacht maar, wacht maar, alles komt goed*" ("Be patient, and everything will be all right in the end")—not in the sense of sentimental songs saying that the hereafter will compensate for what one has missed during one's lifetime or, worse, for what one has suffered unjustly, but in the sense of "God is great and we know him not" (Allard PIERSON's favourite text) or of "God is

---

[6] W.B. KRISTENSEN, "Het boven-ethische in de godsdienst", in: *Symbool en werkelijkheid*, Arnhem, 1954, p. 41.

mighty and does not despise any; . . . he does not keep the wicked
alive, but gives the afflicted their right'' (xxxvi 26 and xxxvi 5). In
other words, there will be a change of fortune, matters will take a
turn for the better, and there will be a reward: "(the oppressed) will
complete their days in prosperity'' (xxxvi 11). I have already said
that Job does not say anything in reply to this. I should think that
starting from what he has said thus far, one cannot possibly assume
that he changed his mind on account of Elihu's speech.

Elihu continues, and in the last poem that he is made to say
he provides a magnificent elaboration of the theme of God's greatness and mystery. The poem sings of thunder, rain, cold, heat,
darkness, and light. It seems to be a prelude to the last voice we
hear, that of God himself (chs. xxxviiif.): a visionary description
of creation, nature, the earth, the sea, the stars and the animal
world.[7]

This poem asks the question, "Where were you, man, when God
created all things?'' The basic elements of creation, of which man
himself is a part, are shown to him, but he cannot penetrate or understand them. For that, he is too small *qua talis*. How then can
he ever expect to understand his own fate? The image of God in
this poetical section of the Book of Job is quite different from that
of the narrative in the beginning of the book. There the divinity of
the King who is free to give and to take away was dependent ulti-
mately on the sincerity of the faith of his servant Job. Without Job's
unfailing piety the Adversary would have won and God would have
been dethroned, or he would at least have had to share power with
satan.

In the description of God in the last poems, in which the poet
makes God himself speak, God is God by virtue of his own power.
He shows this power in creation, in the form of life of which man
is also a part, but his power is totally independent of man, even of
those humans who keep the ethical law which is imposed on them
and whose religion is disinterested. God is a suprapersonal quantity,
unfathomable for man. The poet makes Job see and feel that quantity, for the mystery of life lives in him, too, however tiny and finite
he may be. But the poet offers no doctrine or argument with respect
to that God by which God might be checked or defined.

How does Job react? Does he retract?

---

[7] The special questions evoked by chs. xlf. are not discussed here.

IV

I am now coming to the text indicated in the title of this lecture, xlii 6, in which many people find the answer to this question.

The friends have stopped speaking. Job carries on longer, but after the first poems that the poet makes the new character of Elihu say, he, too, falls silent. The friends were getting repetitious and in my opinion Elihu does not really bring up any new aspects either. His first poems are all variations on what the friends had already said in their own ways. And if Job had replied to these poems, his answer would in all probability have been a variation of what he had already argued at great length and with varying emphasis. He might have repeated what can be found in the poem of ch. xix: that he is convinced with the certainty of a visionary that one day somebody will be standing on his grave and state authoritatively that he was just, that he was in the right. *Veritas filia temporis*. Perhaps he would also have appealed again to what he calls his witness in heaven (xvi 19ff.), at which PEDERSEN rightly comments: "His claim cannot perish; it is greater than himself."[8]

Someone who knew both the poems and the narrative about Job with the happy ending made an effort to tie the two together. He was no poet and narrates in his own language and with the colour of his own faith how God, after speaking to Job—i.e. after the poems about the greatness of creation—, addresses Eliphaz in anger. He upbraids him and his two friends for speaking improperly about God. Job was right and God will punish the friends. They may, however, evade their punishment by offering a sacrifice and asking Job to intercede for them. And this is what they proceed to do.

This narrator places Job in the succession of great believers such as Moses and Samuel who can avert God's anger in precarious situations.[9]

Just before this section, in which God clearly chooses Job's side, there is a short poetical passage that contains two lines (vss 3a; 4) describing man's smallness in the style of God's poem in chs. xxxviiif., asking how anyone could obscure (?) (God's) counsel or instruct him. They are probably a quotation of xxxviii 2f. The

---

[8] Johs. PEDERSEN, *Israel: Its Life and Culture*, vol. II, London-Copenhagen, 1926, pp. 366f.
[9] Cf. the author's *De voorbede in het Oude Testament*, Leiden, 1943.

remaining lines are presented as Job's answer to God. The first is
Job's recognition of God's omnipotence (xlii 2). The second part of
vs 3 is also best understood as a recognition and even as a praising
of God's miracles, which are beyond Job's grasp. The third line (vs
5) is of a visionary nature: up to now my faith in you was based on
the report of others, I believed in a doctrine, but now I have seen
you, now you have shown me your miraculous power, your creation, of which I am myself a part.

> I knew of you only by report,
> but now I see you with my own eyes.

Then follows the last poetical verse:

> ^{c}al-ken $^{\jmath}$æm$^{\jmath}$as w^{e}niḥamtî
> ^{c}al-^{c}āpār wā$^{\jmath}$epær

Most translations and commentaries see this text as Job's capitu-
lation:

> Darum widerrufe ich
> und bereue in Staub und Asche.[10]

(Therefore I yield, repenting in dust and ashes.)

Similar renderings can be found in the *Leidse Vertaling*[11], in the
translation by L.H.K. BLEEKER[12], in that of the Dutch Bible Society, J.H. KROEZE's commentary[13], and in EHRLICH's *Randglossen*[14].

Frequently an object is supplied for the first verb and sometimes
also for the second one. This is already the case in the LXX (''therefore I despise *myself*''), and also in Symmachus and in the Vulgate
(*ipse me reprehendo*). We find the same thought in the Authorized
(King James) Version: ''Wherefore I abhor *myself*, and repent in
dust and ashes'', which is in complete agreement with the translation found in the Dutch *Statenvertaling*.

The Targum chooses another object for the first verb: ''Therefore
I despise *my riches*.'' Following the Jewish commentator IBN EZRA,

---

[10] G. FOHRER, *Das Buch Hiob*, Gütersloh, 1963.

[11] *Het Oude Testament, opnieuw uit de grondtekst overgezet en van inleidingen en aan-
tekeningen voorzien door A. Kuenen, I. Hooykaas, W.H. Kosters en H. Oort*, Leiden: Brill,
1899/1901.

[12] L.H.K. BLEEKER, *Job* (TeU), Groningen-Batavia, 1935.

[13] J.H. KROEZE, *Het boek Job* (KVHS), Kampen, 1960.

[14] A.B. EHRLICH, *Randglossen zur hebräischen Bibel* VI, Leipzig, 1913, p. 343:
''$^{\jmath}$m$^{\jmath}$s, absolut gebraucht, ist = ich widerrufe.''

who adds the object "all my words", STEUERNAGEL (in KAUTZSCH-BERTHOLET) has: "Drum widerrufe ich (was ich geredet habe)".[15] The Dutch *Willibrordvertaling* goes even further, saying, "I retract all, I regret all, sitting down in dust and ashes."[16]

It is clear that according to all these translations (and many more could be mentioned here) Job retracts. They consider the narrator, who by making God say that Job was right and that the friends were wrong linked the collection of poems with the happy ending of the story, to be mistaken. The majority, however, are not always right.[17]

It is worth one's while to have a closer look at some of the ancient translations. As we have seen, in the Septuagint the Greek-speaking Jewish community added an object to the first verb: ἐφαύλισα ἐμαυτόν—"I despise *myself*." They also added a second verb meaning "and I am melting, pining away", which must be the rendering of a Hebrew variant *ʾæmmas*, which looks and sounds almost the same as the first (*ʾæmʾ as*), and is therefore probably to be considered as an alternative reading. This second reading is preferred by some modern translators[18] and in the New English Bible.

The second Hebrew verb is rendered in the Septuagint as ἥγημαι

---

[15] Cf. Also H.TH. OBBINK: "Daarom herroep ik wat ik heb gesproken, ik verootmoedig mij in stof en asch" (*Het Oude Testament (Verkorte Uitgave)*, Leiden, *1942*), and LARCHER in the *Bible de Jérusalem*.

[16] *De Bijbel uit de grondtekst vertaald: Willibrordvertaling*, Boxtel: Katholieke Bijbelstichting, 1975: "Alles herroep ik, over alles heb ik spijt, neergezeten in stof en as."

[17] This also applies to the commentaries. With regard to much-used dictionaries like GESENIUS-BUHL, BROWN-DRIVER-BRIGGS, and KÖHLER-BAUMGARTNER, one should note that for the first verb GESENIUS-BUHL gives the meaning "Widerwillen geg. etw. haben, davon nichts wissen wollen, verachten, verwerfen", indicating for Job xlii 6: "s.v.a. widerrufen?". BROWN-DRIVER-BRIGGS offers the meanings "reject, despise", without suggesting a specific meaning for the text under discussion: the latter is mentioned among the cases in which the verb occurs without an object in the meaning "despise". However, in the first edition of 1953, KÖHLER-BAUMGARTNER indicates as the first meaning of the verb "ablehnen, widerrufen" (without a question mark but only for Job xlii 6); BAUMGARTNER's new edition of 1974 had moved the verse to the head "Verschiedenes": "verwerfen des früher Gesagten durch Widerruf." The second verb (*nḥm* niph.) is rendered in GESENIUS-BUHL as "es sich leid tun lassen", and as "Reue empfinden" for Job xlii 6 and Jer. xxxi 19. BROWN-DRIVER-BRIGGS lists our verse among the texts in which the verb is translated as "be sorry, rue, suffer grief, repent" and takes it to be parallel to the first verb. KÖHLER-BAUMGARTNER (1953) assumes that the original meaning of both niph. and pi. is "seelisch erleichtern" and mentions our verse in a special section: "nif. 3. abs. bereuen", without adding other references. (Cf. the new edition of 1983, s.v. *nḥm*, nif. 1c (*translator's note*).)

[18] M. BUTTENWIESER, *The Book of Job*, Cincinnati, 1922, [2]1925; F. STIER, *Das Buch Ijjob*, München, 1954; H. RICHTER, *Studien zu Hiob*, Berlin (GDR), 1959.

δὲ ἐμαυτὸν (γῆν καὶ σπόδον): "I regard myself as (dust and ashes)." This is something quite different from "doing penance" or "feeling remorse". The Aramaic paraphrase or Targum of Job from Qumrân—which in the first part of this verse has something like *melting* (being poured out), too, and has a second verb that can be translated as "to crumble, to fall apart" (to be solved or boiled)—renders the last part of the verse as "to become dust and ashes". Again there is no question of penance or remorse.[19]

E. KÖNIG's translation of this verse is "Deshalb verwerfe ich meine bisherige Stellungnahme und bereue sie um 'Staub und Asche' willen."[20] The object he adds to the first verb and his translation of the second verb are borrowed from IBN EZRA, and in his explanation of "dust and ashes" he also stays close to this Jewish commentator. He interprets "dust and ashes" as "futility", as man's smallness and mortality. This interpretation is in keeping with that of the Septuagint. A. DE WILDE, too, follows this line, translating the slightly modified Hebrew text as "Deswegen erkenne ich meine Nichtigkeit an und halte mich für Erde und Staub."[21]

In the most popular Aramaic translation the line runs as follows: "Therefore I despise wealth and comfort myself for my sons, who

---

[19] See the *editio princeps* by J.P.M. VAN DER PLOEG and A.S. VAN DER WOUDE, *Le Targum de Job de la grotte XI de Qumrân*, Leiden, 1971, which has the translation "C'est pourquoi je suis épanché et dissolu, et je suis devenu poudre et cendre", and the edition by Michael SOKOLOFF, *The Targum to Job from Qumran Cave XI*, Ramat-Gan/Jerusalem, 1974, which has the translation "Therefore, I am poured out and boiled up, and I will become dust and ash." In this connection I should like to mention specifically Dr. E.W. TUINSTRA's dissertation, *Hermeneutische aspecten van de Targum van Job uit grot XI van Qumrân*, of which (for reasons unknown to me) no commercial edition has been published, and which was only distributed in stencilled form on a limited scale. Dr. TUINSTRA, who was given permission to use the original editors' transcription, translates the Qumrân text as follows: "Daarom ben ik uitgegoten en ontbonden en geworden tot stof en as." He follows the traditional rendering of the Hebrew text and considers the Qumrân text as a lament which shows a striking correspondence with Ps. xxii 15a (14a), rather than as a form of penitence. "Door op deze wijze Jobs antwoord aan God af te sluiten, doet de vertaler Job niet uit het strijdperk treden als iemand die herroept en berouw heeft, maar als de lijdende rechtvaardige, die in uiterste vertwijfeling verkeert" (TUINSTRA, *Hermeneutische aspecten*, p. 44). Concerning the translation of the Septuagint, which he calls a feebler toning down of the Hebrew text, he concurs with G. GERLEMAN, *The Book of Job*, Lund, 1946, p. 55f.: "There is a distinct tendency to tone down and suppress the defiance motif in the LXX portrayal of Job."

[20] E. KÖNIG, *Das Buch Hiob*, Gütersloh, 1929, pp. 450f.

[21] A. DE WILDE, *op. cit.*, p. 396.

are dust and ashes.'' ''Dust and ashes'' are here related to Job's dead children. This implies that, like the addition of ''wealth'' to the first verb, this explanation is derived from the narrative of the beginning of the Book of Job.[22] By indicating a caesura after the second verb, rabbinic punctuation connects ʿal to ''dust and ashes'', suggesting the meaning ''*sitting on* dust and ashes''. The addition of the word ''sitting'' seems obvious, especially if we remember that in ii 8 the narrator describes Job as ''sitting in the ashes'', although there it does not say ''*on* dust and ashes'', but just ''*in* the ashes''.

Apart from the incompleteness of the second part of the sentence as indicated by rabbinic punctuation, there are other reasons to assume that the Septuagint and the Targum, and also the early Christian Syriac translation, are right in not separating the Hebrew words *nḥm* and ʿal. This combination occurs seventeen times in the Old Testament and means to comfort oneself, to be consoled, to close a period of mourning, to rise above, to resign oneself to, to abandon, to accept, to leave behind.[23]

Fourteen times God is the subject of *nḥm* ʿal, reconsidering the disaster or the punishment he imposed or taking away the prosperity he granted (Ex. xxxii 12, etc.). Other subjects are David abandoning the mourning for Amnon's death (2 Sam. xiii 39); Rachel refusing to be consoled for and resign herself to the loss of her sons (Jer. xxxi 15); Pharaoh accepting his defeat, comforting himself ''for all his multitude'' (Ez. xxxii 31); a number of survivors who are consoled for the catastrophe in which their people died (Ez. xiv 22). Job xlii 6 also belongs to this category of texts: Job abandons ''dust and ashes'', i.e. he closes the period of mourning for the disasters that struck him.

If the Septuagint was right in interpreting ''dust and ashes'' as an image of the futility of human life, then the meaning of the second part of the sentence might be: I resign myself to that futility, or, to put it more actively: I stop thinking about it, I accept the fact that as a human being I am a finite, futile creature. There are a few texts in the Old Testament that suggest the meaning of finiteness and

---

[22] For the reading of 11QTgJob, see above, p. 12, and n. 19.

[23] One of these seventeen texts, Ps. xc 13, probably offers an example of an abridged formulation: ''Put an end to (the disaster with which you struck) your servants.'' If one will not accept this explanation, ʿal must have the same meaning as ʾæl, which is not uncommon. For the 47 occurrences of *nḥm* niph. the LXX uses as many as sixteen different verbs.

futility. Abraham dares to speak to God, although he is only "dust and ashes" (Gen. xviii 27); and "to return to dust" is a term for "dying" (Isa. xlvii 1; Job xxxiv 15 with ʿal; Gen. iii 19; Job x 9 with ʾæl. This usage also occurs in Qumrân literature. (See G. WANKE's summarizing article in *THAT*). I prefer the meaning "to comfort oneself after a period of mourning" on the basis of the texts that I mentioned above and especially on the basis of the construction of the poetical text under discussion. The first verb is an imperfect form continued by a *waw*-perfect consecutive. In this kind of construction the two verbs are closely related and should both be translated as a future or present tense. The second verb is often a continuation of what is indicated by the first, e.g. "You will eat and be full" (Deut. viii 12); "I shall be with you, and you will defeat Midian" (Judg. vi 16). The object of the second verb may be implied in the first one, "I shall hunt out and take them" = "I shall hunt them out and take them" (Am. ix 3).[24]

One goes into and out of mourning. To go out of it and consider the period of mourning as closed is not the same as being compensated for or denying the loss one has suffered: it means to live on, to turn a new page in the book of one's life. *nḥm* pi., "to comfort", always implies the opening of new perspective, while *nḥm* ni., "to comfort oneself", "to be consoled", refers to one's living on with what has struck one and to a new future in spite of it. When used of God, *nḥm* ni. means to stop a catastrophe that came from him, and not: to deny or regret it, but to give the person who was struck by it new chances of life. In *le temps d'un soupir* (1963), Anne PHILIPPE finishes her description of her husband's death and her mourning as follows (she is speaking to her deceased husband): "Je sais que la vie me passionne encore. Je veux me sauver, non me délivrer de toi." Job feels no remorse, but he bears his cross and is given the perspective of a new life. As so many translations, the Syriac translation is an interpretation rather than a literal rendering, but it goes to the heart of the matter with "therefore I am silent and rise again from dust and ashes." Syriac uses the same (verbal) stem as Hebrew and in Syriac literature this verb is also used to refer to the rising from the dead, the resurrection into life, the awakening from sleep, the continuation of life.[25] A possible objection to the line of thought

---

[24] Cf. P. JOÜON *Grammaire de l'hébreu biblique*, 2nd ed., Rome, 1947, § 119.
[25] See R. PAYNE SMITH, *Thesaurus Syriacus*, s.v. *nḥm*. The meaning of the ethpa.

followed in the Septuagint seems to be that the second verb does not continue the idea expressed in the first. A similar objection may be raised against the usual translation: to retract and repent. The order of these verbs ought to be reversed. Just as the second verb (*nḥm ⁵al*) does not mean "to repent", but "to change plans", "to abandon", so the first verb (*m²s*) does not mean "to retract". It rather means "to reject", "to despise", "to repudiate", "to have had enough of". The line of thought is clear here: to have had enough of something and therefore think no more about it. The meanings of the verbs employed make it unlikely that the phrase "dust and ashes" refers here to man's futility. The verse under discussion opens with the word "therefore", and it would help us to understand the meaning of this verse if we could find an answer to the question "why?". In the preceding verse, quoted above, Job says that he has seen God. This is the poet's expression of Job's experience at the divine description of creation and natural life, in which stanza after stanza illustrates the difference between God and man. The first verse of these poems says, "Then the Lord answered Job out of the tempest, and said"—but they do not reply to Job's lament, and his complaint is dismissed. As so often in the Bible, "He answered and said" means nothing more than "He addressed". Even if it is true that man is in no way able to do what God once did and is still doing in the earth's life, it *is* revealed to him that this is so. The poet makes Job conclude from this that he, too, is part of this divine creation. The miracle of God's omnipotence is shown to him. Job had heard the theory that God punishes the wicked and blesses the faithful. Had not his honoured position been an indication to him, too, of the fact that this doctrine about God was correct? However, it falls to pieces and is not put together again, neither by some form of recovery and compensation, nor by a promise. The only thing that happens to Job is this vision. However one sees this, it explains *how* he gets the spiritual force needed to overcome the numbing power of his incomprehensible suffering. Job does *not* retract. His friends, the troublesome comforters, are *not* proved right. If this Job, the main character of the collection of poems, has seen God's unfathomable greatness, then all moral theories about him fade into nothing. God

---

is defined as follows: "resuscitatus est, revixit (super pulverem et cinerem), revivam". But (solely) with reference to the text under discussion: "poenitentiam egi". Cf. HIERONYMUS: "et ago poenitentiam in favilla et cinere."

comes to him from another direction than whence he felt himself struck by unjustified afflictions. His sufferings are not gone, but at least he is able to accept life again, now that he has seen the greatness of God. He feels that he is part of the miracle of life:

> Therefore I have had enough of it all and leave dust and ashes behind.[26]

V

The narrator of the story about the honest and god-fearing Job bearing his afflictions provided a sequel in which he is compensated for the losses he suffered. This ought to satisfy our sense of justice, but we cannot quite place the Job who has ''new property and equally numerous offspring'' of the end of the narrative.

> Is er een wisseling van leed en luister
> gelijk van licht en donker, dag en nacht?;
> doch keert wel iemand ooit waar hij begon?

(Do sorrow and splendour take turns,
just as do light and darkness, day and night?;
but does anyone ever return whence he came?)

—as we may say after the poet H. DE BRUIN. The narrative has several climaxes, but the happy ending is not one of them. The poet of the other Job does not judge the events that can happen to one from man and his values. For him life is related to matters that reach far beyond man's existence, understanding and personality. Even beyond honesty and religion, although admittedly these are and will always be matters that people cannot lose without doing harm to

---

[26] In *VT* 26/3 (1976), pp. 369–371, Dale PATRICK suggests the translation: ''Therefore I repudiate and repent of dust and ashes'', which is close to that given by me. My point of view (which developed independently of PATRICK's study) attaches more weight to certain aspects of the history of textual transmission and exegesis to which PATRICK pays insufficient or sometimes inadequate attention. In a reaction to PATRICK's article, L.J. KAPLAN reminds us of the explanation given by MAIMONIDES (*VT* 28 (1978), pp. 356–358). A. DE WILDE informs me that G. BICKELL, *Das Buch Job*, Wien, 1894, p. 5, renders the final stanza ''wörtlich'':
Durch Hörnsagen hatte ich von dir gehört,
nun aber hat mein Auge dich gesehen;
darum tröste ich mich
und bin resigniert, trotz Staub und Asche.

their souls and the societies they live in. The poet successfully paints a greatness that may make us shiver, that reminds us almost cruelly of our futility, a greatness and wisdom which man can see without ever penetrating it, and is so absolute that we can relativize our own lives and fates.

I may have been able to elucidate the meaning of the last poetical verse of the Book of Job (xlii 6), but I still agree wholeheartedly to what H. DE BRUIN makes Job's *Nakomeling* (descendant) say:

> Jobs kindren zijn beschroomde theologen
> en weten niet zoveel als men verwacht,
> ondanks de trek van Jobs beproefd gelaat.

(Job's children are bashful theologians,
and do not know as much as one expects,
despite the lines in Job's afflicted face.)

21

SUR LA MASSORE DE 2 SAMUEL I,23

De ce passage, un verset de la complainte de David sur Saül et Jonathan, la version des Septante offre une leçon plus longue que voici

Σαοὺλ καὶ ᾿Ιωναθάν, οἱ ἠγαπημένοι καὶ ὡραῖοι, οὐ διακεχωρισμένοι·
εὐπρεπεῖς ἐν τῇ ζωῇ αὐτῶν, καὶ ἐν τῷ θανάτῳ αὐτῶν οὐ διεχωρίσθησαν

Cette amplification qui opère une manière de redoublement vise
manifestement à donner un certain balancement à la phrase. La
traduction n'en reste pas moins conforme à la répartition des termes
dans le texte massorétique qui les groupe de la façon suivante

"charmants dans leur vie et non séparés dans leur mort".

La Peshitta et le Targum présentent la même lecture que le texte
massorétique. Quant à la Vulgate, elle lit aussi de même mais ajoute
l'adverbe *quoque*

"amabiles et decori in vita sua, in morte quoque non sunt divisi".

Ainsi elle ne traduit pas le suffice du terme *mort*.

Les anciens commentateurs s'inspiraient de cette répartition des
termes dans leur interprétation. Ils voyaient dans le premier
membre un éloge tout à l'honneur de David, car l'appréciation d'un
ennemie est une vertu rare. "Hostem laudare rara est virtus", a
écrit sur ce verset Pierre Martyr (1500–1563), "haec et piorum
modestia, ut spectent, si quid in hostibus suis occurrat laudabile: a
peccatis vero avertunt oculos". Le second membre, "et dans leur
mort, ils ne furent pas séparés", est considéré comme un hommage
à Jonathan, accusé, suivant certains, d'avoir conspiré contre son
père.

Par contre, les nouvelles versions adoptent à peu près unanime-
ment une coupure des mots autre que celle des massorètes. Ils trans-
portent le *zāqēf qāṭon* du mot *beḥajjēhèm* sur le mot précédent *hanne ᶜī-
mîm*. La *Revised Version*, il est vrai, a conservé la césure de la massore;
d'autre part, elle fait des mots "favoris et charmants", qui constituent manifestement une apposition, des adjectifs attributs. Voici
son texte

"Saul and Jonathan were lovely and pleasant in their lives and in their
death they were not divided".

La Bible de Segond, édition 1953, traduit d'une manière analogue

"Saül et Jonathan, aimables et chéris pendant leur vie, N'ont point été séparés dans leur mort".

Ces versions constituent, autant que je sache, des exceptions. Les autres traductions récentes que j'ai pu consulter modifient toutes la répartition massorétique des termes. Parmi beaucoup d'autres, je mentionne S.R. Driver, *Notes on the Hebrew Text and the Topography of the Books of Samuel*, Oxford 1890, 2nd ed. 1913, p. 238; H.P. Smith, dans la série *International Critical Commentaries*, Edinburgh 1912, p. 263; W. Nowack, *commentaire*, Göttingen 1902, p. 154; A. Schulz, *commentaire*, Münster, Westfalen, 1920, vol. II, p. 17; la traduction de Buber-Rosenzweig; *The Revised Standard Version*, New York 1952, éd. 1965; *La Bible de Jérusalem*, Paris 1956; *The New American Bible*, 1969, 1970; *The New English Bible*, 1970, qui porte

"Delightful and dearly loved were Saul and Jonathan, in life, in death, they were not parted".

Ce déplacement de l'accent a aussi pénétré dans l'apparat critique de la Bible de R. Kittel. A première vue la modification de sens qu'il entraîne paraît être une amélioration. Smith, *op. cit.*, parle même à ce propos d'un rétablissement de l'ordre naturel des termes et du sens de la phrase.

Il est certain que l'expression "dans la vie et dans la mort" est, de nos jours, tout à fait habituelle. Elle provient vraisemblablement non de notre texte dans sa nouvelle lecture mais des mots très connus de Paul dans l'*Epitre aux Romains* XIV, 8

"dans la vie comme dans la mort, nous appartenons au Seigneur".

Nous nous servons couramment de l'expression "dans la vie et dans la mort" pour signifier "à toujours et sans séparation". On comprend donc: Saül et Jonathan ne furent jamais séparés. Ils ont vécu ensemble et ont péri ensemble, dans la même bataille.

Toutefois, cette nouvelle traduction laisse diverses difficultés sans solution. Premièrement, on peut conclure des anciennes versions qu'antérieurement à l'accentuation des massorètes, leur manière de couper le texte était déjà en usage. En second lieu, je ne vois personnellement aucune raison sérieuse de suspecter une inexactitude dans l'accentuation massorétique ici. En faveur du déplacement de l'accent opéré par les nouveaux traducteurs, il existe bien un argument mais contestable. On estime que l'expression "dans la vie et dans la mort" est une expression connue et claire et l'on lit dans le verset 23 deux ou trois courtes propositions: Saül et Jonathan ne furent jamais séparés; ils sont plus prompts que des aigles; ils sont plus vigoureux que des lions. Toutefois, on ne fournit aucune explication de l'accentuation massorétique.

Il m'apparaît bien au contraire que nous avons une raison de douter de la justesse de ce déplacement d'accent dans le fait que l'expression "dans la vie et dans la mort" ne se rencontre nulle part en langue hébraïque. Pour autant que je sache, il en va de même dans les autres langues sémitiques. Les termes de vie et de mort ne se rencontrent jamais qu'en opposition comme dans *Dt.* XXX,19; *Jér.* XXI,8; *Prov.* XVIII,21.

Comment donc devons-nous traduire et comprendre ce verset si nous respectons l'accentuation des massorètes? On pourrait le faire de la manière suivante

> "Saül et Jonathan, chéris et charmants dans leur vie,
> et dans leur mort non séparés,
> étaient plus prompts que des aigles,
> plus vigoureux que des lions".

La phrase verbale "et dans leur mort ils ne furent pas séparés" peut fort bien être considérée comme une prolongation de la phrase nominale mise en apposition aux noms propres, "Saül et Jonathan, les (héros) chéris et charmants dans leur vie". Une pareille combinaison de phrases nominales et verbales n'est nullement inconnue en langue hébraïque, voyez par exemple *Es.* XL,22 ss. Ainsi donc, la complainte déplore la mort du roi et du prince héritier, tués dans la bataille. Le chagrin s'accroît à l'évocation des qualités guerrières des deux héros car l'arc de Jonathan et l'épée de Saül ont été vantés au verset 22. Puis vient l'éloge de leur promptitude et de leur vigueur. Leurs noms reçoivent alors successivement deux appositions formant un douloureux contraste: ils étaient charmants et chéris du peuple lorsque, durant leur vie, ils revenaient triomphants des combats, mais ils ont maintenant succombé dans la bataille, vaincus par l'ennemi, ce qui est le thème essentiel de la complainte. Le deuil est d'autant plus douloureux que le roi et le prince héritier ont tous deux péri, unis dans leur mort. Il n'existe plus d'avenir pour la maison de Saül. Leur gloire évoquée par les

mots "chéris et charmants" qui dépeignent la vie, contraste dure-
ment avec leur chute: le souverain et son successeur ont succombé,
avec les mots qui peignent la mort.

En conclusion, il paraît vraisemblable que l'accentuation massorétique a fixé le vrai sens du passage et que les anciennes versions
et explications du texte étaient sur une meilleure voie que nos
traductions actuelles.

22

LA SYNTAXE DU VERSET QUATRE DU PSAUME VINGT-DEUX

L'article, si riche de substance, de Henri Cazelles sur "La Titulature du Roi David", paru dans *Mélanges bibliques rédigés en l'honneur d'André Robert*, montre qu'il existe au verbe *zmr* un sens militaire.[1] Concernant le même texte traité par H. Cazelles, à savoir 2 Sam. xxiii 1 – 7, une autre étude a paru récemment dans le *Svensk Exegetisk Årsbok*, 41 – 42[2], due à Tryggve N.D. Mettinger, où il rapproche *zmr* d'une racine signifiant "protéger".

A ce propos il traite du sens de Psaume xxii 4. Ce verset, si l'on se conforme à la lecture des Massorètes qui mettent l'*atnach* sous *qādôš*, doit se traduire

> Pourtant, tu es le Saint,
> siégant sur les louanges d'Israël.[3]

Il est possible, cependant, de transférer l'*atnach* sous *yôšēb* et de traduire

> Pourtant tu es le Saint qui trône,
> toi qui es les louanges d'Israël

---

[1] Travaux de l'Institut catholique de Paris 4, Paris, 1956, pp. 131 – 136. Par la suite une grande attention fut donnée à l'hypothèse d'une racine *dhmr*, e.a. par S.E. Loewenstamm, "The Lord is my strength and my glory", *V.T.* xix 4, 1969, pp. 464 – 470; S.B. Parker, "Exodus xv 2 again", *V.T.* xxi 3, 1971, pp. 373 – 379 et *id.* "Jezebel's reception of Jehu", *Maarav* i 1, 1978, pp. 67 – 78. Auparavant, T.H. Gaster avait proposé le syntagme *zmrt*, Exod. xv 2, interprété d'après la racine arabe *dhamara*, protéger, *Expos. Times* xlviii, 1936, p. 45. Dans le même périodique, xlviii, 1937, p. 478, D. Winton Thomas remarquait que déjà Elieser Ben Yehuda avait émis cette hypothèse dans *Thesaurus totius hebraitatis et veteris et recentioris*, Berlin-Jérusalem, 1908 – 1959, 3e volume, p. 1363, *s.v. zmr, zimrat*: Siegreicher, victorieux, victor. Voir aussi D.W. Thomas, "The Language of the Old Testament" dans *Record and Revelation*, Oxford, 1938, p. 395. Il est surprenant que Gaster, dans *Expos. Times*, xlix, 1937, p. 189, revenant sur ce sujet, mentionne que I. Zolli, dans *Giornale della Societa Asiatica Italiana*, 1935, p. 290, l'a devancé dans l'identification de *zmrt* avec la racine arabe *dhamara*, mais ne mentionne ni Ben Yehuda ni Thomas. L'article de Cazelles comporte une série d'interprétations de 2 Sam. xxiii 1 – 7 et de divers autres textes qui garde une valeur permanente.

[2] 1976 – 1977. "The Last Words of David", a Study of Structure and Meaning in ii Samuel 23:1 – 7, by Tryggve N.D Mettinger, pp. 147 – 156. Son excursus sur Ps. xxii 4 se trouve à la page 151.

[3] Mettinger cite la *Rev. Stand. Version*, "yet thou art holy, enthroned on the praises of Israel".

en voyant dans *t^ehillôt yiśrā'ēl* une désignation de Dieu.[4]

Mettinger, quant à lui, juge cette désignation étrange et suppose qu'elle provient d'un *zmr* qui fut compris d'après *zmr* = "chanter". Sans le dire explicitement, Mettinger suppose donc un texte prémassorétique portant un *z^emīrôt* qui avait originellement le sens de "guerrier" ou de "protecteur" d'Israël.[5]

A mon avis, Mettinger n'a pas tout à fait tort d'estimer étrange une désignation de Dieu par l'expression "les louanges d'Israël", ou "la louange d'Israël". Le fait que cette traduction fut adoptée très tôt, dont témoins la Septante et la Vulgate, n'enlève rien à son caractère étrange. B. Duhm de son coté avait déjà qualifié d'obscure la traduction "toi qui habites les louanges d'Israël".[6] Le fait que divers traducteurs proposent des modifications, comme il ressort d'additions différentes: *au-dessus, au milieu de, dans* (les louanges d'Israël)[7], confirme l'opinion trouvée chez Duhm et chez Mettinger.

Tout en admettant la possibilité d'une modification du texte, il me paraît cependant nécessaire d'examiner la syntaxe du passage avant de proposer une modification. Joüon prête peu attention au *pronomina separata*.[8] Gesenius-Kautzsch les mentionne comme une exception fictive à la règle que le pronom séparé indique le nominatif et le pronom suffixe le *casus obliquus*.[9] Par insistance, le pronom figurant en *casus obliquus* est répété comme sujet d'une phrase in-

---

[4] Conformément à la Septante et à la Vulgate e.a. E. Osty, 1971; H. Gunkel, commentaire, 1926; R. Schwab, dans le texte marginal de la Bible de Jérusalem, 1956; New American Bible, 1970; J.P.M. van der Ploeg, Commentaire, 1971; Jewish New Translation, 1972; A New Translation for Worship, London, 1977.

[5] *Op. cit.*, p. 151, "If we follow the MT which has the atnach below *qādôš* the rendering should be "yet thou art holy, enthroned on the praises of Israel" (RSV). Yet there is something to be said in favour of the suggestion to move the atnach to *yôšēb* and interpret the verse "yet thou art enthroned in holiness, thou the praises of Israel", in which case *t^ehillôt yiśrā'ēl* designates God. My suggestion is that this strange designation should then be regarded as the result of deriving *z^emīrôt yiśrā'ēl*, known to us from ii Sam. 23:1, from *z.m.r* I."

[6] Commentaire, *Die Psalmen*, 1899, p. 68, "sitzend auf den Lobliedern Israels. Der Sinn dieses Satzes ist mir ebenso dunkel, wie die Ausdrucksweise anstößig."

[7] *^cal*, au-dessus, upon, über, boven, Targum, Midraš; J. Olshausen, 1853; Joh. Dyserinck, 1877; R. Kittel, 1922; éd. Zwingli, 1942; F.M.Th. Böhl, 1946 etc. *b^e*, la version syriaque, "qui trônes dans votre louange"; au milieu des louanges etc., D. Martin, 1828, L. Segond, 1953. Caractéristique pour un temps passé est l'opinion de J. Wellhausen, "Die Gottheit thront nicht über den Rauchsäulen des Altars, sondern über den Gebeten Israels –", *Israelitische und Jüdische Geschichte*, 6e éd. Berlin, 1907, p. 211.

[8] P. Joüon, *Grammaire de l'hébreu biblique*, 2e éd. Rome, 1947, par. 146 e 1).

[9] W. Gesenius—E. Kautzsch, 24e éd., Leipzig 1885, par. 121, 3.

dépendante et sans attribut. Exemples: ''Bénis-moi, moi aussi'',
Gen. xxvii 34b; ''Moi, mes mains ont étendu les cieux'', Es. xlv
12b.[10] Un pronom ainsi mis en tête se lit aussi en Ps. xliv 3, ''toi,
de ta propre main'' (traduction de Dhorme), soit relatif à ''ce que
tu as fait'', verset 2, soit à ''tu as dépossédé des nations . . .'', verset
3; Deutéron. x 21, que je paraphrase, ''ta louange, elle concerne lui,
ton Dieu''; Jérémie xvii 14b, ''car ma louange, c'est toi''; et Mich.
v 1, ''Quant à toi, Bethléem . . ., de toi sortira . . .''.

Le verset quatre du Psaume xxii appartient à ce genre de syntaxe,
si l'on ajoute le mot *bāk* qui paraît être tombé par haplographie,
puisque le verset 5 commence par ce petit mot. En conséquence, on
aboutit à la traduction suivante,

> Et c'est toi, le Saint qui trône,
> les louanges d'Israël (se portent) sur toi.

Au lieu de *trôner* on peut aussi lire *résider*, soit comme un roi, soit
comme un juge. B. Duhm fut le premier à ma connaissance, qui ait
supposé une haplographie.[11] On trouve la même supposition chez
Ed. Dhorme[12], ''. . . [vers toi] vont les louanges d'Israël''. Le dis-
cernement du type de syntaxe du verset quatre du Ps. xxii fait super-
flu les modifications mentionnées ci-dessus.

La traduction ici proposée est proche de celle de la *New English
Bible* de 1970, (laissant de coté la lecture *ba-qôdeš*, suivante la version
grecque, qui ne regarde pas le sujet de cet' étude),

> ''And yet thou art enthroned in holiness,
> thou art he whose praises Israel sings''.

La traduction ici proposée s'accorde avec le contexte: en toi nos
pères eurent confiance; ils eurent confiance et tu les as délivrés. La
plupart des psaumes comportent des louanges dont Dieu est le sujet.
Les fidèles chantent *sur* leur Dieu, à cause de ses bienfaits envers son
peuple.[13] C'est que les fidèles espéraient par leurs louanges éveiller
leur Dieu et attirer sur eux sa bénédiction.

---

[10] Voir aussi A.R. Davidson, *Hebrew Syntax*, 3e éd., Edinburgh, 1902, par. 1,
avec quelques exemples du phénomène non relevés dans Gesenius-Kautzsch.

[11] *Op. cit.*, p. 68.

[12] *La bible*, édition Pléiade, Paris 1959, p.931, texte et note.

[13] Voir mon ''Cantate domino: an erroneous dative?'', conférence faite à Cambridge, 17 juillet 1979, parue dans *Oudtestamentische Studiën*, vol. xxi, 1981, pp.
55–67.

23
SOME OBSERVATIONS ON DEUTERONOMY VI 4 AND 5

> Dorothy's faith supplied all that Mr Casaubon's words
> seemed to leave unsaid: what believer sees a disturbing
> omission or infelicity? The text, whether of prophet or
> of poet, expands for whatever we can put into it, and
> even his bad grammar is sublime.
>
> George Eliot, *Middlemarch*

In archaeological excavations stones from an earlier level or suitable ones from elsewhere are sometimes found re-used in later buildings. In the same way there are lines in texts handed down to us which are clearly at variance with their context. Their syntax and content, or both, provide a reason for special study and, like archaeology, the unknown factors can be so challenging that scholars arrive at contradictory explanations. Moreover, when such passages have acquired an established place in religious practices—no rare occurrence, the unknown capable of more than one interpretation is atractive—it does not make a study of them any easier.

It is thus that the fourth and fifth verses of Deuteronomy vi are foreign elements in their context. LOHFINK, who wrote a valuable monograph on the fifth verse, "You must love the Lord your God with all your heart and soul and strength", and discussed the word 'ḥd in *Theologisches Wörterbuch zum Alten Testament*[1], speaks of "die Einsamkeit von 6,4b.5", "eine nicht historische Jahweprädikation, anschließend eine Formulierung des Hauptgebots. Kein Rahmen, keine Kommentierung, nichts."[2] Although he observes that verse 4 is not a stock expression in Deuteronomy or with the deuteronomic writers, contrary to the often cited verse 5, yet he takes it that the the two verses form a unity. He considers the fifth verse to be connected to the Decalogue by the use of the verb 'hb, and that Yhwh is the only one for Israel who is addressed as in the love lyric. Eduard NIELSEN too, who wrote a particularly instructive article a short while ago in which the history of the explanation of the passage was also attended to[3], accepts a close relation between verses 4 and 5.

---

[1] N. LOHFINK, *Das Hauptgebot*. Eine Untersuchung literarischer Einleitungsfragen zu Dtn. 5–11. Rome 1963; and 'ḥd in *ThWzAT*, Stuttgart 1971.

[2] *Das Hauptgebot*, p. 163f.

[3] Eduard NIELSEN, " 'Weil Jahwe unser Gott ein Jahwe ist' Dtn. 6,4f." in *Fest-*

According to him, verse 4 can only be understood in relation with verse 5. He attaches great importance to the influence of the northern Isrealite conception of a marriage relation between Yhwh and his people, compare the book of Hosea, a relation in which the Canaanite was excluded.

In early Christian circles, the undivided love of God was made equivalent to love of one's neighbour by attaching to verse 5 the end of verse 18 in Leviticus xix, "and you shall love your neighbour as yourself". This union of two biblical texts must have something to do with the occurrence of the verb w'hbt in both texts. The absence of verse 4 in the answer to the question about the most important commandment in Matth. xxii 37—comp. Luke x 27—indicates that this verse was not taken as a commandment. The parallel text in Mark. xii 29b, however, does consider it as a commandment and this is in accord with Jewish usage, where the recital of verse 4 is called "the acceptance of the yoke of God's sovereignty".[4] The independent character of verse 5 towards what follows, indeed with the whole of Deuteronomy, emerges in the Greek version by the rendering of lbb. διανοία is unusual as rendering of lbb, usual is καρδία, see already verse 6 of the same chapter and too the eight cases in which the same expression occurs in the characteristic repetitive style of Deuteronomy. Our place Deuteron. vi 5 stands alone with its rendering διανοία. The quotation in the three gospels as well as the text of the manuscripts on which Rahlf's edition of the Septuagint is based read καρδία.[5]

The paraphrase "the acceptance of the yoke of God's sovereignty" of the recital of verse 4 in Jewish religious practice may be taken as coming conscious of what were one's obligations by birth. What Christians call embracing Christian belief, a conversion to what, by nature, one is not, can in Jewish belief better be called a return to God's people, to whom by birth one had already belonged. In the period of normative significance for shaping Jewish belief—a

---

schrift Zimmerli, Göttingen 1971, pp. 288–301. Cf. too B. GERHARDSSON, *The Testing of God's Son*. An analysis of an early Christian Midrash. Lund 1966, pp. 71ff. GERHARDSSON's main concern is the fifth verse of Deut. vi.

[4] Berakot ii 5.

[5] Cf. J.W. WEVERS, *Deuteronomium*, Septuaginta Vol. III, 2. Göttingen 1977, p. 120, and his monograph, *Text History of the Greek Deuteronomy*, Göttingen 1978, pp. 59 and 61.

mixture of national and religious feelings—kingship was a phenomenon of the past. The attempt to make "a kingdom of priests",
Exod. xix 6—a post-exilic passage, I think—did not last long. The
people became a community and leadership fell into the hands of
prominent rabbis, often divided among themselves about the difficult issue of their relationship with and resistance to the population
amidst they were living and not least to foreign rule. To become
aware of belonging to the community of Yhwh is called the acceptance of the yoke of God's sovereignty: the acceptance of duties, laws
directly and indirectly regarded as the will of their God. This is the
origin of the idea "holy scripture", the traditional texts which
seemed more permanent than either country or sanctuary.

Early on verse 4 of Deuteron. vi was considered of fundamental
significance in Jewish belief. It was at a later date that the twice daily
recitation of this verse was extended to include verses 5–9 of the
same chapter, the verses 13–21 of chapter xi, and the verses 37–41
of Numbers xv.[6] The first line, Deuteron. vi 4, remained the most
important. Should the believer happen to fall asleep after the recitation of this line, he had still fulfilled his religious duty. The custom
to write the last letter of the first and of the last word of this verse
with a big character is general in the masoretic manuscripts. Its explanation: write (and read) šm^c, "listen" and not šm', "perhaps";
'ḥd and not 'ḥr, "an other" seems to be a frank joke. The custom
does not help to fix syntax or meaning of the line.

Verse 4 and verse 5 took a prominent place in the religious life of
Christians as well as Jews but the independency of the verses remained distinct. Both LOHFINK and NIELSEN distinguish no separate
independency in the verses. They think that verse 4 has to be interpreted from verse 5. Yet it seems to me that, apart from the differences distinguished between these two verses in both Christian and
Jewish practice, there are some other aspects which make an original
unity of these lines uncertain.

In verse 4b, Moses the speaker identifies himself with the people,
the community of Israel, who are being addressed. He says: "*our
God Yhwh*". This identification occurs more in the first chapters of
Deuteronomy, i 6. 19. 20 ii 33. 36. 37 iii 3 iv 7 v 2. In the fifth verse
of chapter vi however, Moses used the typically deuteronomic appel-

---

6 A fourth extension with Numb. xxiii 18–24 was not adopted for practical reasons, Ber. 12b. Cf. further Sukka 42a and Ber. 13b.

lation which occurs 214 times in Deuteronomy: "*your* God Yhwh". Obligations are laid down as divine laws by the special servant of Yhwh. If verses 4b and 5 had originally been a unit, then one would also expect "*your* God Yhwh" in verse 4b, or "*our* God Yhwh" in verse 5, whom *we* ought to love with *our* whole strength.

Verse 4b has a very short sentence structure and those who think that they know its meaning describe the verse as a credo in the form of an exclamation. Verse 5, on the contrary, expresses broadly that Israel must follow their God with an individed heart. The structure of the sentence differs considerably to that of verse 4b.

It is clear that the beginning of verse 4, "Hear, O Israel", does not belong to verse 6ff. It is not likely that it is only serving verse 4b, for why should the teacher—the expression is a didactic one—demand to be heard and to be obeyed while he includes himself with those whom he is instructing? "Hear, O Israel" must either refer to verses 4b and 5, or to verse 5 alone.

Can verses 4b and 5 belong together in line with known Hebrew syntax? If we take verse 4b as a nominal sentence, the answer is in the affirmative, for it is not unusual to continue such a sentence with *waw perfect*. DAVIDSON remarked in this connection[7]: "the causal connection also may be very slightly expressed". From his examples may be mentioned Gen. xx 11,"—there is no fear of God here and (therefore) they will kill me"; Ruth iii 9, "I am your maidservant Ruth, therefore spread thy shirt"; 2 Kings ix 26, "I saw the blood of Naboth and his sons yesterday, therefore I will requite thee". If verses 4b and 5 have such a sentence structure and we take the significance of verse 4b to lie in the statement that only Yhwh, as the one "father", "husband", or "king", has authority, we can render 4b and 5 as one sentence, as NIELSEN does[8]: "Weil Jahwe unser Gott ein Jahwe ist, sollst du Jahwe, deinen Gott, lieben von ganzem Herzen, von ganzer Seele und mit aller deiner Kraft".

However, by doing this the differences mentioned above between the verses 4b and 5 are not solved. If verse 4b and 5 did not originally belong together, there is reason to suppose that verse 5 may be the continuation of 4a, "Hear, O Israel". *Waw perfect* sentences also occur after imperatives. Of the fourteen cases given by DAVIDSON[9] I

---

[7] A.B. DAVIDSON, *Hebrew Syntax*, Edinburgh 1902. Par. 57, Rem. 1.
[8] *art. cit.*, p. 297.

quote 1 Sam. viii 22, "Hearken to their voice—Take them at their word, *NEB*—and make them a king"; 1 Sam. xv 3, "Now go and smite Amalek and destroy all what they have". I take it that Deuteron. ix 1 – 3 is also an example of this sort of sentence structure. The same didactic term[10], šm⁽ yśr'l, is followed in this passage by a description of what was discovered in the land to which the people comes by crossing the Jordan: excessive strong people in impregnable cities. These descriptive sentence are continued by a *waw perfect* sentence, wyd⁽t, which indicates to what Israel must listen—"Hear, O Israel"—and in what it must put its trust, "you will experience" that your God Yhwh will let you conquer. The syntax of Deuteron. vi 4 and 5, I think, confirms an original independency for verse 4b and verse 5, and makes it likely that verse 4a, "Hear, O Israel", and verse 5 belong together.

The oldest preserved form of verse 4 is that of the Papyrus Nash, a fragment probably originating in the second half of the first century after Christ.[11] The page comes from Egypt and contains the decalogue in a form showing variation both from the texts in Exod. xx and Deuteron. v, and agreeing in a number of places—but not everywhere—with the reading of the Septuagint. The last legible lines contain the reading, in agreement with the Septuagint version, of Deuteron. vi 4 and the first letters of verse 5. It is not my intention here to go into the question of lettering, dating, or the text itself, for I only want to observe what has already long been pointed out, that the combination decalogue-Deuteron. vi 4f. indicates the possibility that the papyrus text was used for teaching purposes. One of my former students, J. SCHONEVELD, once examined the possible points of connection of Deuteron. vi 4f. to the liturgy.[12] He contrasted the tradition of the temple service preserved in the Mishna tractates Tamid and Berakot. In Tamid v 1 it was decreed that the recital of Deuteron. vi 4f. by serving priests must take place in a priests' room after the recital of a blessing and the decalogue, while in Berakot i 4 and ii 2 the recital of Deuteron. vi 4f. must be preceded by two

---

9 DAVIDSON, *op. cit.*, Par. 55a).

10 M. WEINFELD wrote illuminatingly about the term under the headings 'rhetorical technique' and 'didacticism' in his *Deuteronomy and the Deuteronomic School*, Oxford 1972, pp. 175f. and 304ff.

11 Cf. P. KAHLE, *Die hebräischen Handschriften aus der Höhle*, Stuttgart 1951, pp. 5ff., discussing W.F. ALBRIGHT's earlier dating, *JBL* 1937, pp. 145ff.

12 1958.

blessings and not by the decalogue. The Talmud, jer. Berakot 12a, reports that the decalogue had to be removed from the series of texts to be recited because of a quarrel of the heretics. The heretics declared nothing to be essential in the law but the Ten Words.[13]

According to the Mishna tractate Tamid, the recital did not take place during the ritual of sacrifice but between temple rites in a side room. It seems clear that Deuteron. vi 4f., like the decalogue, was regarded as independent material ascribed to the priestly liturgy.

It has been observed about Deuteron. vi 4b—most recently by Nielsen[14]—that *qua* form it is close to the community avowal of faith as expressed in hymns and prayers. The Book of Psalms which frequently uses the expression "our God Yhwh", does not, however, have it in the same construction or in a comparable one. Understandably it is the word 'ḥd that has been carefully examined. Once again I refer to LOHFINK's and NIELSEN's studies and also SAUER's contribution covers the ground lucidly.[15] Unquestionable is its meaning in a large majority of its occurrence the numeral *one*. Yet it must be acknowledged that the word sometimes needs a futher epithet to acquire its more close meaning. Thus could be said of the term in Deuteron. vi 4b—to use a late term of the same stem—: it is 'ḥwd "mysterious", "veiled", "closed up".

Quell has given a lucid survey of the difficulties confronting the translator of Deuteron. vi 4b.[16] He ends his article as follows: "Der Befund ist also von der Art, daß es nicht möglich ist, den Sinngehalt dieser Worte in einwandfreier gedanklicher Schärfe zu bestimmen. Diese Tatsache in Verbindung mit dem rhythmischen Schwung der Sprache und der unverkennbaren Größe des Gegenstandes der Aussage macht die Worte zu einem in seiner Art einzigen Zeugnis der gehaltenen und doch unruhvoll drängenden Kraft des Jahweglaubens." Indeed, a beautiful and profound, theological packing, but of what? The packing is at the same time suggestive and concealing. VON RAD, on the contrary, sharply formulated the

---

[13] Cf. I. ELBOGEN, "Bemerkungen zur alten jüdischen Liturgie", in *Festschrift Kaufman Kohler*, Berlin 1913, p. 79.

[14] *art. cit.*, p. 289.

[15] G. SAUER, *Theologisches Handwörterbuch zum Alten Testament*, I, München 1971 *s.v.*

[16] G. QUELL, in *Theologisches Wörterbuch zum Neuen Testament*, III, Stuttgart 1938, pp. 1079f.

meaning of the words[17], which were for him apparently not obscure: "Die Zentralisationsforderung läßt sich somit leicht als die ganz unmittelbare Konsequenz aus dem gewichtigen theologischen Satze von dem einen Jahwe (Dt. 6,4) verstehen, der die ursprüngliche Fassung des Dt feierlich und programmatisch eröffnet hatte". It is not unusual to make a virtue of necessity when studying the Old Testament: obscure texts gain deep theological explanations. This has been promoted here by the significance attached to the passage in Jewish religious practice.

'ḥd in Deuteron. vi 4b belongs, I think, to the cases wherein the numeral needs an epithet to understand its meaning. Without aiming at completeness the following quotations may illustrate the gradations that ought to be made in the rendering of the term.

Gen. xl 5, xli 11, the butler and the baker of the king of Egypt dreamed in *the same* night. The Pharaoh dreamed twice, Gen. xli 1ff., but Joseph said, verse 25, it is *the same* dream, *the similar sort of* dream. Gen. xi 1, the whole earth had *the same* language, used *the same* words. Numb. xv 16, *the same* law and *the same* ordinance shall be for the Hebrews in Palestine and for those who do not belong to their families but are sojourning with them. Hos. ii 2, the people of the South and the people of the North, the Judeans and the Israelites, shall appoint *the same* head. Ezek. xxxiv 23, *the same* shepperd. Zeph. iii 9, *a similarly motivated* service of Yhwh.

Gen. ii 24, a man leaves his parents and cleaves to his wife, they form *a close unity*. 1 Kings v 2 enumerates Solomon's provision for *a whole day*. Gen i 5, usually rendered the first day, but no ordinal numeral is used: the meaning is *a complete* day and in the sequel of the chapter the second, the third etc. complete days are meant. One can paraphrase: a day *on its own*. Thus are the Hebrews a people *on its own*, independent, 2 Sam. vii 23, parall. 1 Chron. xvii 21. Manoah, Judg. xiii 2, Elkanah, 1 Sam. i 1 are called: a man *on its own*, probably meaning that they are independent, not longer belonging to the household of their parents, and no slave.

Zech. xiv 7 and 9 belong to the same category, I think. The day on which there will be neither cold nor darkness and always life-giving water, will be *a complete* day, a day *on its own*. Then Jerusalem's enemies will be destroyed and the name of Yhwh *on its own*,

---

[17] G. VON RAD, *Theologie des Alten Testaments* I, München 1957, pp. 224ff.

yhwh 'ḥd, is sufficient to indicate that there are no powers nor threat of war against the city. Yhwh on its own, without appositions to his name that might be considered as a limitation of his power and influence, Yhwh who is the union of all divine might, He will become the Lord of the whole land.

From the meaning of a variety of gradation of 'ḥd, and from the only occurrence of the term yhwh 'ḥd besides Deuteron. vi 4b in Zech. xiv 9—assuming that my suggestion about the meaning of this text is right—I venture to paraphrase Deuteron. vi 4b as follows: (the term) *Yhwh our God* (means) *Yhwh on its own*.

Verse 4b might have been a more or less technical remark, reflecting a similar hope as the man possessed who wrote the visionary ideas of Zech. xiv. This suggestion does not explain the odd place at which the words are incorporated into the text. The factor of fortuity of the masoretic text-form deserves here attention, the more because verse 5 also is a *corpus alienum* in its context.

24

PSALM 81.6a
Observations on Translation and Meaning of One Hebrew Line

Introduction

Although the meaning of the separate words in Psalm 81.6a is more or less certain, there exists much uncertainty about the sentence as a whole, which is apparent in the diversity of translations and explanations. The ancient versions, the expositions in midrashim, commentaries of former and recent centuries, and translations and explanations of the last century all reflect learning and ingenious imagination. They affirm at the same time how difficult it is to reach a reasonable understanding of the sentence. Any new study of the line bears out this statement, and my attempt, a re-evaluation of some old ideas together with some new ideas, will be no exception.

Psalm 81.6a has two parts, עדות ביהוסף שמו and בצאת: על ארץ מצרים, which belong together. I will begin with the second part.

Psalm 81.6aβ

The verb יצא connected with Egypt (מצרים) recalls the post-biblical phrase for the exodus from Egypt, the deliverance from bondage, יציאת מצרים. The usual construction is the verbal form followed by the preposition מן. However, Psalm 81.6 reads על. Driver assumes that the Hebrew preposition also means 'from', on the ground of Keret II vi 9, where he translates '(the plague) from ('al) (his head)'.[1] This assumption is shared by M. Dahood and used in several places, including our Psalm verse.[2] The Greek and Latin versions read ἐκ and de, but it seems improbable that their *Vorlage* read מארץ. Rather, it seems probable, I think, that they took ἐκ and de in agreement with the standard connection which also occurs in the Book of Psalms (e.g., Ps. 114.1, בצאת ישראל ממצרים). Their explanation of the whole line leads to the equating of Joseph with Israel, the people that went forth from Egypt. The Syriac version considers the preposition על

similar to אל and ל, as is the case in a late phase of the Hebrew language. The Aramaic paraphrase seems to suggest a reading of 'to go from (gaol)' as well as the meaning 'to rule over', probably hinting at Genesis 42.6 (שליט על). This version does not equate Joseph with the people but considers Joseph to be a personal name, the hero of the Joseph story in the book of Genesis.

Besides Psalm 81.6, the phrase יצא על occurs in Genesis 19.23; Zechariah 5.3; Genesis 41.45; Esther 1.17; and 2 Kings 24.12. Genesis 19.23 causes no problems to the translators. The Greek rendering is ἐξέρχομαι ἐπί, the Syriac and Aramaic is npq ʿl, and the Latin is *egressus est super*. Modern translations present the same picture, 'to rise on' or 'upon', 'se lever sur', and 'aufgehen über'.

In Zechariah 5.3 the prophet Zechariah likens the sallying forth of the curse over the country to the rising of the sun on the land. It is translated as ἐκπορεύομαι ἐπί, npq ʿl, *egredior super* in the ancient versions, and also, without any essential difference, in the modern translations as 'to go out over', 'se répandre sur', and 'ausgehen über'. The curse goes out over the face of the whole land and is a power executing judgment.

In Genesis 41.45b the phrase is ויצא יוסף על ארץ מצרים. The Syriac and Aramaic version both maintain the preposition, rendering npq ʿl. The Targum adds explicatively, *šālîṭ* (cf. Gen. 42.6), which can be compared with the addition in the Aramaic rendering of Psalm 81.6. The Greek version, with the exception of the Mss O⁻⁵⁸ ⁷² and Syh, where ἐξέρχομαι ἐπί is the rendering of יצא על, does not translate the phrase. The Vulgate reads *egressus ad*.

Those who omit Genesis 41.45b, in agreement with the Septuagint, consider the phrase a miserable variant of v. 46b ('and Joseph went out from the presence of Pharaoh, and went through all the land of Egypt') or think that the phrase found its place in the text by accident. Some scholars emend the text, reading ויסב את[3] or ויצו.[4] Ibn Ezra's explanation, 'Joseph's name went out, i.e. he became famous', may have influenced Vatablus and his school in Paris, where we find *egressus est fama Ioseph* explained with *notus fuit in tota illa regione*.[5] Related ideas are found in Ehrlich's *Randglossen*, 'die Verbreitung von dessen (Joseph's) Kunde' and in Speiser's Genesis commentary, 'And Joseph became known through the land of Egypt', with the note that the precise meaning is uncertain.[6] Both of these interpreters draw upon Esther 1.17, where the term יצא על in their opinion means 'to spread, become familiar'. Soferno's explanation (sixteenth century), 'to go out as ruler', is related to Paulus Fagius' paraphrase *suâ pompâ procedebat, cum magnificentia quadam et majestate declarabatur esse princeps*. A similar explanation can often be found in modern translations and commentaries. Ed. König translates, 'und Joseph zog aus über das ganze Land Ägypten dahin',[7] and explains the sentence with, 'Dasz er "auszog" (45b) bedeutet soviel wie: als seinen Herrschaftsbezirk einnehmen (vgl. das *yāṣā'* in Ps. 19.5 und 81.6)'.[8] The Dutch Bible Society Translation (1951) adds between brackets 'als heer', as ruler ('en Jozef ging uit, [als heer] over het land Egypte'). L. Köhler translates, with a question mark, Genesis 41.45 and Psalm 81.6 with 'Verfügung haben über', W. Baumgartner tranlates יצא as '(z. Inspektion) bereisen', and L. Segond's translation has 'partir pour visiter'.[9] The New Jewish Translation (1967) reads, 'Thus Joseph emerged in charge of', the NEB (1970) has 'And Joseph's authority extended over', and the Roman Catholic Dutch Translation (1975) reads 'Zo kreeg Josef volmacht over'. The meaning of על as 'over' can be found in the renderings of the Revised Version (1884), the Revised Standard Version (1951) ('went out over') and in de Fraine's commentary (1963) ('trok uit over').

In this discussion of ways of translating Genesis 41.45b, B. Jacob's major work on the book of Genesis must be mentioned separately.[10] Jacob's commentary appeared in 1934 and is often neglected in the discussion. He translates literally, referring to Genesis 19.23, 'und Joseph ging auf über das Land Ägypten'. His explanation starts from Joseph's elevation, and, in his opinion, Pharaoh's gift, the daughter of the priest of the sun-god to be Joseph's wife, confirms the supposition that Joseph received the title of king, 'sun of the country'. To support this, Jacob refers to Amarna letter 107, ln. 9. Jacob may have over-estimated the influence of the idea of the rising of the sun in his explanation of the pericope. However, his emphasis on the royal position, Joseph awarded with royal power, seems right. Recently, Jacob found an enthusiastic supporter in E.I. Lowenthal, who renders Psalm 81.6a as 'And Joseph shone forth over the land of Egypt'.[11]

Other scholars translate the phrase יצא על with 'partir pour'[12] or 'put circuler au'.[13] The meaning of the preposition (על) is then considered to be equal to אל and ל, as is true of a later phase of the language.

The phrase under discussion should be considered, in my opinion, in relation to the decrees of the Pharaoh concerning Joseph. Joseph

becomes the second in command in the country. He is to be in charge
of the food rationing and is to be the ruler of the whole country. The
symbols of his authority are a signet ring of the Pharaoh, royal
garments, a golden chain, a chariot (second to the king's chariot), and
a special salutation to be used by the population; moreover, he has
the absolute right of say concerning the people, a new name, and the
daughter of a priest as his wife. V. 45b now summarizes this
inauguration by the statement, 'Thus Joseph rose over the land of
Egypt', i.e. became Egypt's highest authority next to the Pharaoh.
Furthermore, the passage is part of a story. The narrator put words
in Pharaoh's mouth in order to explain the reason for Joseph's
unbelievable elevation. Joseph is a man with the spirit of the Gods,
and with that quality he is the most discreet and most wise man in his
empire (vv. 38, 39). Redford, in his thorough study of the Joseph
story, speaks rightly of an investiture with a 'superlative tenor'.[14]

As was noted above, both Ehrlich and Speiser support their
explanation of the phrase in Genesis 41.45b by referring to Esther
1.17. Esther 1.17 in the Septuagint reads διηγεῖσθαι, ('to describe, set
out in detail'). The Syriac and Targumic renderings of the text
maintain the sense of the Hebrew phrase with *npq ?*. The Vulgate,
however, reads *egredior ad*. Vatablus' *divulgabitur* and Drusius' *fama
facti* are paraphrases which are commonly found in modern translations and explanations as 'become known to', 'sera connue de', and
'bekannt werden'. Nevertheless, some translators keep to the original
sense of יצא.[15] It is evident, however, that all consider the preposition
עד equal to אל or ל, an opinion more easily accepted because of the
late date of the book of Esther.

There are, I think, some arguments for an explanation of the scene
in the story of Esther in accordance with the literal meaning of the
phrase יצא על, as I have tried to demonstrate in the texts treated
previously. Queen Vashti's refusal to come to the party of her
husband, the king, became not only *known* to all women but became
authoritative in the world of the women. Therefore, it seems possible
to paraphrase the Hebrew text as follows: 'her word will rise over
them', i.e. will take the lead and set the fashion in the world of
women. Hence, as a translation of the passage (v. 17) I venture to
present, 'For the queen's word will exercise an influence over all
women, causing them to look with contempt upon their husbands,
since they will say, "King Ahasuerus commanded Queen Vashti to be
brought before him, but she did not come"'.

The ancient versions of 2 Kings 24.12 render עַל יָצָא with 'to go to', ἐξέρχομαι ἐπί, *npq l*, and *egredior ad*. The Targum maintains the preposition עַל but considers it to be equal to אֶל or לְ. Nicolaus of Lyra (fourteenth century) and a Lapide (seventeenth century) explain *dedidit se in potestatem victoris* by referring to the prophet Jeremiah's advice to leave the city and to go out to the Chaldeans (Jer. 38.2; *ex concilio Jeremiae*). The rendering of 'to go unto' is widely used in our translations and commentaries.[16] Other scholars go one step further and translate 'to give oneself up to'.[17] Josephus' tendentious use of the pericope in *The Jewish War* (VI.103ff.) furnishes proof of the antiquity of this application of the text. He speaks of

> a splendid example before you in Jeconiah, king of the Jews. He, when the king of Babylon made war on him through his own fault, of his own accord left the City before its capture, and with his family submitted to voluntary imprisonment rather than surrender these holy places to the enemy and see the House of God go up in flames. For that he is celebrated by all Jews in the sacred record, and memory, flowing through the ages eternally new, passes him on to future generations immortal.

Josephus mentions this as a splendid example, even if it were dangerous. He adds, 'But I can guarantee your pardon from the Romans'.[18]

It is certain that in Josephus' time the preposition עַל had been used interchangeably with the prepositions אֶל and לְ. Josephus' usage of 2 Kings 24.12 was based on his personal attitude in the turmoil of his days. *The Jewish War* is doubtless the apology of a man who has placed himself on the Roman side. Therefore, I doubt whether we can use his rendering of Jehoiachin's conduct as an argument for an emendation of the Hebrew text (אֶל instead of עַל) or for a late date of the text, thus ascribing it to the period in which the language did not distinguish עַל from אֶל.[19] One need only note that in 2 Kings 18.18, 31, יָצָא אֶל has been used for 'to go forth to'.

It is beyond the purpose of this article to discuss text and meaning of the passage 2 Kings 24.8ff. It suffices here to recall that there are differences between the traditions preserved in Kings, Jeremiah, and the Babylonian texts about the conquest of Judah and Jerusalem by the Babylonians. Moreover, the text in 2 Kings 24 is evidently a composite from different sources. V. 10 speaks about the servants of Nebuchadnezzar, and v. 12 speaks about the king himself. In addition, Klostermann has already called attention to the disparity in time between vv. 12a and 12b.[20] It seems possible to assume that 'the king of Babel', mentioned without the name of the king, originally meant 'the servants of Nebuchadnezzar', corresponding with v. 10. The confusion in the passage gives occasion, I think, for supposing more than one attack on the city.

If we stick to the meaning of יצא על, as demonstrated above, it is possible to translate and explain 2 Kings 24.12a as follows: 'And Jehoiachin, Judah's king, had a stronger position than Babel's king' (i.e. the Babylonian attacker). Judah's king rose over, or had the power to oppose, the unit of the Babylonian army. Accordingly, this first line of the verse would then be a reminiscence of an unavailing attack. A later attack, however, led to the downfall of the town and the deportation of the king, his family, his servants, and his officials.

We return to the phrase בצאתו על in Psalm 81.6. The Greek and Latin versions understood Israel to be the subject of the infinitive construct of the verb יצא. The name Israel could indicate the Northern tribes, or perhaps only Ephraim and Manasseh, the 'sons of Joseph', or all the twelve tribes. The Syriac and Aramaic versions, however, consider Joseph, the hero of the story in the book of Genesis, as the subject of the phrase. This interpretation is based on Genesis 41.45 and appears already in Midrash Rabbah on Numbers 7.49. The Midrash explains the particular spelling of Joseph's name (see discussion below) as an indication of Joseph's divine power. Through this power Joseph knew the seventy languages, which is the midrashic explanation of Psalm 81.6b. Simeon de Muis, whose commentary on the book of Psalms appeared in Paris in the first part of the seventeenth century, observes about the argument that Joseph is the subject of the phrase, 'Non omnino rejicienda est haec opinio'. Muis himself, however, considers God to be the subject, an opinion borrowed from David Kimhi. This explanation occurs also in other commentaries and may date back to the Midrash Rabbah on Qoheleth. There, the Joseph of the story in Genesis belongs to the string of persons who have been pursued and therefore are chosen by God, 'And God seeks what has been driven away [= pursued]' (Eccl. 3.15). Joseph was pursued by his brothers, and the Holy One, blessed be He, chose Joseph, and, as it is said, 'He appointed it in Joseph for a testimony, when He went forth against the land of Egypt' (Ps. 81.6).[21] A similar line of thinking frequently occurs in recent times.[22]

From an early date until the present, references to God's punish-
ments of the Egyptians (Ex. 7–12) have been used to explain Psalm
81 as the establishment of a feast in remembrance of the deliverance
of the people of Israel from bondage in Egypt. Exodus 11.4 is often
the basis for the main argument, but the Hebrew phrase used in it is
יוצא בתוך מצרים, not יצא על. Also, Isaiah 19, which describes the coming
of Israel's God to disturb Egypt, does not use our term but the verb
בוא. And Exodus 15.25, which concerns the establishment of rites
(חק ומשפט) connected with the miracle of sweetening the bitter water
of Marah, does not contain a remembrance of God's sallying forth
against Egypt or any word akin to Psalm 81.6.

In the Hebrew Bible we do not have the idea of God sallying, or
going forth against Egypt, or going to Egypt; and Joseph, the hero of
the story in Genesis, did not go to Egypt of his own free will but was
taken down to that country (Gen. 39.1; cf. 37.28). He never sallied
forth against Egypt. If we respect the Hebrew text, it is inevitable, in
my opinion, to translate the phrase of Psalm 81.6 (בצאתו על ארץ מצרים)
with 'his rising over the land of Egypt'. The sentence is directly
alluding to the story of Joseph, to Joseph's power, and to the
authority awarded him by the Pharaoh (Gen. 41.45).[23]

A further consideration in Psalm 81.6 is the preposition ב in בצאתו.
It has generally been rendered as an adjunct of time (cum, when,
quand, da/als); however an exception is A.R. Johnson's rendering.
Johnson thinks that the preposition in this context has a causal force.
He translates, 'Because of His sallying forth against the land of
Egypt'. The rendering because is to express the great divine act of
salvation—according to him the theme of the whole poem—'in
freeing the Hebrews from the tyranny of their Egyptian taskmasters
and their recognition of the fact that as a result He and He alone
should be the God of Israel'.[24] Apart from this argument derived
from the context, demonstrated in a masterly fashion but in my
opinion not wholly convincing, there are other reasons to prefer the
causal meaning of the preposition in the phrase under consideration.
In syntactical studies little or no attention is given to a causal
meaning of ב. Gesenius-Kautzsch has one line in a paragraph on beth
instrumenti, 'cf bĕ propter, Gen 18.28, 19.16'.[25] Joüon observes that
the preposition rarely has 'une nuance proprement causale'. In this
context he mentions the cases of Genesis 19.16, Exodus 16.7, and 2
Chronicles 28.6.[26] However, more places such as Genesis 29.20 and
Exodus 16.8 can be added. The construction of these phrases is

similar to Psalm 81.6, which is, in my opinion, another case of the same syntactical feature. I base my supposition that Joseph, the hero of the story in Genesis, is the subject of the phrase צאתו על ארץ מצרים on the fact that Joseph was elevated to and entrusted with a position of ultimate authority over Egypt by the Pharaoh who saw that the future of his throne and his country depended on the man who possessed divine power, and whose shrewdness and wisdom were beyond everyone else's. The election of Joseph by God in Psalm 81 goes hand in hand with the purport of the story-teller. This brings us to the first part of v. 6a.

Psalm 81.6aα

Joseph's adventurous career in Egypt from prisoner to acting king, from eliminated member of the clan of Jacob to rescuer and indisputable head of the family, is in my opinion the source of the second part of the Hebrew line under discussion. The names of Joseph's Egyptian sons are Palestinian names, and outside the story there is not the slightest trace of an Egyptian origin or Egyptian sojourn for the tribes of Ephraim and Manasseh. The silence of the rest of the Hebrew Bible on the subject of the Joseph story has but some late exceptions.[27] One of the exceptions is Psalm 81.6 of which Redford cautiously observes that the text is 'obscure'. He states, 'the antiquity of a "statute" (an allusion to the covenant relationship?) is somewhat connected with Joseph's "going forth over Egypt" (cf. Gen. 41.46—read v. 45)'.[28]

The first part of v. 6a is עדות ביהוסף שמו. The phrase שים ב has been rendered in the ancient versions with 'to place in'. However, the Targum reads 'to place upon'. The midrashic explanation, 'because he did not draw near to the wife of his master', is an allusion to the Joseph story, in agreement with the Aramaic rendering of the second part of the line. The idea of commitment, a precept laid on and considered obligatory, is implied in עדות, μαρτύριον, testimonium, and sāhādûtā'. The term is used in different contexts and hence we find a variety of renderings such as testimony, decree, law, solemn charge, and, recently, covenant, pact. Covenant or pact is proposed by J.C. Greenfield in a study on 'Stylistic Aspects of the Sefire Treaty Inscriptions'. Greenfield reads the Sefire inscription I A line 7 as śmw 'dy' 'lhn, and observes, 'This idiom is the equivalent of Akkadian ādē šākānū and Hebr. śym 'dwt. An interesting example is 'edut biyhōsēp

śāmō, "He (God) made a covenant (or pact) with Joseph (= Israel)"
(Ps. 81.6)'.[29] Neither Greenfield nor Fitzmyer, who adopted the
meaning of Greenfield, give arguments for their translations of שׂים
ב עדות with 'conclude a treaty (or pact) with'.[30]

Psalm 78.5 (ויקם עדות ביעקב ותורה שם בישראל) seems to be close to
Psalm 81.6. The two verbs in Psalm 78.5 used in parallelism mean 'to
erect, establish', probably originally to erect stelae, stones, tablets,
commemorative columns, with texts recalling names or precepts.
Remembrance does not mean only sentiments about the past, bygone
events, deceased persons. Memorials also serve to speak of everlasting
authority.[31] עדות and תורה are also synonyms in Psalm 78.5. תורה in
this poem has been used in parallel with 'the words of the deity'
(v. 1), the story of God's wonderful acts (vv. 4, 7 and cf. vv. 12ff.),
and ברית, covenant (v. 10). If vv. 5 and 6 of Psalm 81 belong together,
עדות is parallel to חק and משׁפט (v. 5). Among the acts of God to be
commemorated, Psalm 78 mentions the wonders of the splitting the
sea (Ex. 15.8) in v. 12 and the signs, the plagues 'set in Egypt'
(שׁם במצרים) in v. 43. Here, the plagues are given in an order different
from the tales in Exodus. The Joseph story, however, is not quoted in
the long poem. The exclusive Judean character of the poem is evident
in the lines, 'He rejected the tent of Joseph; he did not choose the
tribe of Ephraim; but he chose the tribe of Judah, Mount Zion which
he loves' (vv. 67f.).

The phrase שׂים ב occurs nearly a hundred times in the Hebrew
Bible. Almost everywhere the preposition in this phrase is a *beth
locale*.[32] In a number of places *beth locale* is followed by a geographic
name, the name of a town, a country, or a land.[33] In Psalm 78.5 the
names Jacob and Israel are used in connection with the phrase שׂים ב.
So, names of a tribe or a land wherein a decree is promulgated, or a
law enacted, can be rendered with 'the territory of . . . '

The reading ביוסף (ביהוסף) is unique in the Hebrew Bible. Greenfield's
position would lead to an emendation (שׂם instead of שׂמוֹ or to a
reading of שׂמוּ, which makes the subject a plural form, the Gods. His
explanation of the name Joseph as synonymous with Israel may be
right but leaves open whether Israel indicates the northern kingdom,
or all the tribes of Israel, the dream of some post-exilic circles (see
Jer. 31 and Ezek. 27) and post-biblical literature.[34] In addition, there
are cases where the name Jacob is similar to Judah. As an example,
the wording of Psalm 77.16, the redemption of 'the sons of Jacob and
Joseph', suggests a reference to the southern and northern kingdoms.

Furthermore, in Psalm 80.2 the phrase 'O shepherd of Israel' is paralleled by 'thou who leadest Joseph like a flock', and both terms indicate the same God. Finally, according to style and purport, both poems belong to post-exilic times.

Given this post-exilic setting, one must also remember that the idea of Joseph's right of primogeniture (1 Chron. 5.1, 2) has been handed down in history with a Judean revision. However, this passage in Chronicles still preserves evident traces of an existing hope of restoration of the independence of the people with the House of Joseph as its centre. The Joseph story itself can be characterized as an encouragement during hard times. The story might have had its origin and setting in circles which nourished hopes of a restoration with the name Joseph as the focus and with aspirations entertained through pictures of an imaginary past. Most of the Hebrew texts, collected and revised, enlarged and rewritten, in order to encourage the remnants of the people in Palestine and elsewhere, have a Judean tendency, but there are scattered fragments wherein non-Judean, sometimes even anti-Judean, ideas are preserved. It seems certain, I think, that the Joseph story of the book of Genesis belongs to these texts, albeit that the composition we have also has a Judean recension.[35]

The word order of the phrase in Psalm 81.6, Joseph before the verb, must indicate the emphasis on the name. Combining this with the frequently used phrase שׂם ב, leads to a rendering, 'It was in (the territory of) Joseph that he instituted it as a testimony'. Moreover, instead of 'the territory of', 'the house of' or 'the flock of' or 'the tent of' can be substituted by those who do not like the supremacy of the Judean leaders and reject an equation of Joseph with Judah.

The object of the verb שׂם, described in v. 5 as a statute for Israel, as an ordinance of Jacob's God, will be חג. Eventually it will become יום חג (v. 4), the cultic feast, a day of loud singing, shouting, and music produced by several instruments (vv. 2-4). It is probable, therefore, that v. 6a belongs to the preceding verses (2-5).

Conclusion

The translation and explanation presented here, partly reconstructed out of the history of our discipline and partly the outcome of some new research and some imagination, also solves, I think, the riddle of the unique spelling of the name Joseph. The attempts to read in the spelling of the name *yhwsp* the divine name *yāh* or *yāhû*, in order to express God's reward for Joseph's piety and moral firmness (midrash on Lev. 17.3), or Joseph's divine wisdom made public in his ability to understand foreign languages (midrash on Num. 7.49), do not convince modern interpreters.[36] The assumption of text corruption by pure accident may not be out of the question, but an explanation on the ground of a reasonable hypothesis is preferable. I venture to suppose that the spelling is intentionally manufactured to suggest an alternative reading, namely Jehudah instead of Joseph.

The unique spelling would then be an indication of Judean opposition to those believers who nourished hope of a restoration of the House of Joseph. It would be at the same time an example of the narrow horizons of the scribes and those who recited the sacred songs in later times. A real radical change was no longer allowed. Moreover, a confusion about the meaning of the second part of the line, a remembrance of the Exodus story instead of the Joseph story, might have been of some influence.

Finally, it is worth remembering that a part of the people expected that the Messiah would come forth out of the House of Joseph. Psalm 81.6 could have been a witness of their faith.

NOTES

1. G.R. Driver, 'Hebrew Roots and Words', *Die Welt des Orients* I, 5 (1950) 406-415; idem, *Canaanite Myths and Legends* (Edinburgh: T. & T. Clark, 1956); and idem, 'Review of A.L. Oppenheim, editor-in-chief, *Assyrian Dictionary*, vol. 16, 1962, pp. xv, 262, Oriental Institute, University of Chicago', *JSS* 9 (1964) 346-50.

2. M. Dahood, *Psalms*, 3 vols (AB 16, 17, 17A; Garden City, New York: Doubleday, 1966-1970). In vol. 3, p. 396, Dahood gives a summary of all the cases.

3. J. Olshausen, *Die Psalmen* (Leipzig: S. Hirzel, 1853), 340.

4. See E. Kautzsch, *Die Heilige Schrift* (Tübingen: J.C.B. Mohr, 1910); *Die Heilige Schrift* (Zürich: Zwingli-Verlag, 1907-1931), known as the 'Zürcher Bible'; and recently, A. van Selms, *Genesis* (Nijkerk: G.F. Callenbach, 1967), vol. 2, p. 215.

5. Quotations from biblical commentaries prior to 1700 are taken from M. Polus (Matthew Poole), *Synopsis Criticorum* (Frankfurt: B.C. Wustii, 1694).

6. A.B. Ehrlich, *Randglossen zur hebräischen Bibel*, vol. I (Leipzig: J.C. Hinrichs, 1908); E.A. Speiser, *Genesis* (AB 1; Garden City, New York: Doubleday, 1964), 311, 314.

7. Why König and other scholars (see J. de Fraine, *Genesis* [Roermond en Maaseik: J.J. Romen, 1963]; the New English Bible [1970]; and Dutch Roman Catholic Translation [1975]) add 'ganze' ('whole') remains unexplained.

8. Ed. König, *Genesis* (Gütersloh: C. Bertelsmann, 1925), 697.

9. Ludwig Koehler and Walter Baumgartner, *Lexicon in Veteris Testamenti Libros* (Leiden: E.J. Brill, 1953); W. Baumgartner, *Hebräisches Lexikon zum Alten Testament* (Leiden: E.J. Brill, 1974); and L. Segond, *La Sainte Bible* (Paris: La Société Biblique, 1953).

10. B. Jacob, *Das erste Buch der Tora, Genesis* (Berlin: Schocken Verlag, 1934).

11. E.I. Lowenthal, *The Joseph Narrative in Genesis* (New York: Ktav Publishing, 1973).

12. Roland de Vaux, *La Sainte Bible* (Paris: Editions du Cerf, 1956) (= La Bible de Jérusalem); and E. Osty, *La Bible, Genèse* (Paris: Editions Rencontre, 1970).

13. E. Dhorme, *La Bible* (Paris: Bibliothèque de la Pléiade, 1956).

14. D.B. Redford, *A Study of the Biblical Story of Joseph* (SVT 20; Leiden: E.J. Brill, 1970), 87.

15. A. Barucq in *La Bible de Jérusalem* (1956), has 'ne manquera pas de venir à la connaissance de'; and W. Dommershausen, *Die Estherrolle* (Stuttgart: Katholisches Bibelwerk, 1968), 31, has 'wird zu (aller Frauen) hinausgehen'.

16. The following are a more or less representative sample: O. Thenius, *Die Bücher der Könige* (Leipzig: Weidmann, 1849), 449; A. Klostermann, *Die Bücher Samuelis und der Könige* (Nördlingen: C.H. Beck, 1887), 486; I. Benzinger, *Die Bücher der Könige* (Freiburg: J.C.B. Mohr, 1899), 197; The Leiden Translation (1899); O. Eissfeldt, 'Die Bücher der Könige', in *Die Heilige Schrift des Alten Testaments*, ed. E. Kautzsch and A. Bertholet, 4th edn (Tübingen: J.C.B. Mohr, 1932); and The Dutch Bible Society Translation (1951).

17. Revised Standard Version (1951); de Vaux, *La Bible de Jérusalem* (1956); John Gray, *I and II Kings*, 2nd edn (London: SCM, 1970), 759f.; and E. Osty, *Premier et Deuxième Livre des Rois* (Paris: Rencontre, 1970).

18. Quotations from Josephus are from G.A. Williamson (trans.), *Josephus, The Jewish War* (rev. edn, Harmondsworth, Middlesex: Penguin Books, 1970), 333.

19. Josephus' examples, which he borrows from the Bible, are wholly determined by the author's aim in writing his *The Jewish War*, which was certainly not a historical, and still less a textual, piece of work.

20. Klostermann, *Die Bücher Samuelis*.

21. This translation is that of A. Cohen, *Ecclesiastes* (London: Soncino Press, 1939; 3rd edn, 1961).

22. See the marginal readings in Revised Version and the Revised Standard Version. See also F.M.Th. Böhl, *De Psalmen* (Groningen: J.B. Wolters, 1947); the Dutch Bible Society Translation (1951); R. Tournay and R. Schwab in *La Bible de Jérusalem* (1956); J.P.M. van der Ploeg, *Psalmen* (Roermond en Maaseik: J.J. Romen, 1973); E. Osty, *Le Livre des Psaumes*, 2nd edn (Paris: Rencontre, 1971); the Dutch Roman Catholic Translation (1975); and A.R. Johnson, *The Cultic Prophet and Israel's Psalmody* (Cardiff: University of Wales Press, 1979), 6ff.

23. The Latin texts of this verse (Ps. 81.6) are often literal renderings of the Hebrew. See Johannes Calvin's commentary of 1557, where he has *quum egressus est super terram Aegypti* (A. Tholuck [ed.], *Ioannis Calvini in Librum Psalmorum Commentarius* [Berlin: Apud Gustavum Eichler, 1836]); and Benedictus Arias Montano's commentary (1573) where he has *cum exiret ipse super terram Aegypti*. However, these literal renderings do not mean their explanation is acceptable. Ed. König in his explanation of Genesis (1925) mentions 'more or less taking as his dominion, compare Ps. 19.5 and 81.6', but he forgot this observation in his later (1927) commentary on Psalms. See König, *Genesis*, and idem, *Die Psalmen* (Gütersloh: C. Bertelsmann, 1927), 332f.

24. Johnson, *Cultic Prophet and Israel's Psalmody*, 6ff.

25. E. Kautzsch (ed.), *Wilhelm Gesenius' Hebräische Grammatik*, 24th edn (Leipzig: F.C.W. Vogel, 1885), 366ff. In a more recent edition it reads under *beth pretii*, a variety of *beth instrumenti*, 'also, in a wider sense, Gn 18.26, *bĕ* for the sake of; 1 S 3.13' (E. Kautzsch [ed.], *Gesenius' Hebrew Grammar*, trans. A.E. Cowley, 28th edn [Oxford: Clarendon Press, 1910; 16th repr., 1982], 380).

26. P. Joüon, *Grammaire de l'hébreu biblique*, 2nd edn (Rome: Pontifical Biblical Institute, 1947), §170j, p. 524.

27. As an example one can observe Ecclus 49.15 where it says, 'and no man like Joseph has been born'. For studies of such post-biblical material, see Redford, *Study of the Biblical Story of Joseph*, p. 249, n. 2. In addition, add H.W. Hollander, 'Joseph as Ethical Model in the Testaments of the Twelve Patriarchs' (Ph.D. dissertation, University of Leiden, 1981).

28. Redford, *Study of the Biblical Story of Joseph*, 248-49.

29. J.C. Greenfield, 'I. Stylistic Aspects of the Sefire Inscriptions', *Acta Orientalia* 26/27 (1965f.), 9.

30. J.A. Fitzmyer, *The Aramaic Inscriptions of Sefire* (Rome: Pontifical Biblical Institute, 1967), 12f., 16f., 32, 60.

31. See P.A.H. de Boer, *Gedenken und Gedächtnis in der Welt des Alten Testaments* (Stuttgart: W. Kohlhammer, 1962).

32. Once it is a *beth temporale*, 1 Kings 2.5, 'to shed blood in time of peace'.

33. Aram-Damascus (2 Sam. 8.6; 1 Chron. 18.6); Edom (2 Sam. 8.14);

Shechem (Josh. 24.25); Bethel and Dan (1 Kings 12.29); Samaria and Damascus (1 Kings 20.34); Jerusalem (2 Kings 21.4); and Egypt (Ex. 15.26; Jer. 32.20; Ezek. 15.26; Ps. 78.43).

34. Note that the Sefire inscriptions translated with 'to conclude a treaty' (I A line 7, I B line 6) are not constructed with the preposition *beth*. Thus, they cannot be taken as a similar phrase to the Psalm text.

35. See Redford, *Study of the Biblical Story of Joseph*, 244ff.

36. Elision of the *he* from an original form *yĕhōsēp* is not a plausible theory. H. Bauer and P. Leander, *Historische Grammatik der hebräischen Sprache des Alten Testaments* (Halle: M. Niemeyer, 1918-22), 229, explain *yĕhūkal* (Jer. 39.3) as a 'Neubildung' of an original form ('Ursemitisch') *yūkal* (Jer. 38.1), being the usual form in biblical times. Both forms of the same name are *hapax legomenon*. *yōsēp*, however, is a regularly used form, even outside the Joseph story. For obvious reasons Bauer and Leander do not adduce the spelling *yĕhōsēp* as an example of an original, vanished form of the name Joseph.

BIBLIOGRAPHY OF THE PUBLICATIONS OF
P.A.H. DE BOER

This bibliography omits only some minor book notices and some publications of a more popular nature. Abbreviations are used according to 'Schwertner' (*Theologische Realenzyklopädie, Abkürzungsverzeichnis*, 1976). The articles included in this volume are indicated with an *.

1936

1. "De 'theologie' van het Oude Testament", *VoxTh* 8, pp. 49–53.
2. "Litteratuur over het Oude Testament", *JEOL* 4, pp. 191–3.

1938

1. *Research into the Text of 1 Samuel i–xvi* (Amsterdam)—dissertation at Leyden University.
*2. *Het koningschap in oud-Israël* (Amsterdam)—inaugural address at Leyden University; English translation "Kingship in Ancient Israel" in this volume.

1940

1. *De boodschap van het Oude Testament* (Assen)—see also 1946.
2. Review of F. Rosenthal, *Die aramaistische Forschung seit Th. Nöldekes Veröffentlichungen* (Leiden, 1939), *JEOL* 7, pp. 399–402.

1941

1. *Genesis ii en iii, het verhaal van den Hof in Eden* (Leiden).
2. "Genesis xi 1–9", *NThS* 22, pp. 304–9.
3. "1 Samuel xvii. Notes on the text and the ancient versions", *OTS* 1, pp. 79–103.
4. "Uit den eeredienst van Israël: Jesaja xii", *Weekblad van de Nederlandsche Hervormde Kerk* 25 (28 juni).

1942

1. "Kain en Abel, Genesis iv 1–16", *NThT* 31, pp. 197–212.
2. "Exegese, prediking en kerk", *Weekblad van de Nederlandsche Hervormde Kerk* 26 (2 mei).

1943

1. "Jahu's ordination of heaven and earth. An essay on Psalm viii", *OTS* 2, pp. 171–93—this volume contains essays presented to B.D. Eerdmans.
2. *De voorbede in het Oude Testament, OTS* 3 (Leiden).

1944

1. "Aramaica", *JEOL* 9, pp. 110–6.

1946

1. *De boodschap van het Oude Testament,* revised edition (Assen).
2. "De civitate", *Mededeelingen uit de civitas academica lugduno batava,* No. 1 (October), pp. 3–6.

1947

1. "Litteratuur over het Oude Testament uit de Angelsaksische landen", *NedThT* 1 (1946–47), pp. 110–7.
*2. "Genesis xxxii 23–33. Some remarks on composition and character of the story", *NedThT* 1 (1946–47), pp. 149–63—a paper read to the Society for Old Testament Study at their meeting in Cardiff in 1946.

1948

1. "An inquiry into the meaning of the term *maśśā*'", *OTS* 5, pp. 197–214.
*2. "Some remarks on Exodus xxi 7–11. The hebrew female slave", *Orientalia Neerlandica* (Leiden), pp. 162–6.

1949

1. "Research into the text of 1 Samuel xviii–xxxi", *OTS* 6, pp. 1–100.
2. "Abraham", *HTS* 6, pp. 43–50.
3. "Over de onlangs gevonden hebreeuwse handschriften", *NedThT* 3, pp. 200–4.

1950

1. "Kanttekeningen bij Prof. Vriezen's boek *Hoofdlijnen der theologie van het Oude Testament, VoxTh* 20 (1949–50), pp. 174–80.

1951

1. "De godsdienst van het Jodendom", J.H. Waszink, W.C. van Unnik, and Ch. de Beus (eds.), *Het oudste christendom en de antieke cultuur* I (Haarlem), pp. 433–536.
2. "De functie van de bijbel", *NedThT* 6 (1951–52), pp. 1–9.
3. "Notes on text and meaning of Isaiah xxxviii 9–20", *OTS* 9, pp. 170–86.
4. "Notes on an Oxyrhynchus papyrus in Hebrew: Brit. Mus., Or. 9180 A", *VT* 1, pp. 49–57.
5. "A mistranscription (1QIs^a: Is. xliii 19)", *VT* 1, p. 68.
6. Review of Abraham Levene, *The Early Syrian Fathers on Genesis* (London, 1951), *VT* 1, pp. 318f.

1952

1. "Via media?", *NedThT* 6 (1951–52), pp. 109–11.

1954

1. "Etude sur le sens de la racine *QWH*", *OTS* 10, pp. 225–46.

1955

1. *Gods beloften over land en volk in het Oude Testament* (Delft).
2. "The counsellor", M. Noth and D. Winton Thomas (eds.), *Wisdom in Israel and in the Ancient Near East—Presented to Professor Harold Henry Rowley, SVT* 3, pp. 42–71.
3. "Vive le Roi!", *VT* 5, pp. 225–31.
4. "De gesloten poort", *Kerk en Wereld* 47 (December), pp. 9–10.

1956

1. *Second Isaiah's Message, OTS* 11 (Leiden).
*2. "Naar aanleiding van een inscriptie uit Ṣoᶜar", *JEOL* 14, pp. 117–21—English translation "An inscription from Ṣoᶜar" in this volume.
3. "26 November", *De Gids* 119, pp. 441–43.

1957

1. *Jeremia's twijfel. Rede uitgesproken op de 382e dies natalis van de Leidse Universiteit door de Rector Magnificus* (Leiden)—Rectorial address to Leyden University on February 8.
2. "Texte et traduction des paroles attribuées à David en 2 Samuel xxiii 1–7", *Volume du Congrès: Strasbourg 1956, SVT* 4, pp. 47–56.
3. "Litteratuur over het Oude Testament", *Theologie en Praktijk* 17, pp. 103–12.
4. "Rede, uitgesproken bij de overdracht van het rectoraat", *Jaarboek der Rijksuniversiteit te Leiden*, pp. 87–108.

1958

1. *De zoon van God in het Oude Testament* (Leiden)—English translation: 1973, No. 2.
2. "Enkele opmerkingen over de betekenis van namen in het Oude Testament", *Bijdragen en mededelingen* der naamkunde-commissie van de Kon. Ned. Akademie van Wetenschappen XIII (Amsterdam), pp. 16–24.
3. Review of H.-J. Kraus, *Klagelieder (Threni), BKAT* XX (Neukirchen, 1956), *VT* 8, pp. 221–3.
4. Review of G.M. Lamsa, *The Holy Bible from Eastern Manuscripts.* Containing the Old and New Testaments translated from the Peshiṭta, the Authorized Bible of the Church of the East (Philadelphia, 1957), *VT* 8, p. 223.

1959

1. "A description of the Sinai Syriac Ms. 35", *Essays in Honour of Millar Burrows, VT* 9, No. 4, pp. 408–12.

1961

1. *Het Oude Testament en het Christelijk geloof* (Utrecht)—a paper.
2. "Methode en mogelijkheden en exegese", *Over bijbel en openbaring: studies uit Vrijzinnig-Hervormde kring* (Assen), pp. 23–54.
3. "Een paaspreek", *Over bijbel en openbaring: studies uit Vrijzinnig-Hervormde kring* (Assen), pp. 123–31.
4. "De dood en het woord", *Theologie en Praktijk* 21, pp. 22–5.
5. "De verpakking van harde, naakte feiten", *Theologie en Praktijk* 21, pp. 107–12.

230   BIBLIOGRAPHY

6. Review of G.A.F. Knight, *Christelijke theologie van het Oude Testament* (Utrecht-Antwerpen, 1961), *Theologie en Praktijk* 21, pp. 161f.
7. Review of *Die Religion in Geschichte und Gegenwart*. Dritte, völlig neubearbeitete Auflage, Band I–IV, herausgegeben von K. Galling (Tübingen, 1957–1960), *VT* 11, pp. 462f.

1962

1. *Gedenken und Gedächtnis in der Welt des Alten Testaments* (Stuttgart)—the Franz Delitzsch-Vorlesungen for 1960.
2. Articles in *Phoenix Bijbelpockets*:
   a. "Het begin van de bijbel", I, pp. 71–82;
   b. "Het verhaal van de Hof in Eden", II, pp. 73–83;
   c. "Noach", III, pp. 85–96;
   d. "Abraham, Izaak, Jakob, Jozef", IV, pp. 83–102;
   e. "De Uittocht", V, pp. 61–6.
3. Review of B. Maarsingh, *Onderzoek naar de ethiek van de wetten in Deuteronomium* (Winterswijk, 1961), *NedThT* 16 (1961–62), pp. 144f.
4. Review of C. Moss, *Catalogue of Syriac Printed Books and Related Literature in the British Museum* (London, 1962), *VT* 12, pp. 504–7.

1963

1. Articles in *Phoenix Bijbelpockets*:
   a. "De Tien Woorden", VI, pp. 71–86;
   b. "Mozes' voorbede", VI, pp. 87–9;
   c. "Bileam", VI, pp. 90–3;
   d. "Jozua in discussie", VII, pp. 66–72;
   e. "Simson", VIII, pp. 69–78.
*2. "A Syro-Hexaplar text of the Song of Hannah: 1 Samuel ii 1–10", D. Winton Thomas and W.D. McHardy (eds.), *Hebrew and Semitic Studies Presented to Godfrey Rolles Driver* (Oxford, © Oxford University Press, 1963), pp. 8–15.
*3. "Als David moeste vluchten voor Saul den Tyran ...", *NedThT* 17 (1962–63), pp. 283–97—English translation "When David had to flee from Saul, the Tyrant ..." in this volume.
4. "Confirmatum est cor meum. The Old Latin text of the Song of Hannah", *OTS* 13, pp. 173–92.
*5. "Een verdwenen bijbeltekst", *Theologie en Praktijk* 23, pp. 49–57—English translation "A lost biblical text" in this volume.
6. "26 November 1940: Toespraak op 26 november 1962 in de Pieterskerk gehouden", *Mededelingen uit de civitas academica lugduno batava* 1962–63, No. 2 (januari 1963), pp. 31–5.
7. "Mag ik mij een christen noemen, als ...", *Kerk en Wereld* 55/16, pp. 1f.

1964

1. Articles in *Phoenix Bijbelpockets*:
   a. "Elia", IX, pp. 75–84;
   b. "Hoor, Israël", IX, pp. 90–6;
   c. "Profeet", X, pp. 66–70;
   d. "Amos", X, pp. 91–5;
   e. "Micha", X, pp. 96–101;
   f. "Messias", X, pp. 105–11;
   g. "Jeremia", XI, pp. 77–91;

h. "Jona", XI, pp. 93–102;
i. "Het tweede gedeelte van het boek Jezaja", XII, pp. 97–107.
2. Review of J. Lindblom, *Prophecy in Ancient Israel* (Oxford, 1962), *BiOr* 21, p. 327.

1965

1. Articles in *Phoenix Bijbelpockets*:
   a. "Maleachi", XIII, pp. 75–9;
   b. "Het boek der Psalmen", XIV, pp. 85–92;
   c. "Job, gisteren, heden en morgen dezelfde mens", XV, pp. 109–14.
2. "Once again the Old Latin text of Hannah's song", *OTS* 14, pp. 206–13.
3. "*kh*, 1940–1965", *OTS* 14, pp. vii–x.
4. Review of *Studies on the Psalms* (Potchefstroom, 1963), *NedThT* 19 (1964–65), pp. 313f.

1966

1. Articles in *Phoenix Bijbelpockets*:
   a. "Wijsheid", XVI, pp. 113–21;
   b. "Daniël", XVII, pp. 97–105;
   c. "Esther", XVII, pp. 117–24.
2. "Psalm cxxxi 2", *VT* 16, pp. 287–92.
*3. "2 Samuel 12:25", *Studia Biblica et Semitica Theodoro Christiano Vriezen . . . dedicata* (Wageningen), pp. 25–9.
4. Review of M.H. Goshen-Gottstein, *The Book of Isaiah: Sample Edition with Introduction* (Jerusalem, 1965), *VT* 16, pp. 247–52.
5. Review of K. Galling, *Studien zur Geschichte Israels im persischen Zeitalter* (Tübingen, 1964), *VT* 16, pp. 128–30.
6. "Rede ter opening van de honderdste vergadering van Moderne Theologen op 2 juni 1966 te Amersfoort", *Theologie en Praktijk* 26, pp. 49–57.

1967

1. "*bbrytm ᶜmd zrᶜm*, Sirach xliv 12a", *Hebräische Wortforschung. Festschrift zum 80. Geburtstag von Walter Baumgartner, SVT* 16, pp. 25–9.
2. "Septuagint", *EBrit* (Chicago) 20, pp. 229–30.
3. "Theodotion", *EBrit* (Chicago) 21, p. 992.

1968

1. "Dispersed leaves", *JSS* 13, pp. 33–5.
2. "Hebrew biblical manuscripts in the Netherlands", M. Black and G. Fohrer (eds.), *In Memoriam Paul Kahle, BZAW* 103 (Berlin), pp. 44–52.
3. "The meaning of Psalm lxxiii 9", *VT* 18, pp. 260–4.
*4. "*wmrhwq yryh mlhmh*—Job 39:25", P.R. Ackroyd and B. Lindars (eds.), *Words and Meanings: Essays Presented to David Winton Thomas* (Cambridge: Cambridge University Press), pp. 29–38.
*5. (Together with W. Baars) "Ein neugefundenes Fragment des syrisch-römischen Rechtsbuches", J.A. Ankum, R. Feenstra, and W.F. Leemans (eds.), *Symbolae iuridicae et historicae M. David dedicatae* I (Leiden), pp. 45–53.

1969

*1. "Op zoek naar de betekenis van Psalm 51:6?", *VoxTh* (Assen: Van Gorcum & Comp B.V.) 39, pp. 155–68—English translation "In search of the meaning of Psalm li 6 (4)" in this volume.
2. Review of H. Schmid, *Mose: Überlieferung und Geschichte*, *BZAW* 110 (Berlin, 1968), *VT* 19, pp. 133–5.
3. Review of L. Bronner, *The Stories of Elijah and Elisha as Polemics Against Baal Worship*, *Pretoria Oriental Series* VI (Leiden, 1968), *VT* 19, pp. 267–9.
4. Review of *Proceedings of the XIth International Congress of the IAHR*, 3 volumes (Leiden, 1968), *VT* 19, pp. 269f.

1970

*1. "Some remarks concerning and suggested by Jeremiah 43:1–7", H.T. Frank and W.L. Reed (eds.), *Translating and Understanding the Old Testament. Essays in Honor of Herbert Gordon May* (Nashville and New York, pp. 71–9.
2. Review of H.J. Boecker, *Die Beurteilung der Anfänge des Königtums in den deuteronomistischen Abschnitten des 1. Samuelbuches. Ein Beitrag zum Problem des "deuteronomistischen Geschichtswerks"*, *WMANT* 31, (Neukirchen, 1969), *VT* 20, pp. 379–81.
3. Review of M. Rehm, *Der königliche Messias im Licht der Immanuel-Weissagungen des Buches Jesaja*, *Eichstätter Studien* N.F., Bd. I (Kevelaer, 1968), *VT* 20, pp. 381f.
4. "Genesis 1. Een uiteenzetting", *Theologie en Praktijk* 30, pp. 153–67.

1972

1. "An aspect of sacrifice: I. divine bread; II. God's fragrance", *Studies in the Religion of Ancient Israel*, *SVT* 23, pp. 27–47.
2. Review of H.A. Brongers, *Koningen*, 2 volumes, *POT* (Nijkerk, 1967/1970), *NedThT* 26, pp. 82–4.

1973

*1. "Jeremiah 45, verse 5", M.A. Beek, A.A. Kampman, C. Nijland, and J. Ryckmans (eds.), *Symbolae biblicae et mesopotamicae F.M. Th. de Liagre Böhl dedicatae* (Leiden), pp. 31–7.
2. "The Son of God in the Old Testament", *OTS* 18, pp. 188–207—English translation of 1958, No. 1.

1974

1. *Fatherhood and Motherhood in Israelite and Judaean Piety* (Leiden)—the Haskell Lectures at Oberlin College, Ohio, for 1974.
2. "Een schakel in een ketting. Over vrijheid in oudtestamentisch perspectief", *Theologie en Praktijk* 34, pp. 91–9.
*3. "Quelques remarques sur l'arc dans la nuée (Genèse 9,8–17)", C. Brekelmans (ed.), *Questions disputées d'Ancien Testament*, *BEThL* 33 (Gembloux and Leuven), pp. 105–14—see also 1989.
*4. "1 Samuel viii 16b", *Travels in the World of the Old Testament: Studies Presented to M.A. Beek on the occasion of his 65th birthday*, *SSN* 16 (Assen: Van Gorcum & Comp B.V.), pp. 27–30.
*5. "The perfect with *waw* in 2 Samuel 6:16", M. Black and W. Smalley (eds.),

On Language, Culture, and Religion: in Honor of E.A. Nida (The Hague: Mouton), pp. 43–52.

6. "YHWH as epithet expressing the superlative", *Essays in Honour of Erling Hammershaimb*, *VT* 24/2, pp. 233–5.

7. "Iets over minderheden in het Midden-Oosten", R. Boeke (ed.), *Verder dan de oekumene. Een kwart eeuw verkenning in Nederland van religies der wereld* (Oosterbeek), pp. 55–59.

1975

1. "Preface to the Jubilee Number", *VT* 25/2a, pp. 257–60.
*2. "Egypt in the Old Testament: some aspects of an ambivalent assessment"—lecture delivered in 1975 at the Oxford meeting of the S.O.T.S., not published previously.

1976

1. *Liber Samuelis, Biblia Hebraica Stuttgartensia* 5 (Stuttgart).
2. *Geloof eens voor altijd gegeven of een mogelijke gift in iedere tijd?* Voordracht, gehouden op een bijeenkomst van de Werkgroep voor Moderne Theologie te Utrecht op 17 mei 1976.

1977

*1. "A note on Ecclesiastes 12:12a", R.H. Fischer (ed.), *A Tribute to Arthur Vööbus* (Chicago), pp. 85–8.
*2. "Einige Bemerkungen und Gedanken zum Lied in 1. Samuel 2,1–10", H. Donner, R. Hanhart, and R. Smend (eds.), *Beiträge zur alttestamentlichen Theologie, Festschrift für Walther Zimmerli zum 70. Geburtstag* (Göttingen), pp. 53–9.
*3. "Haalt Job bakzeil? Job xlii 6", *NedThT* 31, pp. 181–94—English translation "Does Job retract? Job xlii 6" in this volume.

1978

1. *Samuel, The Old Testament in Syriac According to the Peshiṭta Version* II, 2 (Leiden).

1979

1. "Honderd jaar 'uit Egypte ...'", P.A.H. de Boer and P.Sj. van Koningsveld (eds.), *Honderd jaar 'uit Egypte ...': Leidse opstellen over de scheiding tussen kerk en staat aan de openbare theologische faculteit* (Leiden), pp. 1–11—paper read to the Oosters Genootschap, Leyden 1976, in commemoration of the hundredth anniversary of the Old Testament chairs in Dutch universities.

1981

1. "Cantate domino: an erroneous dative?", *OTS* 21, pp. 55–67.
2. Review of M.H. Goshen-Gottstein, *Syriac Manuscripts in the Harvard College Library, a Catalogue, Harvard Semitic Studies* 23 (Missoula, 1979), *BiOr* 38, pp. 91–3.
*3. "La syntaxe du verset quatre du Psaume vingt-deux", A. Caquot and M. Delcor (eds.), *Mélanges bibliques et orientaux en l'honneur de H. Cazelles, AOAT* 212 (Kevelaer and Neukirchen-Vluyn), pp. 87–90.

*4. "Sur la massore de 2 Samuel i 23", *Henoch* 3, pp. 22–5.
 5. "Towards an edition of the Syriac version of the Old Testament", *VT* 31, pp. 346–57.

1982

*1. "Some observations on Deuteronomy vi 4 and 5", W.C. Delsman, J.T. Nelis a.o. (eds.), *Von Kanaan bis Kerala, Festschrift für J.P.M. van der Ploeg*, *AOAT* 211 (Kevelaer and Neukirchen-Vluyn), pp. 45–52.
 2. "Numbers vi 27", *VT* 32, pp. 3–13.
 3. Review of O. Keel, *Monotheismus im Alten Israel und seiner Umwelt, Biblische Beiträge*, N.F. 14 (Freiburg, 1980), *BiOr* 39, pp. 158–60.
 4. *Religieuze aspecten van het Palestijnse vraagstuk* (Leiden).

1983

 1. *Religieuze aspecten van het Palestijnse vraagstuk*, tweede, vermeerderde en gewijzigde, druk (Katwijk).

1984

*1. "Psalm lxxxi 6a: Observations on translation and meaning of one Hebrew line", W.B. Barrick and J.R. Spencer (eds.), *In the Shelter of Elyon: Essays on Ancient Palestinian Life and Literature in Honor of G.W. Ahlström*, *JSOT.SS* 31 (Sheffield), pp. 67–80.

1985

 1. *Historisch recht en religie*—unpublished paper.

1989

*1. "Quelques remarques sur l'arc dans la nuée (Genèse 9,8–17)", C. Brekelmans (ed.), *Questions disputées d'Ancien Testament*, *BEThL* 33, revised and enlarged edition by M. Vervenne (Leuven: University Press/Uitgeverij Peeters), pp. 105–14, 216f. (Supplementary Notes by M. Vervenne)—see 1974, No. 3.

Editorial work

Professor de Boer has also been editor of
OTS (Leiden) 1–16 (1941–69);
VT 1–25 (1951–75);
SVT 1–27 (1953–74);
Studia Post-Biblica (Leiden) 1–15 (1959–70);
The Old Testament in Syriac According to the Peshiṭta Version (Leiden) (1959–80);
Phoenix Bijbelpockets (Zeist/Antwerpen) I–XVIII (1963–68);
Monographs of the Peshiṭta Institute (Leiden) (1972–81).

INDEX OF BIBLICAL REFERENCES

238   INDEX OF BIBLICAL REFERENCES

1 Samuel (cont.)

vii 1	11
vii 6	74, 106
vii 11	74
viii	2ff., 7f., 13
viii 5	1
viii 6	1
viii 7	3
viii 11–17	139
viii 11ff.	3
viii 16	139ff.
viii 20	1
viii 22	207
ix	4, 7
ix 2	54f., 57
ix 14	8
ix 16	7, 13
ix 18	8
x	4, 14
x 1–16	4, 7
x 1–11	7
x 9	144f., 147
x 17–24	4, 7
x 22	8
x 24	15
x 25f.	7
x 27	7
xi	3f., 16
xi 1–11	4, 7
xi 7	8
xi 12–15	7
xi 15	4
xii	4, 7, 11
xii 10	106
xii 11	7
xii 12	2f.
xiii	4
xiii 1	59
xiii 2	7
xiii 13ff.	54
xiii 14	130
xiii 19–22	7
xiii 22	144, 147
xiv	5, 14
xiv 1–16	4
xiv 18	14
xiv 24	14
xiv 34f.	14
xiv 35	10
xiv 37	14
xiv 48	170
xv	4, 57
xv 1	3

xv 3	207
xv 9	141
xvi 2	147
xvi 20	77
xvi 22	77
xvi 23	85, 147
xvii 48	144f., 147
xx 12	72
xx 16	72
xx 19	72
xx 20	72
xx 22	72
xx 41	72
xxi	135
xxii 1f.	55
xxii 11	77
xxiv 7	3
xxiv 10	106
xxiv 11	3
xxiv 12	106
xxiv 17	106
xxv 15	129
xxv 20	144f., 147
xxv 39	77
xxvi 9	3
xxvi 11	3
xxvi 21	106
xxvi 33	3
xxvii 8	153
xxviii 7	126

2 Samuel

i	135
i 19ff.	14
i 22	198
i 23	196–199
ii 1	24
iii 15	77
v 7	148
v 9	148
vi 6	77
vi 10	148
vi 12	148
vi 13–15	148
vi 16	142–149
vi 17–19	142
vi 18	16
vi 19	147
vi 20–23	142, 148
vii 1–5	148
vii 1	74
vii 8–11	148
vii 8	13

OUDTESTAMENTISCHE STUDIËN

25. WOUDE, A.S. VAN DER (ed.). *New avenues in the study of the Old Testament.* A collection of Old Testament studies published on the occasion of the fiftieth anniversary of the Oudtestamentisch Werkgezelschap and the retirement of Prof. Dr. M.J. MULDER. 1989. ISBN 90 04 09125 4

26. WOUDE, A.S. VAN DER (ed.). *In quest of the past.* Studies in Israelite religion, literature and prophetism. Papers read at the joint British-Dutch Old Testament Conference, held at Elspeet, 1988. 1990. ISBN 90 04 09192 0

27. DUIN, C. VAN. *P.A.H. de Boer*: select studies in Old Testament exegesis. 1991. ISBN 90 04 09342 7

DATE DUE

HIGHSMITH   # 45220